Frederic Cozzens

Marine Painter

Home From Cathay,
Collection of Anita Jacobsen

Frederic Cozzens

Marine Painter

Anita Jacobsen

ALPINE FINE ARTS
COLLECTION, LTD.
Publishers of Fine Art Books
New York   London

I dedicate this volume to my father, George Vincent Kershaw.

Published in 1982 by:
ALPINE FINE ARTS COLLECTION, LTD.
164 Madison Avenue, New York, New York 10016

ISBN: 0-933516-60-6

Design and photography: Miles Tilton
Editor: Matthew Slatin

This book was produced in Belgium by
Offset Printing Van den Bossche.

Table of Contents

Introduction

In the May 16, 1926 issue of the *New York Times*, there appeared a reproduction of a Fred. S. Cozzens watercolor of the first America's Cup Race on August 8, 1870. Mr. Wilmot T. Cox, a gentleman reader from New Canaan, Connecticut, wrote immediately, "What a delightful marine picture is the reproduction in today's *Times* of Frederic S. Cozzens' watercolor purporting to be a scene of the first America's Cup Race in this country on August 8, 1870. I see that it is dated 1884.

"I saw the race from the steamboat, *Seawanhaka*, in company with the Reverend John Hasgate of St. Paul's School who was staying with us at East Island and also with the Reverend Dr. Ferguson, afterwards rector of St. Paul's School, who was adrift in the Pacific in an open boat after the burning of the ship, *Hornet*.

"I saw the *Cambria* near at hand that day and the rest of the fleet and the picture is stamped in my memory. The *Cambria* had a single spar bowsprit, carried a jib and a forestaysail and a loose footed mainsail. Her jackyard (club) topsail was quite noticeably squareheaded and she had ratlines on her shroud. Altogether, she was a markedly thickset and sturdy looking craft and as different as possible from the big American skimming dishes. I can't place the yacht in the Cozzens watercolor, but she might be the *Idler* or the *Dauntless* or the *Sylvia* (which was painted claret).

"As I remember the weather, there was not much breeze in the morning, but in the afternoon it breezed up from the south and what a picture it was with the wide, flowing and bellying maintop mast staysails! I remember that of the *Dauntless*, especially. The *Magic* certainly did slip in ahead in great shape.

"As we neared Scotland Light, the schooner, *Sappho*, passed us homeward bound from England. My eyes were sharp in those days and I remember, with keen interest that the *Sappho* also carried a forestaysail."

Signed,

Wilmot T. Cox
New Canaan, Conn.

The reproduction of one of Cozzens' watercolors and the letter from a reader evoked some queries respecting Cozzens' whereabouts from some of the yachtsmen who knew him years before. The editor of the *New York Times* assigned one of the writers of that newspaper, Henry J. Brockmeyer, to find the elusive Cozzens. The result was a feature story with pictures about the artist which appeared in the Sunday *New York Times* edition of June 13, 1926. It was entitled: "Cup Race Artist on Deck at 80. Fred. S. Cozzens, painter of yacht contests, hopes to picture the next victory. Criticizes negligent sketching of marine subjects."

The article gives us great insight into his character, personality and attitudes. Even his language is salty. "I am most certainly 'on deck,'" he snapped. Mr. Brockmeyer wrote, "The 100 Guinea Cup, won by the yacht *America* from the British Fleet in 1851 is still the most cherished possession of the New York Yacht Club, but Sir Thomas Lipton looms threateningly in the offing with designs for another *Shamrock* and hence it is likely that Fred. S. Cozzens, the artist, will be called upon, once more, to commemorate in paint another attempt to 'lift the Cup.'"

The article continued, "Mr. Cozzens is eighty years of age. He is still active and has an eye as clear, he believes, and a hand as steady as when he sketched the contenders in the race between the *Puritan* and the *Genesta* forty-one years ago in 1885...In fact, he is now finishing at his studio at 42 Mundy Avenue, Port Richmond, Staten Island, a series of drawings of the International Yacht Races for a member of the New York Yacht Club. 'When I get through with the job,' he says, 'I'll have nothing to do but sketch and paint the next big one'."

He continues, "Many tides have battered against the sea wall at the Battery since Mr. Cozzens dedicated his pencil and brush to painting marine subjects and more particularly to a picture of the history of the America's Cup Races. He hopes to record still another American victory. There is, however, a note of regret in his remarks, 'Yachts are racing machines. They are not worth a darn for anything after the racing is over.

They are not wholesome cruising boats like some of the earlier contenders were.'"

The article continued, "Mr. Cozzens is, or has been, a thoroughly practised yachtsman. His pictures show it. Not a detail in his drawings of a boat's construction but is plain to the naval architect; not a fine line in the graceful sweep of a hull or in the towering 'stick' of the big sloops carrying a smother of canvas but is faithfully set down in pigments true to hue and seemingly alive with the pert flippancy of a gay flapper of the seas."

It is because of the almost photographic truthfulness to details that Mr. Cozzens was aroused to comment, sarcastically, upon a magazine reproduction of a painting of an old clipper ship, the *Thermopylae*. In the phraseology of early days, he referred to her as a "teaship." Seemingly, all vessels that traded with the Orients were "teaships." "And mind you," he said, "the man who drew the picture of the old clipper gave her a brig rig... preposterous!"

"And I notice, too," he added more in sorrow than in anger, "that there is a tendency on the part of some artists to desregard what might be called the national touch in the build and rigging of vessels. More than once I have seen drawings of historic American ships rigged as the English rigged their sails. That is fundamentally wrong. The wonderful records of some of our old ships, if nothing else, should command a careful representation of their lines and rigging."

Recently, Mr. Cozzens completed a painting of the *Oriental*, a teaship, for the Great Northern Railway Company. But his heart and his memories are bound up in the races for the America's Cup.

"I recall, among other things, the intense rivalry between the two schools of yachtsmen in the earlier days," he said. "They argued and contended back and forth over the relative merits of the English cutter type of boat and the shallower American model. The controversy was particularly warm about the time of the *Puritan* and *Genesta* race. During that memorable race,

Roosevelt Schuyler was the New York Yacht Club observer aboard the *Genesta*. The race was twenty miles to windward and return, as I recall it; a run out and a beat back. I was close to the turn and could see all over the *Genesta's* deck and there was Mr. Schuyler amidship with the water sloshing around him. He was soaking wet to the waist. After the race, I asked him how he had enjoyed the trip. 'Fine,' he replied. I asked him if it hadn't been a trifle wet. 'Oh no!,' he said, 'dry as a bone.' The joke in this was that Mr. Schuyler had been a staunch advocate of the cutter type boat, such a boat as the *Genesta*, and he would not admit that his pet theories had received such a knockdown blow. The champions of the American model had contended all along that the cutters were bound to be wet boats and wet boats they were!"

He continued, "In the *Volunteer-Thistle* race, Latham Fish was the American observer aboard the challenger. The Englishmen had a good, fast yacht and they knew it. They were very cocky, Oh! my yes! Some of them affected disdain, which they took no pains to conceal, for the Yankee boat. 'We'll show that old iron pot what we can do,' they boasted.

"Mr. Fish didn't like that kind of talk any too well. 'Excuse me,' said he, 'You call her an old iron pot; but let me tell you that she is the fastest sloop in America.'

"Just before the start of the race, the *Thistle*, jockeying for position at the line, sailed gaily about, presenting a beautiful, sprightly sight while our yacht barely moved through the water. The American skipper wasn't showing all his paces to his opponents so early in the race. But, my boy, fifteen minutes after the boats crossed the starting line, the *Volunteer* was sailing ahead like a ghost and the Englishman who had made the slighting remark about her walked up to Mr. Fish and apologized. 'You said that she was the fastest yacht in America,' he said, 'My stars. She's the fastest yacht in the world!' One of the reasons why we beat the Englishmen in those days was because of the greater efficiency of our sails. The English sails were loosly woven and baggy. Our's were closely woven, taut and flat. Later, the Englishmen saw the advantage in our methods of carrying sails."

The *New York Times* article was accompanied by Cozzens' picture of the first America's Cup Race and a portrait of the artist. The interview clearly shows his understanding and knowledge of all aspects of yacht racing whether he was discussing racing-form hull structure, sail construction or sailor's attitudes, as well as his first-hand acquaintance with the foremost yachtsmen of the time.

The preceeding interview was not the only time that someone was looking for Frederic S. Cozzens, for he had disappeared from view several times. Fortunately, the editor of the *New York Times* was able to locate him in the 1920s to interview him. All during the 1930s the editors of Goodspeed's catalogue, *This Month*, appealed to their readers to find some trace of Cozzens, who they believed had disappeared from sight. "Perhaps we have not looked in the right places, but we have been unable to learn much of Mr. Cozzens' history. If you know of any source of information, whether written or not, please let us know about it." They were keen admirers of his work, and were trying, at that early date, to fill in the missing biographical information about him. A Goodspeed catalogue, issued in 1937 stated, "Speaking of early lithographs, those corking prints must have been made fairly early in Mr. Cozzens' career for we understand that the artist is still painting." There was only fragmentary data known about the elusive Cozzens at that time.

The editors of *This Month* were searching in vain; Frederic S. Cozzens had died in 1928. After his death, there was little interest in his work or in the details of his life. The collecting of shreds and scraps of information from his life fabric has been a long and difficult task. Although a great deal of biographical information is available about his father, the author, Frederic Swartwout Cozzens, there is very little available about Frederic Schiller Cozzens. Even the scanty references that could be gleaned from old books proved, upon close scrutiny, to be inaccurate.

In the absence of facts, many myths grew up about him. For instance, it is believed that he gave up painting in the 1890s to take over his father's wine business. However, we know that his father failed in the wine business in 1868 and died in 1869, so this could not be a possibility. In addition, we have many watercolors dated during this period to prove that he was indeed painting at that time.

Interviews of people who knew him also resulted in contradictions. For instance, all of his grandchildren remember him as an old man who painted in his room all day. It may be true that Cozzens never left his room in his old age, painting there at an easel, but we know from the testimony of many bystanders that Cozzens participated in many of the yachting events and witnessed most of the races that he sketched as a guest on one of the racing boats or on the judge's boat. He often finished his work at home or in his studio, but, in his prime, he worked directly at the scene.

Delving into all sorts of early records established a few vital statistics of the man. We know what he looked like, how tall he was, where he was born, etc., but the only way Cozzens can speak to us now is through his work, his interpretation of the marine scene during his lifetime. It is a panorama that stretches before our eyes, recording the marine and yachting scene from its earliest days until he died in 1928.

Frederic Schiller Cozzens was raised in a cultured milieu. He was the ninth generation of his family in America, after Richard Heywarde, who settled in Rhode Island late in the 17th or early in the 18th century. His grandfather, Frederic Smith Cozzens, was a chemist and his father, Frederic Swartwout Cozzens, was a New York City wine merchant and published author. Raised in an atmosphere of belief in everyman's duty to his world, he spent his entire life doing what he thought was important—creating beautiful pictures.

Frederic Schiller Cozzens, the artist, was born in New York City on October 11, 1846 at #42 Stuyvesant Street. In 1852, when he was six years old, the family moved to Chestnut Cottage in Yonkers, New York. The house overlooked the Hudson River and the Palisades. The Hudson became an important part of young Cozzens' life. A wrecked coal barge, moored close to the bank, made an admirable place to play. There was a smooth, sandy beach in front of the house with a dock, boathouse and small rowboat in which the lad, his brothers and sister spent many happy hours. The artist was raised at the water's edge and knew from experience how the sky and water looked at different times of the day and night. He learned many things from watching the old wooden sloops on the river. From the beach, one could hear the quick rattle of the rings as the sloops reefed their sails before a squall. Early in life, he experienced sights that he portrayed, beautifully, later on. Fred. S. Cozzens, Sr. wrote, "A grey rain curtain was drawn across the river shutting out everything except the spectral masts and spars of a schooner riding at anchor!" Cozzens drew variations of this theme all his life.

Young Cozzens grew up in a home frequented by the literary friends of his father who were active in the 19th century intellectual life in America. William C. Bryan, Fenimore Cooper, Thomas Hicks, William M. Thackery and Washington Irving were frequent guests at his home. There was a wide range of interest in literary, scientific and cultural interests in this background that shaped his interests and personality.

The information about Cozzens' education is sketchy. Aside from a reference to Yonkers #10 School of Prospect Street Hill, nothing is known of his early education. The records do not reveal any preparatory schooling prior to his entrance to Rensellaer Polytechnic Institute in Troy, New York in 1864. Checking into the college archives, we find his registration for the winter session of the 1864/65 school year. It shows that he wrote his name Frederic S. Cozzens Jr; he gave his address as Yonkers, New York, his birthplace as New York City and his birthdate as October 11, 1846. In all, he attended Rensellaer for two full winter sessions and three summer sessions. Although the Alumni Directory, issued in 1929, lists him as an alumnus of the class of 1868, he never graduated. There was no further attendance after 1867. His father failed in business and closed his wine and grocery store in 1868 and this may have caused young Cozzens to drop out of college before graduating.

Although there was no exact record of the courses he took at R.P.I., there was no stress on art. As far as can be ascertained, his college education offered little art training; the emphasis was on mathematics and engineering. He experimented with painting and drawing for his own amusement. There are none of his watercolors on the Troy, New York campus today.

Fred. S. Cozzens, Sr. tried vainly to discourage a career in art for his son. When a friend advised him to let Fred. Jr. work at his hobby rather than a career in engineering, he grudgingly consented. According to Trow's *Directory of New York City, 1872–73*, young Cozzens set up a design studio at 160 Fulton Street in New York City. He obtained work as a piano designer. The 1874–75 directory still listed him at the same address but the occupation had changed from designer to artist. This is the first indication we have of Frederic Cozzens officially calling himself an artist. It wasn't until 1890 that he changed from artist to marine artist.

There are only four photographs of Cozzens in existence. Rensellaer Polytechnic Institute supplied a carte-de-visite picture which Cozzens had given to a fraternity brother, Sam Fields, when they were both students. It shows a tall, slender young man with an erect posture and a head of thick, brown hair. A granddaughter of Cozzens', Marie Simmons, has three photographs of him. One is a formal pose showing him as an older man. This was the one used to illustrate the article in the *New York Times* in 1926. Another is an informal one sitting out in the open fields and a third is a snapshot of him with a pipe in the corner of his mouth.

Old friends and neighbors who remember him described him as shy, aloof and extravagantly formal. He did not deliberately seek anonymity, but his desire for privacy kept him apart. He was an extremely sociable person but he preferred to spend time at home with his family. Although he was often invited to many of the homes and boats of his wealthy friends and patrons, he felt that he could not reciprocate and therefore, it was not proper for him to accept invitations. Cozzens' generation lived by a strict code of behavior, and this added to the aura of aloofness that grew up about him.

It would seem logical for an artist working in the late part of the 19th century in the New York area to belong to one of the many associations that flourished at that time. However, a search for any membership in the American Watercolor Society, the Academy of Art or the American Art Association proved to be disappointing. Cozzens apparently did not belong to any of these associations.

This book has been organized to trace the chronological development of the artist Frederic Schiller Cozzens (1846–1928). The evolution of his art can be easily traced as he carefully dated most of his work. A minute study of this work starts with the earliest watercolors, those done while at college in the 1860s, and continues through his career, to his death in 1928.

Some of his strongest paintings were done as illustration for the book, *American Yachts, Their Clubs and Races* and the accompanying portfolio of prints. He excelled at painting the great sailing yachts with their picturesque sails, but there is also a vast amount of other work, such as the pen and ink illustrations for the book, *Yachts and Yachting*. He painted anything that floated on water from a canoe to a barge or a large intercontinental schooner. He excelled at portraying working craft such as whalers, fishing boats, tugs, pilotboats, liners and sailing and steam pleasure boats and did a serious study of the United States Navy that has never been equalled. Cozzens was a consummate artist who drew every aspect of the marine scene. His career started when sailing ships were still to be seen on the water. His work covered the end of the age of sail and extended into the age of steam. However, Cozzens' great strength is not only in the realistic portrayal of his picture but in his perception of the power of the sea. He never allows you to forget the joys, the thrill and the dangers of being on the water.

In this study of the art of Frederic Schiller Cozzens, the social, psychological, artistic and financial forces that shaped his personality and had a profound effect upon his work are noted. The strong influence of his parents and their friends, his idyllic childhood, education and determination to become an artist, all presaged his serious devotion to painting. His artistic output is examined year by year, the characteristics of his work enumerated and a catalogue raisonné of his complete *oeuvre* allows one to study his entire career.

Winter Session of 1864-65.

Names	Births.	Birth-place	Residences	Time gd
Roswell Emmons Briggs	Oct 11th 1846	New Bedford, Mass	New Bedford Mass	14th Sept
Cornelius Roosevelt	Oct 27 1847	New York. N.Y.	New York. N.Y.	"
Charles Ridgely Schott	Nov. 11th 1847	Baltimore Md	Philadelphia	"
Irving Ariel Stearns	Sep 12th 1845	Gorham N.Y.	Rushville N.Y.	"
James Duncan Reynolds	Aug. 25 1846	Massilon Ohio	Chicago Ill.	"
John Joseph Albright	Jan 18 1848	Etna Va	Scranton Pa.	"
Alter Megear	October 23. 1847	Philo. Penn	Wilmington Del.	"
Joseph Hiram Campbell	March 4th 1848	Backwoods	Ironton Ohio	"
Franklin Develle	July 17th 1847	Rushville N.Y.	Rushville N.Y.	"
Andrew Onderdonk	August 30th 1848	New York City	Sherwood N.Y.	"
Frank Orlando Bennet	October 10th 1846	Bell Port N.Y.	Bell Port N.Y.	"
José Ricardo Nadal	November 19th 1846	Mayagüez. P. Rico	Mayagüez. P. Rico	"
Antonio Emelio Desvernine	June 18th 1846	Havana	Havana	"
Frederic Auguste Apelles	Aug 29th 1843	New York	West Point	"
Ambrose Vincent Powell	May 4th 1847	Laurens N.Y.	Laurens N.Y.	"
William Knight	June 15 1848	Brooklyn	Yonkers N.Y.	"
Frederic Schiller Cozzens Jr	Oct 11 1846	New York N.Y.	Yonkers N.Y.	"
Herman Atwill	Mch 4 1844	New York	New York N.Y.	"
Benjamin Romaine Lawrance	May 10 1846	Marshall Mich.	New York City	"

Small Coastal Schooner,
Courtesy of the New York Historical Society

Frederic Cozzens

The first written mention of Fred. S. Cozzens as a marine watercolorist appeared in the diaries and account books of Samuel Sawyer of Gloucester, Massachusetts. John Wilmerding, in his book, *Fitz Hugh Lane*, quoted from these diaries, "Many artists are regularly appearing at Gloucester. Sawyer noted that in 1863, the marine artist, Fred. S. Cozzens was at #89 Water Street in Gloucester." However, Sawyer must have had his dates in error, as in 1863, Cozzens was a seventeen year old student at Rensselaer Polytechnic Institute and not yet recognized as a marine watercolorist. No examples of his marine work at this early age have been found to date.

Although nothing of a marine nature has been found, Cozzens did some character sketches and street scenes while he was a student at Rensselaer in the 1860s. Eight sketches of his were pasted into a scrapbook that was kept by a classmate, Samuel Fields of Buffalo, a member of the class of 1867. The eight sketches are in pencil or pen and ink, done on tablet paper or on cards, ranging in size from 2½" x 1¼" to 5" x 8". Unfortunately, they are tightly glued to the pages of the scrapbook which is disintegrating from age.

A student *carte-de-visite* picture was given to Fields by Cozzens and was put into the scrapbook. On the back of the picture is a penciled notation, "Made watercolor marine sketches—gave to

S. J. Fields 1868." This, in his own hand, shows that he was doing marine sketches as early as 1868. He signed his picture, "Yours in T.K.O. Fred. S. Cozzens, 1868." This is the first reference that we have of his marine watercolor painting.

The next mention of Fred. S. Cozzens' work was found in the archives of the Suffolk Museum and Carriage House at Stony Brook, Long Island in a reference, dated 1870, to the fact that Cozzens was working on Staten Island at that time, years before he moved there to live in 1881.

About 1870 Cozzens started to do free-lance art work that proved to be the bulk of his output for the next fifty years. This work consisted mainly of commissions for watercolors of privately owned boats, illustrations for newspapers, magazines, his own books and books that others wrote.

In *American Graphic Art*, Frank Weitenkampf wrote, "Fred. S. Cozzens became identified with the sea and its ships." Weitenkampf mentioned *Punchinello*, which was a comic-reader, subsidized by Tweed and published by the Punchinello Publishing Company in 1870. Vol. I covered the time span from April to September 1870 and Vol. II covered the time span from October to December 1879, at which time the magazine failed. There were forty illustrations in the two issues and Cozzens was one of the illustrators used by the magazine. Copies of *Punchinello* show that although the humor magazines of the 1870s did not have the force of sharp satire, they did have splendid illustrations.

Whenever an article on yachting or boating appeared in *Harper's Weekly*, *Leslie's*, *Century* or other magazines, it was usually illustrated by Cozzens. This was a pre-camera age when illustrators were needed to portray the story and give the readers an opportunity to be there at the scene of action and vicariously witness it.

Harper's Weekly used Cozzens' talents often. As early as 1870 he was commissioned to do a number of illustrations for the Cup Races between the yachts *Magic* and *Cambria*. The August,

1870 issue of the magazine featured his work with *The First Attempt of the British to Recover the America's Cup; the Challenger, Cambria, was Badly Beaten.* The part of the race that Cozzens depicted showed the *Cambria* first and the *America* third. Several other versions of this race exist by Cozzens. One is entitled, *The Finish Off Staten Island, 1870.* It shows the *Cambria, Dauntless, America, Idler* and *Magic.* Another version, at the Museum of the City of New York, dated 1870, is of the yachts *Magic* and *Cambria.*

An interesting early Cozzens sepia wash drawing, dated 1873, shows New Bedford seen from the shore at Fairhaven, Massachusetts. In 1871 he also painted watercolors of the race between the yachts *Sappho* and *Livonia.*

The first newspaper mention of his work that has come to light to date appeared in 1875. In the June 19, 1875 issue of the *Daily Graphic,* a New York City newspaper that ran from 1873 to 1889, we find eleven woodcuts that were made from Cozzens' drawings. The caption below the grouping of pictures reads, "Annual Regatta of the New York Yacht Club last Wednesday." They are entitled: *Ah! We'll Catch Them!*, showing a yacht racing far back of the pack; *Steam Yacht Race, Go it! Young 'Un's*, which shows two open boats with steam engines cutting across the bow of a large excursion steamer; *She's*

The Shore at Fairhaven, Mass.
Collection of Thomas B. Card.

Charming, See Her Come Up! referring to a sailboat advancing into the harbor; *Madcap Nearing the Climax*; *Madcap Rounding the Mark*; *Not a Visionary Jib* referring to the yacht, *Vision*; *Rounding the First Spit*; *Neck and Neck*; and *Home Again*, showing a yacht with her sails down in a calm sea. The center and largest picture, *Rounding the Lightship*, was signed. The course of the race was from the new boathouse of the New York Yacht Club at Stapleton, Staten Island to the South West Spit with return. Cozzens captured much of the excitement and joy of boating with this group of drawings.

The *Daily Graphic* issue of November 2, 1875 shows the city of New Bedford, Massachusetts with sketches by "Our Special Artist". The captions below the Cozzens illustrations show the high regard the editors held for his work. The nine Cozzens woodcuts take up a full page of the newspaper; as was the custom of the time, only the center picture is signed. *A Young Whaler* shows a group of children playing in an old whale boat that has been laid up on the shore with one young fellow holding a twig as if it were a harpoon. Below this is a picture entitled, *Old Whaler*. It shows a boy having his backside whaled by his mother, a humorous touch that is not often evident in Cozzens' work. *Epizootic Over the River* shows an ox-drawn fire engine. *Hove Down* and *Caulking and Sheathing* show a whaler on her side being repaired. The central picture is untitled and shows two piers with six or seven storage sheds. One of the whaling ships carries a flag, "T.B." *Wamsutta Mills* shows a large factory and *Just Arrived: Full Cargo* shows a whaling ship coming into port. *Down the River* is another view of the city of New Bedford and there are two city views, *City Hall* and *The Library*. The central picture is well drawn and finished; the others are sketches.

In this period of his artistic career, Fred. S. Cozzens was struggling to obtain commissions. In the year 1876, the entire yachting world was interested in the race between the two yachts, *Madeline* and the *Countess of Dufferin*. The *Madeline*, owned by John Dickerson, then Commodore of the Brooklyn Yacht Club, raced against the *Countess of Dufferin*, owned by a syndicate from the Royal Canadian Yacht Club of Toronto, Can-

Untitled
Collection of Arthur Baker

ada. The race, over the regular inside New York Yacht Club course, was won by the *Madeline*. Cozzens did many versions of this contest and the pre-trial matches.

An interesting scene was done for *Harper's Weekly* of September 27, 1879. It shows the buoy station at Quarantine Landing on Staten Island. It is a busy little scene, seen from a high vantage point, looking past the station with a prominent flagpole on a huge rock, past the many buoys lying on the ground, ignoring the dozen men working in the yard. We see past the launch and side-wheel vessel tied at the station dock, straight to the waters of the Narrows with a sailing vessel in front of the Brooklyn shore. This scene dramatically shows his keen ability to lead the eye into the composition. Fred. S. Cozzens did another Staten Island scene which showed Tompkinsville on the night of May 20, 1879, when an explosion of petroleum occurred on board the bark, *Amalfi*, lying at anchor off Staten Island. A woodcut of Cozzens' version of this scene was later reproduced in *Leslie's Magazine* on June 7, 1879.

In the September 4, 1879 issue of *Harper's Weekly*, one entire page was devoted to Cozzens' drawings of the quarantine station of New York Bay. Every ship that came into New York Harbor was required to weigh anchor in the Narrows before entering the harbor so the quarantine doctor could board the vessel to make sure that no infectious disease was on board. If there was any evidence of cholera, yellow fever or plague, the ship was quarantined in front of the station, which was located on the Staten Island shore. The sick patients were removed from the ship and placed in a hospital on the grounds of the station. The crews of every ship were subject to this examination as well as the passengers of the ships carrying immigrants from Europe to America.

The existence of the quarantine hospital had been a source of irritation to the residents of Staten Island because of the danger of contamination. The shore near the station where the ships were anchored was strewn with filth of all kinds. As the ships lay at enforced anchor, their cargo was unloaded and the stevedores moved in and out of the villages associating freely

THE BUOY STATION, QUARANTINE LANDING, STATEN ISLAND.

LOWER QUARANTINE.

SWINBURNE ISLAND HOSPITAL.

DOCTOR'S BOAT.

UPPER QUARANTINE.

F. S. COZZENS

QUARANTINE, NEW YORK BAY.—DRAWN BY F. S. COZZENS.

28

with the natives. As a consequence, any disease inside the infected ships or within the hospital compound, quickly found its way outside and spread to nearby villages. The residents repeatedly requested the removal of the hospital but all their efforts were in vain.

Finally, in 1857, the people took matters into their own hands and burned the pier that ran into the water from the station to prevent any sick people landing from infected vessels, but the pier was rebuilt. On September 2, 1858, an armed group of volunteer citizens invaded the walled compound and burned every hospital building to the ground. It was then decided that the two islands lying off the shore of Staten Island should be used for the new quarantine station. Hoffman Island (Upper Quarantine) and Swinbourn or Dix Island (Lower Quarantine) became the new homes. Until the buildings could be erected, a floating hospital, called the *Falcon* or *Florence Nightingale*, was used.

The quarantine affair was a hotly discussed issue at this time. It epitomized the attitude of the authorities who disregarded the health and well-being of the entire population by insisting on the continuation of a condition that was obnoxious to them. Ever alert to public issues, *Harper's Weekly* asked Cozzens to do some drawings which would graphically tell the story. Cozzens relished this type of assignment and presented it in novel form: the drawings to be tacked to a board. He curled up the corners of every picture and even drew a realistic tear in one corner.

Harper's Weekly used one entire page to present his four drawings. A tiny one shows the doctor's gig being rowed out to a sailing vessel anchored in the Narrows. The upper fourth of the page shows the floating hospital ship that was used from 1859 to 1863. Cozzens depicted her as a desolate vessel, emphasizing the monotonous large black hull with little or no superstructure. Although there are many sailing vessels in the background, one feels the isolation and apartness of the vessel. The center drawing shows a picture of Swinbourn Island after the hospital buildings had been erected. Cozzens even included a small dory that was used to remove patients from the ship to

GRAIN SHIPS LAID UP IN GOWANUS CREEK—WAITING FOR CARGOES.—Drawn by Fred. S. Cozzens.

the hospital. It had a canopy to protect them from the sun or rain as they were being transferred. The bottom half page drawing shows the water area in front of the quarantine area with many ships waiting for clearance from the doctors. There are sailing vessels as well as a few steam-sail vessels in enforced idleness. A tiny tug pokes her nose between the vessels. One ship lists badly as her cargo is being unloaded. Although the scene is crowded with many ships huddled together, there is an air of dejection and despair implicit in the work. Cozzens used this patient, listless waiting of ships again in 1880 when he depicted the grain ships at Gowanus Creek awaiting cargo.

Harper's Weekly asked Cozzens to make a pen and ink drawing of the Sandy Hook Lightship, which was frequently used as a marker in racing competition. It was used in the September 27, 1879 issue and is recognizable in many of his watercolors of racing scenes.

One of the most interesting events that Fred. S. Cozzens covered for Harper's Weekly was the arrival in America of Cleopatra's Needle, an ancient Egyptian commemorative pillar that had originally been erected by Thutmose III before the gates of the Temple of Heliopolis. In the year 22 B.C. this monumental stone pillar, covered with hieroglyphic writing, was moved from Heliopolis to adorn the Caesareum, which Cleopatra had started to honor her son, Caesarium. In the late 19th century, a movement was started to bring this upright monolith to America to be installed in New York City. The removal from Alexandria to New York City and the transportation by water to its new home was fraught with difficulty. A special ship, the Dessoug, was altered to carry it over the Atlantic Ocean. When this important relic of ancient civilization arrived in America, the boat was dry-docked in Clifton, Staten Island, to facilitate the removal of the huge stone. Cozzens had ample opportunities to see every aspect of its removal from the hold of the ship (by removing plates from the hull) as well as the transportation by barge to New York City and Central Park where it was erected and still stands.

The group of six drawings supplied by Cozzens to illustrate this trip occupied an entire page in the September 8, 1880 issue of *Harper's Weekly*. There is one large central picture of the ship, *Dessoug*, with the obelisk being removed from a hole in the hold of the ship. He did five smaller drawings. *Obelisk in Hold of Dessoug* shows the large stone chained in place. There is a lateral view of the obelisk being removed by crane from the ship. Another drawing shows the copper craws or anchors which secure the stone to its base. The last drawing shows the obelisk being towed up New York Bay. Two tugs are pulling a large barge with the obelisk on its side as five men scamper about the barge at work. The entire group of drawings was captioned, "Removal of the Monolith from Hold."

Fred. S. Cozzens continued to receive commissions from many private individuals as well as newspapers and magazines. James Stillman gave him a commission in the early 1880s to do a painting of the yachts *Wenona* and *Muriel* racing under the Stillman signal. In 1880 he did a watercolor of the steam yachts *Corsair*, owned by J.C. Osborn, and *Stranger*, owned by George Osgood. Both pieces were reproduced in the August 7, 1880 issue of *Harper's Weekly*.

Harper's Weekly kept Cozzens busy in 1880. They used three of his drawings in the October 8, 1880 issue showing three different scenes of the race between the *Madge* and the *Schemer*. The first of the races in American waters with the British-built, Scotch cutter was sailed on September 27, 1880 over the Seawanhaka Course. Cozzens used this first match to illustrate the story. The sails of these two yachts billow in the breeze.

The exhibition records of the American Watercolor Society show that in the year 1880 Cozzens put two of his watercolors into the exhibition: *Morning Off the Isle of Shoals* and *Winter Down The Bay*. The New York Yacht Club exhibits an interesting set of six Cozzens watercolors which now decorate the grill of its clubhouse in New York City. All are dated 1880. Originally, the set of six pictures might have been commissioned by Frank Osborn, the owner of the schooner-yacht *Nettie*, to hang in the cabin of the *Nettie*, because she figures prominently in all six pictures.

LANDING THE BASE OF OBELISK

SHOWING THE ANCHORAGE OF OBELISK TO BASE

OBELISK IN HOLD OF DESSOUG.

F.S.Cozzens

REMOVING FROM THE HOLD.

THE OBELISK—THE PROCESS OF REMOVAL FROM THE "DESSOUG."—From Sketches by F. S. Cozzens.

THE STEAM-YACHTS "CORSAIR" AND "STRANGER."—Drawn by F. S. Cozzens.

The set is actually two three-part sets. Each has a long center picture and two smaller, flanking pictures. One center picture depicts a race with yachts, spectator boats, committee and work boats. The two companion pictures depict other racing events. The second center scene is a panoramic view of New York City and the harbor, seen from the stern of a vessel. It clearly shows Castle William and the Brooklyn Bridge, which was started in 1870 but not completed until 1883. The harbor is filled with craft of all kinds. It is a busy, mural-type picture. This is flanked by a powerful moonlight scene and a cold, winter scene. The six watercolors make a very unusual set of pictures.

The *Nettie* was built by Samuel Hart of Northport, Long Island for Charles Cromwell and had her rigging altered in New London in 1874. She was sold to Frank Osborn in 1878 and was held by him until 1880. She was later renamed *Nokomis*. Cozzens was familiar with the boat; when she was the *Nokomis*, she figured prominently in his famous set, "American Yachts" as Plate 21: *A Misty Morning; Drifting*, showing the *Utowana*, *Nokomis* (late *Nettie*), *Crusader* and *Hildegard*.

Harper J. Russell, in his book, *Early Painters and Engravers of Canada*, mentions a Cozzens watercolor of a ship collision off Newfoundland that was done in 1880. Cozzens also did a fine watercolor of the Robbins Reef Lighthouse with two men in a dory in this same year.

In 1881 another group of Cozzens' black and white drawings were used as a cover for the February 19, 1881 issue of *Harper's Weekly*. The caption was "Ice Yachting on the Hudson" and it shows one large central picture of three men sailing an iceboat. Two smaller drawings below are captioned, *Rearing* showing an iceboat on one side, and *Air Hole* showing two iceboats capsizing while their crews are dumped about. Two tiny vignettes were used to fill in the two upper corners of the front sheet.

A superb watercolor by Fred. S. Cozzens almost certainly depicts November 9, the first day of the 1881 America's Cup race. The first sloop in the painting, displaying her blue and white striped burgee and accurately portrayed with her clipper hull is the *Gracie*, owned by Messrs. Charles R. Flint and Joseph P. Earle. The second sloop, with her red, white and blue burgee and her plumb stem hull, is the *Mischief*, owned by Joseph R. Busk, an Englishman by birth, who was a member of the New York Yacht Club. The third sloop is the *Atalanta*, the challenger from the Canadian Bay of Quinte Yacht Club in Belleville, Ontario, owned by Captain Alexander Cuthbert. The left side of the painting shows the marker boat, the committee boat and the steamer, *Sirius* of the Iron Steamboat Company, which went over the course carrying spectators.

The year 1881 was an important one in the history of the America's Cup races for several reasons. It was the first year that the race was held between single-masted sloops, as op-

Ice Yacht 1,
Courtesy of the New York Yacht Club

Ice Yacht 2,
Courtesy of the New York Yacht Club

Ice Yacht 3,
Courtesy of the New York Yacht Club

posed to the, until then, traditional double-masted schooners. It was the first year that official trial races were held to determine which yacht would be the defender, and the circumstances surrounding the races occasioned several changes in the Deed of Gift (the rules governing future races).

However, perhaps the most fascinating thing about the 1881 America's Cup race was the dramatic story behind the race itself, for although the contenders were the Canadian challenger *Atalanta* and the officially designated defender, *Mischief*, in reality, as Cozzens' painting shows, the contest was between the two N.Y.Y.C. sloops, the *Gracie* and the *Mischief*, with the story being as follows: As the time of the race approached, it was generally felt that the *Atalanta* did not pose a truly dangerous threat, but it was decided to hold a series of three trial races

Ice Yacht 4,
Courtesy of the New York Yacht Club

Ice Yacht 5,
Courtesy of the New York Yacht Club

Ice Yacht 6,
Courtesy of the New York Yacht Club

on October 12, 19 and 20 between the *Mischief*, the *Gracie*, the *Hildegard* and the *Pocahontas* to determine the defender. *Mischief* won the first, which was also the only race in which the *Hildegard* participated. *Gracie* won the second and, from contemporary newspaper reports, seemed to be the favorite of N.Y.Y.C. members. However, in the third race *Gracie* was delayed a full two minutes by an obstinate tug, the *Egbert Myers*, and lost the race to *Mischief*—but by only fourteen seconds. Whereupon, the *Gracie* challenged the *Mischief* to a series of five races to determine the defender; this challenge was not accepted.

It was then decided that the final selection would not be made until the first day of the race itself and that meanwhile, both *Gracie* and *Mischief* were to be held in readiness for the race. The official reason for the last minute decision was consideration of the weather. Nevertheless, the decision in favor of *Mischief* was announced on November 8, although the race could not take place that day because of the heavy fog. The choice elicited considerable controversy because the *Gracie* was generally favored, having won seven out of her last nine contests with the *Mischief*. This drama culminated on the day of the race, November 9. Of her own accord, the *Gracie* went over the course with *Mischief* and *Atalanta*; *Atalanta* rapidly fell far behind and *Gracie* made better time than *Mischief*, who was still, of course, the official winner. However, contemporary newspaper reports included all details of *Gracie*'s performance, right along with those of *Mischief* and *Atalanta*. In a postscript to the race, an indignant letter was sent to the newspapers objecting to *Gracie*'s self-determined participation. It drew the response that in fact, the *Gracie* had fulfilled an obligation in providing yachtsmen and the public with a real contest, which they would have been denied otherwise.

The Museum of the City of New York has a typical Cozzens version of an exciting yacht racing scene showing the yachts *Sappho* and *Livonia*, drawn in 1871. Another yachting scene in the same museum is of the two yachts *Puritan* and *Genesta* dated 1881.

HARPER'S WEEKLY.

A JOURNAL OF CIVILIZATION

Vol. XXV.—No. 1260.] NEW YORK, SATURDAY, FEBRUARY 19, 1881. [SINGLE COPIES TEN CENTS.
[$4.00 PER YEAR IN ADVANCE.

Entered according to Act of Congress, in the Year 1881, by Harper & Brothers, in the Office of the Librarian of Congress, at Washington.

"ROARING"

AIR HOLE

ICE-YACHTING ON THE HUDSON.—Drawn by F. S. Cozzens.

An active portrayal of a tug at work in the harbor was drawn by Cozzens in 1878. The New York Historical Society exhibits a wash and opaque drawing entitled, *River Tow*, which is dated 1879 and shows a paddlewheel towing barges with a man in a dory in the foreground. "No. 6 River Tow" is written in the lower left corner.

In 1882 *Harper's Weekly* reproduced a Cozzens watercolor of an old whaler hove down for repairs near New Bedford. This is a dock scene with many old buildings in the background and nine or ten men working on the hull of the boat. The name beneath is Frederic Swartwout Cozzens, obviously a mistake, since Cozzens Sr. had been dead for many years.

In his book, *Adventures of America 1857–1900: A Pictorial Record from Harper's Weekly*, the author, John A. Kouenhoven, reproduced this picture of an old whaling ship hove down for repairs that had appeared in the 1882 issue of the weekly. These whaling ships were part of the battered remnant of a fleet which had numbered more than four hundred ships thirty years before.

Cozzens also exhibited in the 1882 American Watercolor Society annual exhibition, *A Fair Wind*. The State University of New York has a Cozzens drawing of a girl sitting on a stranded boat, done on the back of a sheet of music. It is a pencil sketch dated July 20, 1882.

The 1883 annual exhibition records of the American Watercolor Society reveal that he exhibited a watercolor that he entitled *A Free Wind*. The Royal Vancouver Yacht Club possesses a Cozzens watercolor of sailing vessels in the vicinity of a lightship that was done in 1883. The Peabody Museum of Salem, Massachusetts has one of his watercolors of the British steamer, *Egypt*, that is dated 1883. She had been built in Scotland in 1871 and was shown by Cozzens running a gale. According to the Bicentennial Inventory of American Paintings compiled by the Smithsonian Institution in 1976, Cozzens also did a watercolor of a sailboat race from San Francisco to Hawaii in 1883. He also drew Admiral Pauling with his staff reviewing the

Fred. S. Cozzens
86

"GRACIE."

Fred. S. Cozzens
86

"MISCHIEF."

United States Fleet off Oyster Bay in the same year. This watercolor is in the Franklin Delano Roosevelt Library in Hyde Park, New York.

The Newport Historical Society has a process print of the steam iron-collier, *Frostburg*, that he drew in 1884. The Annals of American Sport used a centerfold of a Cozzens version of the *Atalanta* that was dated 1883.

Frederic S. Cozzens started on his career as a marine artist in the 1860s. By 1883 he was well-established and was thinking of ways to expand his art work. Starting in the year 1884, he did a tremendous amount of work. He had found a way to popularize his work by making marine watercolors available to the public in sets of lithographs.

The first of these sets of prints to appear was a brilliant series of twenty-six yacht prints published as "American Yachts, Their Clubs and Races" by Charles Scribner's Sons in New York in 1884. They were published in full color facsimile and James Douglas Jerrold Kelley, then a lieutenant in the United States Navy, wrote a separate text describing Cozzens' prints. The book was illustrated with outline sketches of the watercolors in the set of prints.

River Tow

There are twenty-six prints, plus an extra print, in the portfolio. On the verson of each plate is a label which reads, 'Artist's Proof, Number__," containing the number, title, names of the yachts in the plate and the date of the race, i.e. "American Yachts, Plate XII, *Over the Cape May Course* by Fred. S. Cozzens. Facsimile by Armstrong and Company. Copyright 1884 by Charles Scribner's Sons."

Color facsimiles are usually produced in two states. The first state, known as "artist's proof", is the early impression, signed by the artist. These are limited in number and are usually printed on a handmade paper. They also bear the stamp of the Fine Art Guild, the buyer's guarantee that the limited number is not exceeded.

AN OLD WHALER HOVE DOWN FOR REPAIRS, NEAR NEW BEDFORD.—Drawn by F. S. Cozzens.

The second state, or subsequent impressions, known as color prints do not bear the signature of the artist but in other respects are similar to the first. The size stated is exclusive of margins but there is usually a toned border which, when desired, allows for framing close to the artist's signature without showing white.

The prints of the Cup Race winners are matted and the titles are mounted on the mats in an embossed design of oars and steering wheels embossed with an imprint of the mug of the Royal Squadron. They are decorated with blue and gold ribbons.

The prints were published in heavy cardboard mount with extra margins of three to four inches. There was also issued in 1884 a Deluxe edition limited to 250 copies. One of the Deluxe editions is in the Library of Congress.

Lieutenant Kelley's book describes the events shown in each plate. The book also contains a good description of the race and much general information about the history of yachting. It also gives technical descriptions about boats and owners: "Extreme boats will not do for cruising and hence the men who can own but one boat and desire comfort, safety and speed as well, cannot hope to compete with knife edges or skimming dishes which are designed purely for racing purposes."

In the preface, Lieutenant Kelley wrote, "In these pictures of our pleasure fleet, the portrait of no boat has been painted until all possible means tending to accuracy have been exhausted. Whenever possible, the originals have been found, within the year devoted to this art work, they were carefully painted, both under sail and at anchor. Failing this, studies were made of verified photographs and plans and in many cases the finished picture was submitted to the owners of the boats represented, and when the criticism was just, for yachtsmen are not among the keenest critics of their own vessels, these were accepted and the work revised until it received the imprimatur of those most nearly interested. Finally, a number of plates were exposed in yacht clubrooms to the frank and solicited judgment of experienced yachtsmen and the opinions expressed were carefully considered."

Admiral Pauling Reviewing the Fleet off Oyster Bay,
Courtesy of the Franklin Delano Roosevelt Library, Hyde Park

As if to reassure the readers of the artist's integrity, Kelley wrote in another part of the book that the sketches are the result of sincere and honest labor and, that in one sense at least are unlike those poems and pictures dashed off by gentlemen of quality in moments of elegant leisure.

Mr. Cozzens' work included portraits of more than one hundred craft including sloops, steamers, schooners, iceboats, cutters, catboats, pilotboats and yawls. The craft are shown under sail in favorite American waters: New York Bay, Cape May, Sandy Hook, the Hudson River, off New London, Newport, Nantucket, Boston Bay and Marblehead.

Many of the sketches depict Cup Races and other notable events in yachting annals. Plate #25, *Ice Boating on the Hudson,* is catalogued separately. Plate #27 contains pennants.

The editor of *The Month At Godspeeds* wrote, "These splendid pictures of billowing canvas and rolling sea seem to get better each time one looks them. They are mellowing as all good things should. But for all the tides that have ebbed since Cozzens painted these beautiful ships, the thought of the races they ran still excites the mind. We recall stories of monies won and lost, of the winner's thrill and the loser's gloom, of the champagne uncorked and winners and losers engulfed in a golden haze together. The colors are warm and delicate. Cozzens grew up to be one of the finest of all American painters of yachting scenes."

Even the titles of each print stand as a tribute to Cozzens' imagination and verve. They are exceedingly nautical and the name of each watercolor conveys the very spirit of racing: *A Stern Chase and a Long One; Before the Wind; A Breezy Day, Outside.*

This set of twenty-seven paintings are among the strongest paintings the artist produced. Fred. S. Cozzens combined keen observation of shapes and forms and used these boldly as the central theme of his work. Above all, he was able to convey the atmosphere of that precise moment, as well as the thrill and excitement engendered by the event. He created a solid, three-dimensional form of space, light and elements that recreates the scene for the observer. The series is a wonderful panorama that stretches before one's eyes. In this series, Cozzens recorded yachting and sailing from the first Cup Race of the *America* until the year 1884.

Plate #1, *The Early Racers* shows the brave old *America*, winner of the first International Race, August 22, 1851, the *Maria, Una* and the *Ray* of the New York Yacht Club. Regattas and matches were common among the larger yachts and public interest was awakened by the racing of such yachts as the *Maria, Cornelia* and *Una*.

The yacht, *Maria*, named in honor of the wife of John Cox Stevens, was an exaggerated New York sloop built in the Hoboken shipyard of William Capes in 1845. She was the wonder and delight of sailors on both sides of the Atlantic both for her speed and for the experiments made in her design in the interest of all yachting. Capes had embodied in her design and construction more radical innovations than could be found in any other yacht. The owners of the *Maria* often raced the incoming European steamers for enjoyment.

The *Una*, a centerboard sloop, was sixty feet on the water line and was owned by J. M. Waterbury. She was forty-six tons and so speedy that she could make the run from Boston to New York in thirty-two hours. The *Una* was converted into a schooner by the Marquis of Conynham who had bought the boat from the yards of Captain Bob Fish of Pamrapo in 1852. He later shipped her to Europe. The generic name, *Una*, refers to the class of which she was a prototype.

The schooner, *America*, was designed and built by George Steers, for John C. Stevens, Hamilton Wilkes, G. L. Schuyler, James Hamilton, J. Beekman Finley and Edward A. Stevens, all members of the New York Yacht Club. This clipper yacht, winner of the Cup in the great match for all nations at Cowes on August 22, 1851, provided a name for sailing's greatest trophy and agitated the world's most powerful woman, Queen

The Early Racers,
Courtesy of the New York Yacht Club

Sandy Hook to the Needles, 1866,
Courtesy of the New York Yacht Club

Victoria. When the *America* was on the last leg of her race against fourteen British yachts on August 22, 1851, Queen Victoria asked who was in the lead. *"America,"* she was told. Then she asked, "Who is second?" "Ah!, Your Majesty, there is no second," was the answer. *America* had truly outdistanced her rivals.

The history of the *America* is well known. In 1850, an English merchant suggested that one of the fast pilot boats, so popular in America, be sent to England to take part in a yacht race to be held during the time of the great Trade Exposition in London. A syndicate of six yachtsmen commissioned George Steers to build a wooden keel schooner of about 170 tons at the yards of William H. Brown at the foot of 12th Street and the East River in New York City. She was 101 feet long overall and of one hundred and forty-six tons displacement. She carried two masts. Her mainsail was eighty-one feet long and her foremast seventy-nine feet, six inches. They were stepped with a strong rake that was characteristic of the pilot schooners that navigated in and out of New York Harbor. She carried 5,263 square feet of sail in mainsail, foresail and single jib.

The *America* proved to be the most popular yacht ever built. She crossed the Atlantic Ocean in July 1851 to take part in the August 22 race open to yachts of all nations called the First International Race of Cowes, Isle of Wight. The prize was a silver cup valued at one hundred guineas offered by the Royal Yacht Squadron to be held as a world trophy

The course of the original race was round the Isle of Wight inside No Man's Buoy and Sand Head Buoy and outside the Nab Lightship. Fifteen vessels left from the starting line at Cowes; fourteen of these were members of the Royal Yacht Squadron.

The typical American yacht, at that time, was recognized as a boat of light displacement, large sail area and great initial stability with small reserve against capsizing. The yacht, *America*, was radically different from the usual English yacht and she made an unfavorable impression on the British boatmen who were unfamiliar with her design. However, one can refer to Cozzens' line drawing of the *America* used to illustrate *The America's Cup Race*, by Herbert L. Stone, William H. Taylor and William W. Robinson, P. II, to see the graceful form and lines of this racing yacht. She had a long, sharp, lean, concave bow and heavy, raking masts with no topmasts.

It was asking a great deal to have one yacht sail against a whole fleet, especially over a course for a good part of the distance not in open water. One of the London newspapers wrote on the morning of the race, "The course around the Isle of Wight is notoriously one of the most unfair to strangers that can be selected and indeed does not appear to be a good raceground to anyone in as much as the current and tides render local knowledge of more value than swift sailing and nautical skill."

When the boats arrived for the race, *America* was at the line waiting for the starting signal with fourteen English cutters and schooners ranging in size from one at forty-seven tons, the *Aurora*, up to a 392 ton three-masted schooner, the *Brilliant*. The 170 ton *America* was one of the last to get away. In sailing the course, *America* defeated the entire fleet of vessels and was awarded the cup.

In 1857, the owners of the *America* gave the cup to the New York Yacht Club to be held thereafter as an international yachting trophy. Instead of the One Hundred Guinea Cup, it has become known as the America's Cup and is the most coveted yachting trophy in the world. Although it is no beauty, it is typical of the ornate taste of that era. The deed of gift stated that any yacht could challenge for a match with a vessel of thirty to 300 tons. Although some minor rules have been changed as to competition, it remains essentially a trophy for expert yachtsmen and millions of dollars have been spent to "lift" the cup from the New York Yacht Club where it remains.

The history of the America's Cup encompasses the history of naval architecture as well as the sport of racing. The yacht came to epitomize the finest racing craft sailed in a spirit of sportsmanship in competition. The *America* did much to revi-

An Old Rendezvous—New London,
Courtesy of the New York Yacht Club

Off Brenton's Reef,
Courtesy of the New York Yacht Club

talize the design of yachts and gave yachting the greatest impetus it has ever known.

In Plate #1, one is immediately aware of the great esteem and affection that Cozzens felt for the boat; he delineated the *America* much larger than the other boats and her sails and masts were drawn with precision.

Plate #2 shows the great ocean race; *Sandy Hook to the Needles*, December 11, 1866. There are three large sailing ships, an observation boat and a dory in the left foreground. Sandy Hook is in the right background. The picture contains action and excitement. It shows the yachts, *Henrietta*, *Vesta* and *Fleetwing*. The *Vesta* and *Fleetwing* had made a match for a large sum of money to sail across the Atlantic Ocean. It became a stake race when the *Henrietta* was admitted to the contest. No other yachting event awakened so much international interest as this ocean race. The novelty of the match, the magnitude of the prize, the rigorous season of the year and the length of the course all invested the contest with a touch of interest to yachtsmen and to the general public as well.

The *Henrietta* was a keel-type schooner, built for James Gordon Bennett in 1861 by Henry Steers at Greenpoint in New York. She presented a beautiful marine design in her hollow bow, short counter and sailor-like rig.

Fleetwing was a keel-type schooner, built for George Osgood by Van Deusen in 1865 and owned by Robert S. Elliott. She was long and graceful.

The *Vesta* was a centerboard schooner, built by David Carll in 1866 at City Island for Pierre Lorillard. Her quarters were round and her upper spars stood with little rake.

George and Franklin Osgood bet Pierre Lorillard Jr. and others $30,000 that the *Fleetwing* could beat the *Vesta* to the Needles on the coast of England. The yachts were to start from Sandy Hook on the second Tuesday in December, 1866. Part of the conditions of the race were the sails to be carried; these were

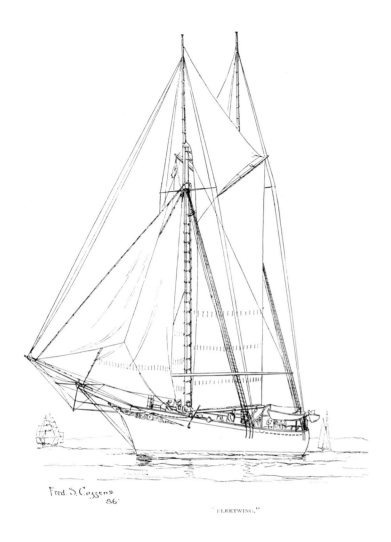

Fred. S. Cozzens
86

"FLEETWING."

mainsails, foresails, jib, flying jib, topsails, fore and main gaff topsails, staysails and trysails. There was also a square sail.

Then James Gordon Bennet, Jr., requested to be admitted to the match, which was to be held on December 11, 1866. On a cool, clear, winter morning, with a fresh northerly wind, the three got away from Staten Island and stood down the Narrows. One disaster struck the *Fleetwing* on December 19th at 9 P.M. In a rising gale with heavy seas running, *Fleetwing* was boarded by a sea over the quarter and the watch on deck of eight men was washed out of the cockpit. Six of them were lost. The yacht broached to, lost her jib boom and lay hove-to for five hours before resuming her course.

The *Henrietta* picked up the Scilly Lights before resuming her course Christmas Eve at 7:45. She had sailed the whole course without a tack and was but eleven miles out from the straight line from start to finish. She passed the *Lizard* at 3 A.M. Christmas morning and at 3:45 she passed the Needles, the winner. The *Vesta* went astray in a slight fog so she did not finish until forty minutes after midnight.

Lt. Kelley described the start of the race, "Tuesday, the eleventh of December 1866 was clear, cool and bright with breeze fresh enough from westward to tumble into foam flags the white caps of the Lower Bay. The yachts lay at anchor and with sails lowered off Staten Island and clustered around them, to accompany them down the Harbor and to send them over the bar with the hearty God-Speed, was a fleet made up of every type vessel our water knew. The excitement of the race had grown day by day and when starting time approached, had reached the high water mark of intensity and earnest hopes. When the tugs towed the yachts toward the Hook, the enthusiasm bordered on summer madness. Cheers rang on cheers, steamers, filled with exultant sympathizers, circled about the racers. Salutes thundered from the government center and from the forts which guard the harbor mouth and from every spire and turret. From the top of the hill-crowned shore, flags waved joyously, dipping in graceful recognition as the yachts slipped through the breezy Narrows." Cozzens has

Rounding the Lightship,
Courtesy of the New York Yacht Club

The Finish off Staten Island,
Courtesy of the New York Yacht Club

caught the excitement of the start of that race. More than one hundred years later, one can still feel the thrill and excitement of the race when looking at the print. The International Races of 1870 and 1871 were the direct result of the great ocean race from Sandy Hook to the Needles that Cozzens has pictured in Plate #2.

Plate #3 is entitled, *An Old Rendezvous, New London*. The waters of Long Island Sound have long been the favorite cruising grounds of vessels owned in the New York area. There is every reason why this should be the favorite sailing resort for it possesses a charming landscape on one side,with deep bays and white beaches on the other. Its surface is dotted with picturesque islands and everywhere, within moderate runs, are beautiful harbors. New London was considered an ideal spot with cool, sea breezes and rock-bound coves.

Cozzens has placed the yacht, *Julia*, in the center, with the yacht, *Valkyr*, in the right foreground and the yacht, *Jessie*, in the left foreground. *St. Mary's* is on the right.

Julia, built in 1854 by George Steers for Mr. Waterbury of the New York Yacht Club, was a centerboard sloop, seventy-seven feet in length. In 1863 she was altered to a keel schooner and she was known, thereafter, as an altered centerboard or keel-type schooner. At last, she received a new name, *Nirvana*. *St. Mary's*, in the background of the scene, was a school ship. *Jessie* was a catamaran owned by Mr. Cartol of Philadelphia. She was built by Farren in Yonkers in 1877 and was considered to be very fast. *Valkyr* was a centerboard cutter. She was a comfortable, fast yacht, owned by J. E. Schermerhorn. She had been built in Greenpoint by Driscoll in 1881 and was fifty-four feet long.

Plate #4 is entitled *Off Brenton's Reef*. It pictures the cutters, *Ileen*, *Wenonah* and *Oriva*. Cozzens Placed the *Wenonah* in the center with the *Oriva* on the right and the *Ileen* in the left background. The race was over an ocean course of 275 miles.

With increasing leisure, more money and a higher appreciation of the mental and physical value of the sport of yachting, there came a desire for blue water cruising and for longer voyages. These begat a taste for sea life, and as rough water and moderate gales taught the deficiencies of our boats, a demand was created for vessels with hard weather qualities. Hence, safer, more seaworthy yachts were required and though many large vessels were built, the popular taste for the sport was made evident in the increase of smaller boats. Then the cutter began to prove its value. Three conditions govern the building and use of a yacht; speed, safety and comfort. All three yachts pictured in Plate #4 were cutters.

The *Oriva* was sixty-two foot class keel cutter with a conventional rig with loose footed mainsails and chain halyards for her jib. She sailed pluckily and intelligently. She had been built by Piepgrass in 1881 and was owned by C. Smith Lee of New York. *Wenonah* was a keel-type cutter designed by John Harvey of England and built by Piepgrass in 1882 for James Stillman of New York. She had Lapthorne sails, was sixty feet on the water line and had the same type of construction as the Harvey Cutters, *Oriva* and *Bedouin*. She placed at the head of all single stick craft in this country. *Ileen* was a keel-type cutter; the most treme cutter yet built in this country. She was seventy-eight feet long and was built by Piepgrass in 1883. She was owned by A. Padelford of New York. Cutters had long been popular in England with yachtsmen and now this type of boat was beginning to become known and appreciated in this country.

Plate #5 is called, *Rounding the Lightship* and Cozzens crowded it with sailing craft and excursion boats. A stern view of the yacht, *Fanny,* is presented as she spreads her sails to move quickly. *Gracie* is pictured in the center of the scene and *Rover* can be seen coming into view on the right. This plate shows the crack American sloops rounding the lightship.

The victories of the yacht, *Gracie,* outnumber those of any other single-masted vessel afloat in these waters. She was a seventy-nine foot long, large and shallow centerboard sloop, built at Nyack, New York by Polyhemus in 1868. She raced in the

In the Narrows—A Black Squall,
Courtesy of the New York Yacht Club

Running Out—New Bedford,
Courtesy of the New York Yacht Club

cup race trials at Newport with the yachts, *Hildegard, Pocohantus* and *Mischief*, when the *Mischief* defeated her. She was lengthened twice and completely rebuilt by David Carll with double headsail rig. She was owned by C. R. Flint and J. P. Earle of New York.

The yacht, *Fanny,* was a seventy-two foot, large centerboard sloop, designed by Richmond of Mystic, Connecticut in 1876. *Fanny* was famous not only for the speed of the boat but for the excellent seamanship of her crew. Owned by W. R. Travers of New York who regularly raced her with the yachts, *Mischief* and *Hildegard*, in 1885, she was in the Autumn Regatta with the schooner, *Zinga* and the sloops, *Rebecca* and *Mannering.*

The yacht, *Rover,* was a centerboard sloop built by Piepgrass in 1880 for W. E. Iselin of New York in Greenpoint, New York. She was 45.6 feet overall in Length.

Plate #6 was named by Cozzens, *Second International Race, The Finish off Staten Island, Magic* defeating *Cambria*, August 8, 1870, showing *Cambria, Dauntless, Idler, Magic* (late *Madgie*)".

The race for the possession of the challenge cup took place on the eighth of August, 1870 and throughout the country there was the greatest interest manifested in the result. The course was from the Anchorage to the buoy off the South West Spit, passing the lightship and returning the same way. The day opened overcast and gloomy and soon after daybreak, heavy rain clouds brooded threateningly over the bay; but by nine o'clock the sky shone bright and clear and a bright and cheery southerly breeze blew bravely landward. They sailed "with a fresh breeze from south-by-east to southward with smooth water."

It was emphatically a holiday and though our lower bay had seen a grander array of contesting yachts before, in regular regattas of the home club, never before was there such a gathering of gleaming canvas and representation craft. Excursion boats overburdened every ripplet of water not occupied by the contestants, fruiters and pleasure boats. There were also peaceful inland watercraft, even up-river schooners and lumbering loggers sharing in the general desire to be a part of a memorable yachting day.

There were, in all, eighteen starters. *Alarm* was at the extreme eastern end of the line of yachts and *Widgeon* next, followed by the *Sylvie, Dauntless, Tarolinta, Halcyon, Madgie, Idler, Rambler, Phantom, Fleetwing, Madeleine, Calypso, America, Tidal Wave* and *Cambria,* to the *Alice* which led the extreme western end.

The contender, *Cambria,* was a keel schooner of the deep, narrow English type owned by James Ashbury. The course for the contest was set after lengthy negotiations. The *Dauntless,* owned by James Godon Bennett, agreed to race the *Cambria* from Daunt Head in Ireland to Sandy Hook. The *Cambria's* top sails were the first sighted twenty-two days later and she sailed across the finish line first. A loud wail went up from the American public. The *Cambria's* owner was the given the option of sailing for the America's Cup in one race over the club's regular course in New York Bay against the club's entire fleet. Thus, twenty-three were pitted against one.

The little *Magic,* one of the smallest in the squadron, favorably placed on the Bay Ridge Shore with a strong ebb tide under her, was able to lug well down through the Narrows and gained the lead. A dozen competitors rushed the America and gave her a rousing cheer as she flew by the forefront like a great sea bird. They all rushed for the Sandy Hook lightship. The schooner, *Magic,* rounded the lightship first. *Cambria,* the English challenger, was nearby.

During the match over unfamiliar water, the *Cambria* could not be expected to win. She finished in tenth place, twenty-three minutes after the leader, *Magic.* Thus, the first attempt to lift the cup failed. It was the last time that a challenger was asked to race against the entire fleet. This practice was decided to be unfair and unsportsmanlike and was discountinued.

The finish of that race has been immortalized by Cozzens. In Plate #6, he shows the finish off Staten Island with the *Magic*

Off Soundings—A Smokey Sou'wester,
Courtesy of the New York Yacht Club

Robbins Reef—Sunset,
Courtesy of the New York Yacht Club

rushing across the line in the fastest time ever made over the course. The stately schooner, *Dauntless*, passed by the marker next. The schooner, *Idler*, finished third and the *America* fourth.

Plate #7 was called, *In the Narrows, A Black Squall in New York Bay*; it shows a bad knockdown showing the sloop, *Active*, the catboat, *Dora*, the schooner, *Rambler* and the schooner, *Wanderer*.

It is in the unexpected squall that danger lies for the yachtsman. No waters are safe from squalls. On the afternoon of July 20, 1876, the schooner, *Mohawk*, lay at anchor, abreast the New York Yacht Club clubhouse on Staten Island. The weather had been threatening all during the day. Many light squalls had passed over. The owner of the *Mohawk*, William Garner, his wife and a party of friends, were on board, when a sudden squall struck her right abeam. She lurched and her cabin filled with water. She sank with five persons lost. No yachtsman could forget this tragedy.

On June 15, of the next year, one of the most remarkable regattas of the New York Yacht Club was sailed. The race was made exciting from the very start. At the beginning, a sudden shift of wind, changed as if by magic the positions of the competitors, pushing those in the rear to the front at once. The varying strength of the wind in different parts of the bay sent some of the lucky ones bowling seaward·while others lay almost becalmed. Once outside the Hook, the breeze piped so merrily that the leading yacht was rounding the lightship before the last went past the buoy in the South West Spit and finally the culmination for such a marvelous day—there was a squall at the finish which was without parallel in such competition.

Only eleven yachts entered the contest that day but among them were the keel-schooners, *Wanderer, Rambler, Restless,* and *Nettie*. Also in the race were the second-class schooners, *Comet* and *Peerless*, the double-hulled, *Nereid*, the first-class sloop, *Vision* and the second-class sloops, *Ariadne, Active* and *Windward*.

Lt. Kelley wrote, "On the way home, the *Vision* was in the van followed by the *Comet*, *Wanderer* and *Rambler*. Halfway up to Lower Bay, the breeze suddenly shifted to the northwest and the weather quarters grew hoarse with wind and black brooding squalls. Over Staten Island there bent a dense and smoky arch of black through which a lurid glare of lightning flashed at times making the pall clinging to the slopes of the Island. The forts on either side were silhouetted against threatening clouds which every moment darkened at their base and grew, until their summits that had carried a golden lining from the sunshine behind, faded into the somber arching of the sky.

"Far up the Narrows, every sail was scurrying to a safe anchorage and as the racers roared along the foaming course, the squall became blacker and rushed faster vieing with the boats which should first reach the finish line off Staten Island. Into the darkness the yachts sped; the *Vision* flying rather than sailing; next the *Comet* tore past, foresail and flying jib coming down by the run as she crossed and behind her, not a hundred yards distant and going like Tam O'Shanter with the devil after him, came the *Wanderer* and *Rambler*.

"In an instant there was a flash of vivid, lurid brightness, followed by a moment of intense silence; so quiet, indeed, was it that the creaking of the blocks and the strain of the sheets could be heard and then, with a roar and a bellow, the bursting squall struck them both and lee-rails under, they staggered like stricken deer in a tangle of brake. The *Wanderer* reeled as if hurt to death, her bulwarks going under and the water flooding her breast high in the gangways; but down rattled the flashing sails and righting herself, defiantly, she stood there, quivering and palpitating, daring the fury of the storm—a perfect sea picture.

"The *Rambler* behind her keeled over until half her deck was submerged, while off to leeward, like the wounded wing of a seabird, flamed up in the darkness the huge main topsail of the *Wanderer*.

"In that instant, the lightning broke from the storm clouds sweeping to leeward and as the thunders from their bosoms

Around Cape Marblehead,
Courtesy of the New York Yacht Club

Over the Cape May Course,
Courtesy of the New York Yacht Club

awoke the rumbling echoes of the hill, the rain fell in torrents and then the sky grew clear and all the land and the sea were smiling, in the sunshine of the summer day."

Plate #7 shows all the action and excitement of that moment. It is a superb example of Cozzens' ability to catch and recreate a moment, a feeling, a mood.

Plate #8, entitled, *Running Out, New Bedford*—is a sweepstake race off New Bedford, showing the schooner, *Peerless*, the steamer, *Ruth*, the sloop, *Metric*, and the sharpie, *Roslyn*. The New Bedford Lighthouse can be seen in the background.

Peerless, shown in the left of the scene was built at Brooklyn in 1872 by Poillon Brothers and "is a tidy schooner just outside the limits where the sloop rig is banned, for her sixty-six feet upon the water line take her out of that debatable ground where, in vessels of our type, schooners should begin and lesser vessels end."

Ruth was a centerboard schooner, built at Noank by Palmer for Mr. Watson of New York in 1881. She was a beauty on the water. She is the largest boat in the scene. *Metric*, placed in the right foreground by Cozzens, was a fast sloop that had already made a name for herself among the small flyers of the Eastern Yacht Club. *Roslyn* is faintly seen in the right background. Lt. Kelley described the main characteristics of a sharpie. "The sharpie is supposed to date from 1835 and owes its existence to the oystermen of Connecticut, who originally pursued their calling in log canoes but were forced by the want of proper trees to resort to a flat-bottomed boat, which was rockered or rounded up at both ends. This was sometimes known as a skip-jack but Mr. Clapham of Roslyn, has introduced the nonpareil type in which the bow is immersed with the view of obviating the spanking or hammering of the flat floor when the boat is driven in rough water. The *Roslyn* had a sharp bow and a square transomed stern. The sails are of leg-of-mutton cut and they are extended by a horizontal sprit. Sandbag ballast is used and the boats are remarkably fast both on the wind and off. *Roslyn* was launched for Franklin Osgood by Clapham of Roslyn in 1883."

"INTREPID."

Plate #9, entitled, *Off Soundings; A Smoky Sou'wester*, shows the cutter, *Bedouin*, at the left of the scene, the schooner, *Intrepid*, in the center and the steamer, *Namouna*, at the right.

Among the most successful cruising boats of this era, one had to count the *Namouna* and the *Intrepid*. The latter was a keel-schooner, a cruising schooner of one hundred and sixteen feet overall in length, designed by A. Cary Smith for Lloyd Phoenix in 1878 with many notable changes in detail of hull and rig. She was a seagoing schooner of beautiful, underwater lines and graceful hull with a dashing, thoroughly fit man-of-war look about her from truck to keelson. She was properly a cruising boat and had travelled abroad and to the West Indies but had given a splendid account of herself in the few trials and races that she had entered. She had been built by Poillon Brothers of Brooklyn. The yacht, *Bedouin*, owned by Archibald Rogers, was built by Piepgrass in Williamsburgh from designs by Harvey and was eighty-three feet overall in length. She had made a good record for herself and her type in the Seawanhaka sloop and cutter races of 1882. The yacht, *Namouna*, was owned by James Gordon Bennett and was an iron, three-masted, screw schooner of 845 tons. She had been built in 1882 by Ward Stanton of Newburgh, New York to take the place of the *Polynia*, which had not developed the speed desired by her owner. Her performance proved her to be a speedy, seagoing craft and her beautiful model reasserted the claim that the American ship designers could build the best and the most graceful ships in the world.

The sloop, *Gracie*, and the American cutter, *Bedouin*, raced the *Priscilla* and the *Puritan* trying out in a Goelet Cup Trial off Newport in August of 1885 when the *Puritan* was chosen to defend the Cup against the British cutter, *Genesta*.

In Plate #10, *Robbins Reef*, off Staten Island is New York Harbor; "A Scrap among the Little Ones," Cozzens shows the yacht, *Albertina*, the largest yacht in the scene, at the left of the picture. The *Albertina* was the late *Susie S.* The yacht, *Lady Emma*, is in the center. She (the late *W. R. Brown*) was a small, shallow, centerboard sloop. The *Valiant*, a cutter, and a canoe, *Lita*, are in the right. This is a peaceful yachting scene painted at sunset.

By Sou'west Spit,
Courtesy of the New York Yacht Club

Moonlight on Nantucket Shoals,
Courtesy of the New York Yacht Club

The *Albertina* and *Lady Emma* are very good examples of the small, centerboard yachts which raced in American waters. Both boats are of the same general dimensions and are in marked contrast to the little cutter, *Valiant*.

The *Albertina*, built by Mc Giehan of Pamrapo in 1871, was owned by I. Smith of Brooklyn. The *Lady Emma* was a centerboard sloop built by H. Smedley of Brooklyn in 1874 and owned by E. L. Israel of New Orleans.

Robbins Reef is a lighthouse in the Upper Bay of New York harbor. It is off the northwest corner of Staten Island at the head of the Kill Van Kull, the body of water separating Staten Island from New Jersey. It is a busy waterway. According to an article in the *Staten Island Historian* in the July 1978 issue, Robbins Reef had been a detriment to navigation because it was in the direct and well-travelled route to Manhattan. In October 1835, the brig, *Chieftain*, went on the rocks at the reef in thick weather. Then, on March 2, 1838, the *Samson*, one of Captain Oliver Vanderbilt's ferry boats, broke open on the rocks as the tide fell. It was decided that a light was needed and on July 21, 1838, work began on the Robbins Reef Lighthouse. The name of the reef was of Dutch origin derived from "Robyn's Reft," meaning seal banks. Before a stone could be laid, Haselron and Warren, who were the contractors, had to remove great quantities of sand, mussels and snags which had found their way to the reef over the years.

The ship, *Henry Kneeland*, on its way to New York, proved the necessity for the accelerated completion of this lighthouse when it struck the reef in August of 1838. The lighthouse was finally in operation in 1839. In 1884 it was replaced with an iron substructure which is currently in operation.

Cozzens often used this particular light in his work. He lived on Staten Island and the light was, and still is, very visible to the inhabitants of the island. The lighthousekeeper or tender, rowed to Staten Island in a small rowboat for daily provisions.

Plate #11, *Around the Cape, Marblehead*; the crack yachts of New England showing the *Fearless, Gitana, Mona, Shadow* and *Fannie*.

Lt. Kelley wrote, "Of the yachts so cleverly painted by Mr. Cozzens, it need only be said that their records speak for them."

Mona was a narrow, deep-draft cutter with knife edge proportions that could be sailed by a small crew and knocks about the coast easily. *Hera* was a keel sloop and *Fannie* a catboat, named in honor of Fannie Herreshoff. *Fearless* was an old comfortable centerboard schooner that had been built in Bath in 1870 and had a comfortable history in American yachting. *Shadow* was a crack centerboard sloop built by the Herreshoffs. *Gitana* was a keel schooner built at East Boston in 1882 by Lawley of South Boston for J. Pfaff of Boston, who was, at that time, the commodore of the Boston Club.

At the time the book, *American Yachts, Their Clubs and Races* and the set of prints was published, there were fifteen regularly organized yacht clubs, cruising and racing in the waters to the northward of Cape Cod. Midway between Boston and Cape Ann Lights, Salem Bay opens into the land with an entrance four miles wide between Gale Head and Marblehead. On the shore lines of this deep, irregular indentation are the towns of Manchester, Beverly, Salem and Marblehead. Cozzens and Lt. Kelley were well aware of the large number of New England yachtsmen who sailed from the Boston, South Boston, Lynn, Dorchester, Eastern, Beverly, Jeffries, Quincy, Haverhill, Salem Bay, Cape Ann and Hull Yacht Clubs.

Plate #12, called *Over the Cape May Course*, with the working schooner, *Sharpshooter*, the pilotboat, *Negus*, the working schooner, *Reindeer*, the schooners, *Clio*, *Enchantress* and *Dreadnaught*.

The Regatta of 1873, open to all yachts, pilot boats, fishing and working boats, was over the Cape May Course which stretched to and south'ard well clear of the Jersey shallows, in waters which deepen a fathom to the mile, down to the lightship on the Five Fathom Bank, off the Delaware Capes and then home again. The race was to be run October 9, 1873 for a prize cup of the value of one thousand dollars to be run from an anchorage off Owl's Head, New York Harbor to and around the lightship in the Five Fathoms Bank off Cape May,

Lying-to off George's Bank,
Courtesy of the New York Yacht Club

A Stern Chase and a Long One,
Courtesy of the New York Yacht Club

New Jersey and return to the Sandy Hook lightship. Eighteen boats were entered; six were yachts, seven were pilotboats, four were working schooners and one was a smack.

Enchantress was a splendid keel schooner built by Captain Bob Fish in 1870. *Cilo* was a yacht modelled by William Townsend in 1873, a centerboard schooner. *Dreadnaught* was a keel-type, large, schooner-yacht.

The October day of the race was bright and beautiful. The air was pure and fresh. Overhead was a sky of the deepest blue without a single cloud to mar the breezy water sparkling in its sunshine. There were thirteen starters. The yachts were *Enchantress, Alarm, Dreadnaught, Clio* and *Eva*. The pilotboats were #2, *Edmund Blunt*, #10, *Widgeon*, #1, *T. S. Negus*, #4, *Mary E. Fish* and #7, *J. E. Elwell*. The working schooners were *W. H. Van Name, Reindeer,* and *Sharp Shooter*. The fishing smack was the *Wallace Blackford*.

This was a race thrown open to the competition of sailers of every degree, a contest hitherto narrowed to a class favored by fortune. This was a race of 300 miles, where the skill of crews was important, when subtle knowledge of rip tides and eddies may tell more than power of boats. *Clio* got away first. Kelley described it, "As the squadron passed the point of the Hook, it formed the finest marine picture the Bay has ever known for if the sea tossed turbulently, the wind was fresh and fair, and when the regatta steamer turned slowly landward, the schooners had squared away to the southward and, hull-down on the verge, were fading with glittering sails into the afterglow of a glorious day.

"When the ships passed the lightship, a wind was blowing half a gale so that Nils Olsen, who had been sent to the Cape with instructions to board the lightship in order to get the times of the passing yachts, was unable to make her, for the sea was such that no ordinary boat could have a fair chance in it.

"When the day broke, *Enchantress* was leading with all sails reefed by the wind and she drifted past the lightship first. It was ten hours before any more of the boats came into sight. First was the pilotboat, *Negus*, of the New Jersey fleet. Then the pilotboats, *Widgeon*, *Fish*, *Elwell* and *Blunt*, the schooners *Dreadnaught*, *Van Name* and finally, the yacht, *Clio*. The *Enchantress* won the cup.

"The victory of the *Enchantress* was one that ranks equally with that of any yacht in our waters, for it sailed splendidly under circumstances that were sufficient to test any boat and crew in the yachting world. The records of the *Negus* and *Widgeon* were equally admirable and proved that good seamanship in staunch, well-built boats will tell in contests even against those extreme models and equipment deemed essential to racing success."

Cozzens' picture is filled with billowing canvas. A sidewheel steam-sail is in the right background. There is excitement and tautness in the air.

Plate #13 is entitled, *By Sou'west Spit*, an excursion of the fleet on Decoration Day showing Class D and Class E sloops and schooners. These include *Roamer*, *Crocodile*, *Clytie*, *Grayling* and *Fanita*.

One of the most popular races for cabin yachts began at an imaginary line between the club steamer and Fort Wadsworth, went to Buoy Number Ten on the South West Spit, thence and around Buoy Number Eight and a Half thence to and around Sandy Hook lightship and returned over the same course. It was a thirty-seven mile run of good, inside yachting work.

One of the schooners entered in the race was *Grayling*, a ninety foot centerboard schooner, modelled by Phil Ellsworth for Latham Fish of the Atlantic Yacht Club. She was built by Poillon Brothers in 1883 and carried no inside ballast. Shortly after she had been put into commission, she was struck by a heavy squall and capsized; but she was raised and repaired to sail again. She was wide and shoal with the old sloop rig. Cozzens pictured her in the center background.

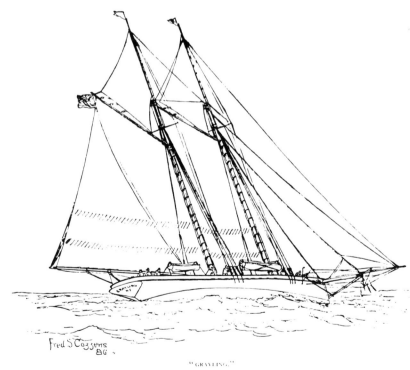

Fred S Cozzens 86

"GRAYLING."

A Breezy Day Outside,
Courtesy of the New York Yacht Club

Crossing the Line,
Courtesy of the New York Yacht Club

Clytie, a centerboard schooner, built by Ketchum in 1877 for A. P. Stokes of New York was a rather deep, early-type yacht. Cozzens placed her in the center left foreground, larger than any other yacht in the picture.

Fanita, a fifty foot sloop, had been built at Young at Greenpoint for G. J. Gould. A good boat, she was fast, safe and roomy. Cozzens pictured the *Fanita* at the extreme right.

Crocodile, was a centerboard sloop built by Poillon Brothers of Brooklyn for J. G. Prague of New York. *Roamer* was a centerboard sloop built by Mumm of Brooklyn in 1883 for J. W. Cooper of New York. Cozzens placed the *Crocodile* and *Roamer* side by side in the left background of the scene.

Plate #14 is called *Moonlight on Nantucket Shoals*; sailing by moonlight showing the steamer yacht, *Ibis*, the steamer yacht, *Tidal Wave*, the schooner, *Estelle*, the sloop, *Sagita* and the schooner, *Aeolus*.

Nantucket Shoals is the name given to the large extent of sandbanks and rips which extend to the eastward and south eastward of Nantucket Island. They are feared by the coaster who leaves the pleasant waters of the Sound for the boisterous open by a gateway which no one may approach without the utmost care. There are quicksands of varying depths so vexed by swirls of current and so shifted by every gale that blows that many a veteran pilot had found them a grave. The depth of the water varies from 6 feet to 4 fathoms and all the bars have specific names to define their general location.

But Nantucket Sound has in its eighteen miles of length, wide and deep channels through which skilled pilots can, in good weather, carry vessels without danger.

Tidal Wave, pictured by Cozzens in the left background of the scene, has been described as a "snake with a frog in her belly." She had been designed by Schank of Nyack in 1870 and had sailed in the Cup Race of 1870 with *Dauntless*, *Rambler*, etc.

Ibis, a wooden screw steam yacht, had been built by Hoagland in 1873 and altered to steam in 1875. Cozzens' picture of the *Ibis* is very tiny, in the far right distance.

Estelle was a centerboard schooner, built by Richards of Norwalk in 1874. She is pictured as the largest yacht in the center of the scene by Cozzens.

Sagita, a centerboard sloop, built in Islip, Long Island by Smith for H. C. Ward of New York, was pictured by Cozzens in the right foreground. One has a good picture of her deck and crew.

Aeolus, a centerboard sloop built in Patchogue, Long Island by Wood in 1881, was pictured in the far right distance.

Plate #15 is called, *Lying-to off George's Banks*, showing the schooner, *Norseman* and the schooner, *Atalanta*. Cozzens has given us an excellent picture of two sturdy yachts lying-to off those shoals which are so dangerous to mariners approaching our coast and to the unfortunate fishermen who are yearly offered up as a dreadful tribute to the fury of the Georges. These shoals are formed by a dangerous sand ridge, which is just one hundred miles from Cape Cod. The shoalest part is near the eastern end, and in 1821, this end was said to have as little as three feet of water on it. The bottom shifts constantly. A nasty dangerous sea is kicked up by these shoals. If ever the weather is bad and one is caught off it in a gale, every precaution should be taken. Not that good, large sea boats, like the yachts in the plate are liable to suffer, nor even staunch fishing vessels; but smaller craft, with insufficient crews and equipment and particularly the dories used in fishing need expect no mercy.

Still, vessels as small as these dories have lived out the furious gales beating upon its shoals and fog-ridden water. George's Banks was a famous fishing ground and many of Cozzens' work boats were pictured at this location.

The yacht, *Norseman* is pictured in the center of the scene, pulling away from the viewer. She was a keel schooner built in Brooklyn by the Poillon Brothers in 1881 for Ogden Goelet of New York.

Minot's Ledge Light,
Courtesy of the New York Yacht Club

America's Cup,
Courtesy of the New York Yacht Club

The yacht, *Atalanta* was a centerboard schooner, built by David Carll of City Island in 1873 for W. R. Vermilye of New York. She is pictured in the right background with two unidentified sailing craft.

Plate #16 is entitled, *A Stern Chase and a Long One*, June 1876. It shows the *Countess of Dufferin (now Countess)*, *America*, *Grant* and *Madeleine*.

The year 1876 was a centennial year. Two beautiful yachts, the *Madeleine* and the *Countess of Dufferin* came up to the starting line that year. *America* also raced, as did the revenue cutter, *Grant*.

Madeleine was one of the fastest yachts ever built. She had been built as a sloop by Kirby at Rye, New York for John Dickerson in 1868 but was changed into a schooner. Her size and style are very evident in the Cozzens drawing in Plate #16 showing her graceful lines and sails. She had a clean, buoyant bow, cradled under the forefoot and her stem rose with a gentle slant or curve from the water.

The *Countess of Dufferin* was not an American yacht. She had been built by Cuthbert of Toronto in 1876 as a centerboard schooner. Her lines differed from the traditional American yacht lines. She had an exceedingly long bow and straight, or upright, stem rising from the water to her knighthead. She had an overhanging stern, and depended more for her speed on her bow, hoping to open the water easily, than on the after part of her hull, where the dead drag is. All of these features are evident in the Cozzens drawing.

The day of the race dawned grey and foggy so the competition started from Buoy #5$^1/_2$ for an outside race. Soon after nine o'clock a light, southerly air lifted the curtain of fog and the yachts, under tow, started for the mark, accompanied by the *America*. Both boats crossed the line nearly together. The *Madeleine* took the lead. At the finish, the *Madeleine* crossed the line first, *America* second and the *Countess of Dufferin* third.

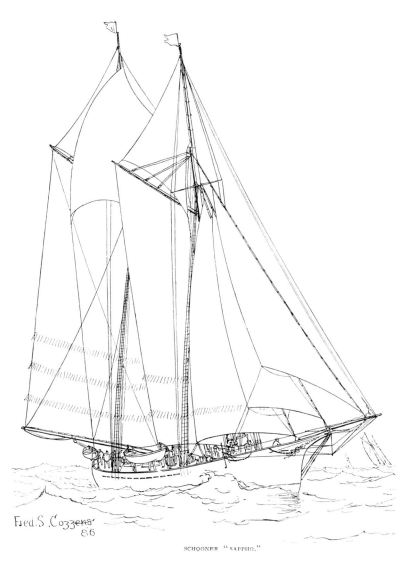

Fred. S. Cozzens
86

SCHOONER "SAPPHO."

Cozzens called Plate #17 *A Breezy Day, Outside*. He pictured the schooners, *Columbia* and *Palmer* and the world famous racer, *Sappho*.

The Long Island coast has been a famous yachting ground for craft of every size and here in the picture which Cozzens has painted with so much spirit, we see on the left the yacht, *Columbia*. She was a centerboard schooner, built by Van Deysen in 1871 at Chester, Pennsylvania for F. Osgood of New York. She was the successor of the *Magic*. She received important alterations by Carll at City Island in 1883.

In the center of the scene, Cozzens placed the yacht, *Sappho*, a keel schooner of 135 feet. Built by Poillon Brothers of New York in 1867 for William P. Douglas of New York, she had gained the attention of the world by her performances. She won eleven out of twenty-four starts or races. Four of her victories were in international races and in one of her famous ocean passages, on April 28, 1872, under three-reefed foresail, she made the extraordinary run of 318 miles in sixteen days, three hours and twenty-six minutes. She was modelled by Townsend and built by Poillon Brothers and later altered in 1869, by Robert Fish. Then her successful racing career began.

Palmer, the yacht on the extreme right of the scene, was a centerboard schooner, 110 feet in length, built by Byerly and Sons of Philadelphia in 1865 for R. Stuyvesant of New York. Her first appearance was in a match race against the *Henrietta*, on October 16, 1865, when the *Henrietta* beat her by twenty-one minutes over a course to the lighthouse and back. She had entered in many of the races and regattas on the Atlantic seaboard.

This is a fine yachting view of these admirable boats with every sail pulling.

Plate #18 is entitled, *Crossing the Line, New York Bay*. It shows the centerboard sloop, *Coming*, the centerboard schooners, *Montauk* and *Comet*, and the keel sloop, *Kelpie*.

A Misty Morning—Drifting,
Courtesy of the New York Yacht Club

In Down East Waters,
Courtesy of the New York Yacht Club

Montauk, pictured by Cozzens in the center of the plate, was a noted yacht of 103 feet built by Poillon Brothers in Brooklyn in 1882. Many experienced yachtsmen believed her to be the best schooner in American waters.

The yacht, *Coming,* pictured in the left of the scene, was a centerboard sloop, built by Poillon Brothers in 1869 and rebuilt in 1880. *Coming,* a boat with an enviable record, is especially notable for having ridden out a gale under circumstances which are among the strangest and most exciting in yachting history.

Comet was a centerboard schooner of eighty-two feet built by Smith of Islip, New York in 1874. She probably won more racing silver in her day than any other boat sailed in this country.

Kelpie was an early, keel-type yacht of rather deep, centerboard type, built by Smedley of Brooklyn in 1876. She was a sturdy boat that had been completely altered into a keel sloop. Under her new construction, she was a good all-around boat.

Plate #19, *Under Minot's Ledge Light* shows the schooners, *Tempest,* and *Fortuna,* the sloop *Viva, and* the yawl, *White Cap.*

The New York Yacht Club had six distance courses in New York Bay for racing but many races have been held at other places, notably Glen Cove, New London, Newport and New Bedford. Cozzens has pictured many of these races. Plate #19 shows a cluster of yachts rounding Minot's Ledge Light. Of all the yachts in the picture, *Fortuna* was perhaps the best known. She was designed as a deep-type centerboard keel schooner by Poillon Brothers of Brooklyn in 1883 for H. S. Hovey of Boston. In her maiden race, she broke a record that at one time promised to put her in the forefront of all American schooners.

Tempest was a keel schooner, built at Bath, Maine by Harrington in 1872 for H. F. Whittier of Boston. *Viva* was a keel sloop built by Dyer at Cape Elizabeth, Massachusetts in 1874 for G. W. Benson of Boston. *White Cap* was a keel yawl built by Adams and Story in 1878 at Essex, Massachusetts for D. G. Rice of Boston.

Cozzens' scene is a quiet, peaceful yachting harbor with Minot's Ledge Light in the background.

Plate #20, entitled by Cozzens, *For the America's Cup, The Start*; showing the *Mischief* and the *Atalanta* in the Fifth International Race on November 11, 1881.

The 1881 challenge was received from Captain Alexander Cuthbert, who had designed and built the centerboard sloop, *Atalanta*, for the Bay of Quinte Yacht Club owners in Belleville, Ontario. However, she was plagued by a lack of funds and was not sailed from Lake Ontario to New York by way of the St. Lawrence River and the sea, but was taken to New York by way of the Erie Canal and the Hudson River. The yacht, stripped of her spars, was heeled over as far as possible on the bilge to permit passage through the locks. This was very bad for the boat.

Mischief, an iron sloop owned by J. R. Busk of New York and designed by A. Cary Smith, was chosen to be the defender. She was built deeper than most of the "skimming dishes" with more shape. All of her grace is shown in Cozzens' line drawing that was used to illustrate the book, *America's Cup Races* published in 1970 by the editors of *Yachting Magazine*.

The first race, on November 9, 1881, was started on a fresh southwest wind amid a band of excursion boats following the race over the familiar New York Yacht Club course. *Mischief* finished before the *Atalanta* and *Gracie*. The next race, on November 10, 1881, was over an outside course of sixteen miles to leeward from Buoy number five off Sandy Hook and return. *Mischief* finished the second race thirty-eight minutes ahead of the *Atalanta*.

Cozzens pictured the start of the third and final race which was held off Staten Island. In Plate #20, *For the America's Cup, The Start*, Cozzens placed the *Mischief* in the foreground.

Lt. Kelley described the start of this third and final race, "Just before the start, storm clouds began to gather over the hills

Before the Wind—Newport 1883,
Courtesy of the New York Yacht Club

Under the Palisades,
Courtesy of the New York Yacht Club

and the Island and with such a threatening look that both yachts made preparations for a heavy squall; but with a splatter of rain this burst over and shaking out the reefs, both waited for the preparatory signal. The *Atalanta*, having no windlass, was a long time in picking up her anchor and getting under way and when, at last, she stood toward the line, another light squall knocked her over so far that her lee-rail dipped and her sailing master was forced to take in the gaff top sail which had just been set. Both boats maneuvered a little bit at first, running down to the line and going about. *Mischief* crossed with a good headway and the *Atalanta* a little over minute later." Cozzens caught all the excitement and anticipation of the race.

Plate #21 is entitled, *A Misty Morning, Drifting*, showing the steamers, *Utowana*, *Nokomis* (*Nettie*), *Crusader* and *Hildegard*. "There is nothing more trying to the patience of men who go down to the sea in ships than the enforced idleness of a calm, when hour after hour, often day after day, the changeless minutes crawl, under a hot sun that beats pitilessly from a sky of gleaming steel upon a sea which sears like molten metal. From the yards, the sails hang idly, their reef points flagging like flails upon the sheaves of a ripened harvest," Kelley said.

In Cozzens' tranquil picture, a squadron of excellent boats like *Crusader*, *Nokomis* and *Hildegard* may be rendered helpless despite the best model and seamanship while a sturdy little steamer like the *Utowana* will rush past them as if possessed of a royal road to pleasure.

Nokomis (late *Nettie*) was a keel schooner built in Northport in 1861 by Hart and altered in 1880. The *Hildegard* was a large, seventy foot centerboard sloop yacht that had raced with *Mischief* and *Gracie* and *Pocahontas* in trial races. She had been built in Islip, Long Island by Smith for H. Oelrichs. *Crusader* was a centerboard schooner, built in 1880 by Mumm of Brooklyn. She was ninety-seven feet overall. This scene is an excellent example of Cozzens' ability to set a mood with his calm water and limp, hanging sails.

Plate #22, entitled, *In Down East Waters, Boston Bay*, shows the cutter, *Beetle*, the sloops, *Syren* and *Countess*, the schooners, *Halcyon* and *Phantom* and the steamers, *Adelita* and *Sappho*.

Of all the boats shown in this plate, the *Halcyon* had won the greatest reputation. She was built at Port Jefferson by Harris in 1866 and had an extraordinary sail pattern. Cozzens has placed her in the center of his scene and this sail pattern is very evident.

The *Adelita* was a wooden screw built in East Boston by Lawlor for J.H. Peabody of Boston. The *Phantom*, a famous boat, was built by Van Deusen in 1865 and rebuilt at Noank in 1879. *Syren*, a well-known centerboard sloop, was turned out by Whitman of Brooklyn for L. H. Keith of Kingston, Rhode Island. The *Sappho* was built as a screw schooner in 1879 at Brooklyn by Lennox. The *Beetle* was a new cutter, built by Lawler in 1882 in Boston. The *Countess* was a keel sloop turned out in 1882 by Lawley and Son for Charles Armstrong of Boston. She was a roomy, comfortable boat.

"A light breeze ruffled the surface of the Bay and the innumerable little sailboats that dotted it took the sun and the wind upon their wings—which they dipped almost into the sparkle of the water and flew hither and thither like gulls," is the description of the scene that Kelley pictured for Cozzens' Plate #22.

Plate #23, *Before the Wind, Newport 1883*, shows the schooner, *Social* (late *Cornelia*), the sloops, *Vixen* and *Arrow*, the steamer, *Permelia* (late *One Hundred*) and *Maggie*, a cutter.

There had been a raging controversy as to which made a better yacht, a cutter or a sloop. Kelley differentiated thus, "Accurately stated, the difference between a cutter and a sloop is one of rig, though, by common consent, the terms are now employed to describe differences of type. Broadly defined, an American sloop is a single-masted craft, which is generally under sixty feet long on the waterline, with three feet of this length to one foot of breadth, and with a depth equal to one

Ice Boating on the Hudson,
Courtesy of the New York Yacht Club

Signal Chart,
Courtesy of the New York Yacht Club

third of the beam. The spars consist of a mainmast, a topmast, a standing bowsprit and, usually, of a jib boom. The principal sail is a mainsail, which is short on the head and long on the foot, this last being laced to the boom; next, there is a jib of relatively great size and then a topsail with narrow head and long foot. The hull is low with little freeboard, the entrance is sharp, the greatest beam is carried well aft and the stern is full and short. The advantages are great stiffness and sail carrying power under certain racing conditions, cheap first-cost, very high speed with strong lower sail winds and easy seas and in smooth water handiness in working. The disadvantages are liability to capsize in squalls or due to inattention. As a rule, the sloop is not a good sea boat."

Kelley continued, "The cutter type is found in a narrow boat which, with great length in proportion to beam, and great depth relative to both, carried low down, inboard and on the keel, large amounts of ballast. The stem is straight, and the sternpost rakes and the draft of water forward is about one half of that aft. Amidships, the cutter is rather full and bold, with a low bilge, a fine long entrance and a sharp run, which curves into high quarters. There are four working sails; first a mainsail which is wide on the head and short on the luff or on the part which is made fast to the mast and long on the foot, this last being secured to the boom at the extremities, the canvas sweeping, when not distended, in a graceful curve below the spars; next there is a jib which is hooked to a ring called a traveler, and is hauled out to the bowsprit by a tackle, its head being hoisted by chain halyards, and afterwards set up taut by a tackle; then comes a foresail, which is fitted with hanks to the fore-stay sail; and finally a large square-headed top sail, bent to a yard and set flying, the lower part of the luff being afterwards laced to the foot of the top mast above the cap and to the doublings of the mast.

"The advantages of a cutter are: sea-going qualities of the highest order, speed in all winds and weather and especially in light airs and in strong breezes; safety so pronounced, owing to the great range of stability, as to forbid capsizing; ability to work to windward under all conditions; great maneuvering power, due to momentum, small amount of canvas in proportion to work done and to speed obtained with other types; effective room below and on deck; small crews; handiness of rigging and gear; more nearly equal efficiency as racers and cruisers than any other class; and, finally, a readiness, at all times, to meet any vicissitudes of wind and weather under racing or working rigs."

Cozzens knew every detail of the construction and sail pattern of all the various kinds of craft and truly brought the joy, understanding and delights of racing to the general public by his pictures.

Permilia, the steamer, formerly called the *One Hundred*, had been built by Herreshoff of Bristol, Rhode Island in 1883.

Arrow, built by David Kirby in 1874, had many races with the yacht, *Gracie* at Newport.

Social (late *Cornelia*) was a keel schooner that had been built in Brooklyn in 1873 by McGarrick.

Vixen was a centerboard sloop built by Albertson in Philadelphia.

Maggie was a keel cutter built in England by Hatcher in 1878.

Cozzens pictured the yacht *Arrow* in the center of his scene. Her canvas spreads out in graceful curves. *Vixen* is pictured at the left center and shows her spread of canvas. *Permelia* steams away to the right while *Maggie* and *Social* are shown in the far background.

Cozzens entitled Plate #24, *Under the Palisades*. It shows the steamer *Stranger*, the steamer, *Rover* and the yacht, *Atalanta*.

Stranger was a one hundred and ninety foot boat built by Cramps in Philadelphia in 1880. She was an iron screw boat.

Atalanta, a two hundred and thirty-six foot iron screw boat had also been built at Cramps a year later for Jay Gould of

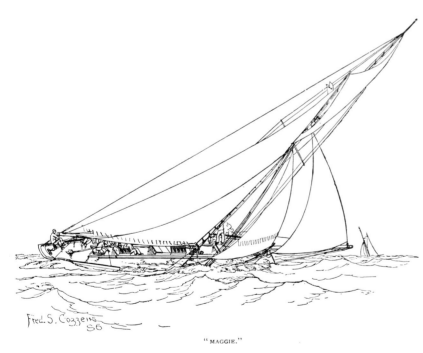

"MAGGIE."

99

New York. She ranked as one of the finest steam yachts anywhere in the world in regard to speed, construction or equipment.

The iron screw steamer, *Rover* was a small boat, built by Gorringe of Philadelphia in 1883.

These boats are shown at anchor under the towering Palisades. Cozzens knew these sharp cliffs well and they often appear as background in his work.

Plate #25 is listed as *Ice Boating on the Hudson*. It shows the sloops, *Avalanche, Gypsie, Icicle, Haze* and *Whiff*, and the iceboat, *Echo*.

Kelley wrote, "The sailing of an iceboat is so totally different from that of the ordinary watercraft that the tarriest of tars would be a double lubber on board, because of the ideas he has to unlearn before he can be in anything but nobody's watch and everybody's way."

The mainsail is nearly always trimmed flat aft, the sheets being hauled taut and well in, unless a beam wind is so strong as to make the yacht slip sideways, or "rear". To get underway, or to fill away, the sheet is flattened aft, and the stern swung aroung until the sails fill. At times, the boat merrily dashes along on her lee runner and rudder. She can be brought back to the ice in two ways: if beating to windward, by luffing; if running, by easing off the sheet. The boat occasionally capsizes.

Ice yachts may roughly be described as a skeleton frame, the chief timbers of which are arranged in the form of a "**T**"; the rig is usually that of a jib and mainsail sloop. The speed of iceboats can be really extraordinary. Boats have been known to attain a velocity of sixty-five to seventy-five miles an hour. The season in New York is limited to twenty favorable days a year.

Kelley wrote, "The iceboat bears the same relation to a water-borne sailing vessel that the light, web-springed trotting wagon does to all other land vehicles; and the iceboat sailor is as much an American institution as the trotting-horse driver."

In this scene, Cozzens depicted the *Avalanche*, a forty-three foot sloop, *Whiff*, a thirty-seven foot sloop, and *Echo*, an iceboat. Nearly all of the boats represented in the plate fly the pennant of the Poughkeepsie Ice Yacht Club. The scene shows two large iceboats and five other boats. Men are figure skating and one can see tracks on the ice denoting the cold atmosphere. These ice yachts often raced the New York Central trains along the shores of the Hudson River for sport.

Plate #26, *Signal Chart*, shows the *Yolanda*, a cutter designed by her owner, Roosevelt Schuyler. She had been built in 1879.

In August 1848, an act of Congress was approved by the president of the United States that said, "All licensed yachts should use a signal of the form, size and color prescribed by the secretary of the Navy." In Plate #26, the private flags and devices of sixty-six yacht clubs are displayed together with the coast or night signals of six of these.

Signals of Yacht Clubs

1	American Yacht Ensign	21	Jeffries
2	Seawanhaka	22	Portland
3	Atlantic	23	Dorchester
4	New York	24	South Boston
5	Eastern	25	Haverhill
6	American	26	Quincy
7	New Jersey	27	Cape Ann
8	Rockaway	28	Lynn
9	Pennsylvania	29	Salem Bay
10	New Brunswick	30	Quaker City
11	Hudson River	31	Jersey City
12	Yonkers	32	Williamsburgh
13	Long Island	33	Knickerbocker
14	Larchmont	34	Madison
15	East River	35	Albany
16	Raritan	36	Narragansett
17	Manhattan	37	New Haven
18	Beverly	38	Bunker Hill
19	Boston	39	New Bedford
20	Newburyport	40	Hull

41 Providence	54 Savannah
42 Mobile	55 Columbia
43 Cleveland	56 St. Augustine
44 Royal Nova Scotia	57 Southern
45 Toronto	58 Baltimore
46 Royal Halifax	59 Charleston
47 Royal Canadian	60 Otego
48 Royal Sail	61 Bohemian
49 Bay of Quinte	62 Oshkosh
50 Royal Bermuda	63 Poughkeepsie (Ice)
51 Buffalo	64 Warwick
52 Oswego	65 National
53 Chicago	

Coston Night Signals

I New York	IV Chicago
II Eastern	V New Bedford
III Seawanhaka	VI St. Augustine

Plate #27, *Near the Finish with the Puritan and the Genesta*, is an extra plate for the America's Cup International Race of 1885.

In 1885 another challenge was received for the America's Cup from the British yacht *Genesta*, a typical, narrow cutter. A group of Boston yachtsmen commissioned Edward Burgess to design a large sloop to defend the Cup. Burgess combined the wider beam and the shoaler hull of the centerboard as they had developed in the New England area with some of the best features of the cutter-type boat. He produced the *Puritan*, a highly successful racer beating the shoal-draft defenders and eventually, the cutter, *Genesta*.

The race between the *Puritan* and the *Genesta* was originally scheduled for September 7, 1885 but took place on September 14. The *Puritan* crossed the finish line first. The next race occurred two days later when there was an autumnal nor'wester blowing. It was a spirited race that ended with the *Puritan* finishing two minutes ahead of the *Genesta*.

Cozzens clearly showed in the extra plate of his series *American Yachts* the narrow English cutter racing against the modernized American centerboard sloop. He named the picture *Near the Finish; Puritan and Genesta*.

In addition to the many watercolors, drawings and outline sketches that Cozzens produced to fill specific orders, he also did a great deal of non-commissioned work. This work had to have a popular appeal and he used various themes for it. One of these, that he used again and again, showed a lighthouse on the shore with a sailing vessel in the center of the scene and a small dory in the left foreground. In one, dated 1885, he turned this theme into an evening setting and placed two men in the stern of the sailing vessel. He constantly drew rescue scenes and beach scenes, with and without boats. One, dated 1885, was entitled *Surf Casting Along the Jersey Coast*. These non-commissioned watercolors were sold wherever he could find a buyer. He left some in an art store in New York City to be sold; or he would sell them to anyone interested in buying an interesting picture. Many of them were untitled, and many, alas, were repetitive.

One of his watercolors that is now hanging in the New York Yacht Club clubhouse is a cup defender of the year 1885 or 1886. It shows a two-masted cutter in heavy swells in a grey-green sea under a blue sky.

The Staten Island Institute of Arts and Sciences lists a woodcut in their collection from a Cozzens drawing that appeared in the *Harper's Weekly* issue of September 3, 1886. It was of the yacht, *Mayflower* off Marblehead, with topmast housed. The woodcut was taken from a pen and ink drawing of the yacht.

A New York City auction gallery recently sold a Cozzens watercolor, entitled, *Putting Out to Sea*, that is dated 1886. The New York Yacht Club has another Cozzens watercolor, dated 1886, of the side-wheel vessel, *Banshee*, shown running the blockade in daylight off Galveston in 1865. Although twenty-one years had passed after the occurrence, Cozzens realistically painted fire exploding in air, shells falling into the sea and men working frantically on deck. Masts of grey vessels in the background dip at strange angles.

According to the reference book, *Appleton's Encyclopedia of American Biography*, published in 1887 by James Bryant Wilson and John Fiske, "Frederic S. Cozzens produced a series of outline drawings of vessels of all kinds comprising steamers from 1819 to the present time, American and English yachts and all varieties of American craft propelled by oar, sail and paddle. These sketches were published in the magazine *Outing* in 1886, preparatory to their appearance in book form under the title, *Cozzens' Outlines*." Herringshaw's *National Library of American Biography*, published in 1909 by the American Publishing Company, also mentions *Cozzens' Outlines* as drawings of vessels of all kinds from 1819 to the present time. Although copies of the magazine *Outing* are available, no trace of *Cozzens' Outlines* has been found in the Library of Congress, Smithsonian Institution or Pre-Union Imprints to date.

The sketches that appeared in *Outing Magazine* consisted of outline drawings of vessels of all kinds, including steamboats from 1819 to the 1880s. The first appearance was in the April 1886 issue in an article by Edward S. Jaffray. It contained fourteen outline drawings of yachts by Cozzens dated 1886. The May issue of *Outing Magazine* contained an article by C.J.C. McAlister. It was illustrated by eighteen outline drawings of yachts by Cozzens, all dated 1886. The June 1886 issue contained Part One of the *History of American Yachting* by Captain R.F. Coffin with thirteen outline drawings of yachts by Cozzens. The July issue contained Part Two of this history and was illustrated with eleven outline drawings. The August issue continued the history and was illustrated with ten outline drawings. The September issue contained Part Four of the history and showed seven outline drawings and two pictures, seemingly in his style but unsigned and undated. The October issue contained Part Five of this history with six of his yacht outline drawings and the November issue concluded with Part Six and four outline drawings and two drawings that were unsigned and undated. Captain Coffin, who was mentioned in *Herring-*

shaw's National Biography as having written an article that Cozzens illustrated, wrote the section of the history of American yachting in the book *Yachts and Yachting*.

The series of articles on the history of American yachting ran in *Outing* from June 1886 in six parts and was illustrated by fifty-one outline drawings by Cozzens. Counting all the articles by McAlister and Joffrey, this brought the total of his illustrations in this magazine in 1886 to a total of eighty-three . Many of Cozzens' illustrations for *Outing Magazine* were later used in his book, *Yachts and Yachting*. The picture of the yachts, *Mayflower* and *Galatea*, that had been used as a frontispiece in the book, *Yachts and Yachting* appeared in the December 1886 issue of *Outing*.

This same year, Cozzens collaborated with J. D. J. Kelley to produce another yachting book, *Typical American Yachts*. It was published by Charles Scribner's Sons of New York. The sixteen illustrations were identical to those used in *American Yachts, Their Clubs and Races*. These include:

A. Plate 1 (In *American Yachts*) *The Early Racers*
B. Plate 2 *Sandy Hook to the Needles*
C. Plate 17 *A Breezy Day Outside*
D. Plate 7 *In the Narrows*
E. Plate 6 *The Finish Off Staten Island*
F. Plate 21 *A Misty Morning*
G. Plate 15 *Lying-to off George's Banks*
H. Plate 22 *In Down East Waters*
I.   Plate 16 *A Stern Chase and a Long One*
J.   Plate 5 *Rounding the Lightship*
K. Plate 19 *Minot's Ledge Light*
L. Plate 20 *For the America's Cup*
M. Plate 9 *Off Soundings*
N. Plate 13 *By Sou'west Spit*
O. Plate 27 *International Race of 1885* (*Puritan* and *Genesta*)
P. Plate 25 *Ice Boating on the Hudson*

The selection of these sixteen scenes out of the original twenty-seven makes one wonder if Cozzens believed them to be superior to the ones that were omitted.

The popularity of Cozzens' yachting watercolors and print sets kept him busy. In 1887 he issued a book called, *Yachts and Yachting* with over one hundred and ten illustrations by Fred S. Cozzens and others. It was published in New York by Cassell and Company with the following articles on various aspects of yachting:

1. History of American Yachting by Captain Roland Folger Coffin. He is also the author of *The America's Cup* and *Old Sailor's Yarns*.

2. *Mayflower* and *Galatea* Race of 1886 by Charles E. Clay

3. American Steam Yachting by Edward S. Jaffray

4. British Yachting by C. J. McAlister

There was also a deluxe edition of this book issued at this time that was limited to 250 copies. One of these editons is in the library of the Staten Island Institute of Arts and Science.

Of the 100 illustrations in *Yachts and Yachting*, seventy-four were done by Cozzens. The other illustrators include Hornelle, McDougal and Bourgain. The humorous pictures of life aboard ship are the only exceptions to the pictures of yachts. All of these are fairly small, detailed line-drawings of various yachts. All are signed Fred. S. Cozzens in the lower left corner. Most are dated 1886, but twelve of the illustrations, from pages 164 to 193, are dated 1888. Under the picture on page 117 is the caption, "Drawn by Cozzens, New York and American Yacht Club." The one exception is the *Mayflower-Galatea* contest which is a black and white reproduction of a watercolor dated 1886. Many of Cozzens' drawings which are used in this book had appeared earlier as illustrations in the April to December 1886 issue of *Outing Magazine*.

The frontispiece shows the *Mayflower* and *Galatea* race of 1886. Three races were scheduled to be held in September of 1886 over the usual inside course of the New York Yacht Club. Cozzens pictured one of these races showing the *Mayflower* crossing the finish line twelve minutes and forty seconds ahead of the *Galatea*. The second race was held on September 11th and was twenty miles to leeward off the Sandy Hook Lightship and return. It was raced with a fine northeast breeze blowing out of the lower bay. Both boats were shown by Cozzens with their light canvas spinnakers, balloon jibs and blue topsails catching the wind. *Galatea* finished thirty minutes ahead of the *Mayflower* in this race. This is a dramatic scene showing men working on the sails and on deck.

On page 11 there is an illustration of W. Edgar's *Cygnet*. It is a careful drawing showing details of the masts and sails as well as a view of the boat as she rode in the water. On page 12 is a sketch of C. B. Miller's *Sybil* showing several men working on board. As H. Wilkes' *Spray* sails past, on page 13, the reader can almost taste the salt spray that she kicks up as she passes John Jay's *La Coquille*. Even the famous *Gimcrack* is shown in New York waters. Coffin traced the history of yachting in his article from the early days to 1870. He included details of all the meets and regattas.

Cozzens drew all the important boats: *Mist*, *Hornet*, the beautiful *Maria*, *Julia*, *Henrietta*, *Una*, *America*, *Alpha*, *Ray* and *Lucky*. Each boat is shown as a central theme. There may be incidental craft in the background, but the drawing is made to show in particular the structure, composition, grace and beauty of the individual yacht.

The second section included the period from 1859 to 1870 when changes were made in the rules to accommodate boats of various sizes. The majestic *Fleetwing* was illustrated by Cozzens as well as the schooner *Madeleine*, making her way through choppy water with ease. The schooners *Sappho*, *Halcyon*, *Dreadnaught*, *Comet*, *Vixen*, *Vesta*, *Wanderer*, *Maud*, *Gracie* and *Enchantress* were all illustrated. Mr. Coffin described the various races that were sailed in this period of American yachting. Cozzens illustrated this portion of the text with his illustrations of boats that had participated in these races. He had drawn

Fred. S. Cozzens 86

SCHOONER "HALCYON."

Blue Fishing,
Collection of Arthur Baker

Hold Fast,
Collection of Arthur Baker

portraits of these yachts before, but these sketches are unique and quite different from his illustrations in *American Yachts, Their Clubs and Races*, when he grouped similar boats together in one scene.

In the International Period, Cozzens sketched the sloop, *White-wing*, originally owned by William and John J. Astor, the sloop, *Fannie*, and the schooner, *Majestic*. The drawing of the *Fannie* is particularly good as the viewer looks down on to the boat. One man crews the tiller while several perch on the rail for ballast and others work amidship. Cozzens had the ability to bring the viewer into the scene he was depicting.

Cozzens drew the schooner, *Palmer*, owned by Rutherford Stuyvesant, as she calmly sails past. *Frolic* romps dead ahead, and *Thetis* has all her canvas up. The view of the *Intrepid* shows her long, narrow hull. *Hope* sits serenely in the water. To overcome the monotony of one line-drawing after another, Cozzens has positioned them in many different angles: approaching or leaving in various directions so that one never tires of viewing the pictures. Each scene is carefully drawn; there is no skimping on details. Each gives the best view of the yacht's basic lines, hull and sail characteristics. The drawings fully differentiate between the various kinds of yachts. He showed the basic differences between a sloop, a yawl and a schooner. This study of the important characteristic lines and rigs of each yacht is called to your attention by his loving delineation. Most of his drawings show the crew working on deck or on the sails. Cozzens was always able to picture the crew of a boat, working realistically at real tasks aboard ship.

As Captain Coffin described yachting in America from 1871 to 1876, Cozzens pictured many of the famous yachts: *Isis*; *Estelle*; *Clytie*; the *Grayling* keeled over as she passes; *Fortuna*; *Adrienne*, pictured in calm water; *Fanita*, as she rushes past in a cloud of sails; tiny *Mischief* rounding a buoy with all hands on deck; *Montauk* serenely spreading her glistening sails.

In the period 1876 to 1885 we find the yachts *Bedouin, Maggie* (with one rail awash) and *Stranger*, which we see from above looking down to details of her deck and superstructure. Cozzens also pictured the *Atalanta* and *Priscilla*.

The second part of the book was devoted to the *Mayflower-Galatea* race of 1886.

The third part of *Yachts and Yachting* concerns itself with American steam yachting and was written by Edward S. Jaffray. Cozzens illustrated it with sketches of the *Corsair*, owned by J. P. Morgan of Highland Falls, New York, the *Camilla*, owned by Col. Frank Brandreth of Sing Sing, New York, the *Atalanta*, owned by Jay Gould of the American Yacht Club, the *Pastime*, *Sentinel*, *Electra*, *Viking*, *Nooya*, *Promise*, *Aida*, *Orienta*, *Radha*, *Polynia*, *Stiletto*, built by Herreshoff, *Namouna*, owned by James Gordon Bennett, showing the symmetry of her lines, and the *Nourmahal*, owned by Mr. William Astor, as well as *Picture* and *Sunbeam*.

"British Yachting" is the title of the last part of the book. It was written by C. J. C. McAlister. Cozzens drew the *Galatea*, *Irex*, *Miranda*, *Uledia*, *Carlotta*, *Dawn*, *Constance*, *Marjorie*, *Ione*, *Diane*, a splendid view of the *Buttercup*, *Samoena*, *Egeria*, *Waterwitch*, *Loma* and the *Gertrude*. He also included drawings of *Tara* and *Queen Mab*.

Cozzens' ships are realistically portrayed, even when in extreme positions such as the *Grayling*, heeled over on her side. They do not sit woodenly on the water. Rigging is shown in detail without disturbing the sense of draft or shape. Photography of that era was not up to the demands of catching a boat in action and a skilled artist such as Cozzens, with an eye for detail and accurate lines, was the only means of recording what the yachts looked like. This study of Cozzens' yachts is a delight to see.

A third and limited "New and Revised" edition of *Yachts and Yachting* was published by Cassell in 1888. It contained over one hundred and thirty illustrations by Cozzens and others.

A Cozzens illustration was used in the booklet put out by Samuel E. Hendricks of 115 Nassau Street in New York City. It was the "Staten Island Athletic Club Decennial Celebration at the Club Grounds, West Brighton, Staten Island, Monday, September 5, 1887, Labor Day." There is a woodcut from a pen

Untitled,
Collection of Arthur Baker

Two-Mast Ship,
Collection of William Sullivan

and ink sketch by Cozzens of the great American yacht *Volunteer*. According to Bales' *History of Staten Island*, the grounds of the Staten Island Athletic Club in 1886 were on Bement Avenue, West Brighton, Staten Island.

In the March 19, 1887 issue of *Harper's Weekly*, Cozzens pictured the start of the *Dauntless-Coronet* race across the Atlantic Ocean. In the May 28, 1887 issue, a Cozzens drawing of the collision of the *Celtic* and *Britannic* appeared. He had redrawn it from sketches of George Rudd, a passenger who was on the *Britannic* during the collision. In the July 30, 1887 issue of *Harper's Weekly*, there appeared another Cozzens drawing, *The Flyers of the Atlantic Yacht Club*, with identification of the yachts below the picture. The yachts *Shamrock*, *Titanic*, *Atlantic*, *Rover* and *Grayling* were shown. This is a busy scene, full of yachts and many other small craft. In the August, 1887 issue, Cozzens pictured a scene, "Interviewing Newfoundland Fishermen as to the Presence of Cruisers Inshore." In the September, 1887 issue of *Harper's Weekly*, there appeared a full page of illustrations by Cozzens of "The Annual Meet of the American Canoe Association." In the September 27, 1879 issue of *Harper's Weekly* Cozzens depicted the Sandy Hook Lightship with a sailing vessel nearby. This lightship was a favorite theme of Cozzens' and he drew many versions of it.

Cozzens also drew many versions of the Cup race between the yachts *Volunteer* and *Thistle*, which took place in 1887. George L. Watson, who had built the old *Madge*, built a new contender, the *Thistle*, to meet the challenge. General Charles J. Paine commissioned Edward Burgess to design a new boat to be built at the yards of Pusey and Jones Company in Wilmington, Delaware. Called *Volunteer*, she was narrower and deeper, as well as longer, than any of her predecessors. Her keel had more curve and she carried 1,171 square feet of sail.

It was decided that the races were to be held over the inside course; one to windward and return outside Sandy Hook and the third, if necessary, to be the triangular outside course. The first race was held on September 28, 1887. The morning broke gray and somber with indications of a fog blown in by a fitful northeast breeze. *Thistle* got a good headstart. The wind headed both boats, and slowly they beat down the channel, tack and tack, the wind gradually working around to the southwest. The excursion boats crossed in on the *Thistle* causing anxiety so that a sign had to be displayed that read, "Keep Astern." *Volunteer* crossed the finish line 20 minutes ahead of the *Thistle*.

On September 29 there was no wind so the race was postponed until the next day. The performance was repeated as the *Volunteer* raced home a mile and a half ahead of the *Thistle*.

The Mariners Museum of Newport News, Virginia, has a marine chromolithograph of this international yacht race entitled *Just After the Start, The First Day*. The original was painted in 1887 and it was lithographed by Armstrong and Company of Boston, printed by Riverside Press of Cambridge and published by C. L. Jones and Company. The Staten Island Historical Society has the same print.

In the February, 1887 issue of *Outing Magazine*, three Cozzens drawings of ice-yachts, dated 1886, appeared in an article entitled "Yachting in Mid-winter" by Charles Ledyard Norton.

Cozzens did many rescue scenes at this time. One of them was turned into an etching by W. Wellstood in 1887. Another etching was made from a dramatic Cozzens watercolor that shows a two-mast sailing vessel breaking apart with a life-saving boat ready to take on a woman with a babe in arms. The captain of the sinking vessel can be seen directing the men. A watercolor, in a private collection, dated 1887, shows a coal burning barge going past the Robbins Reef Light upstream to the Hudson River. Cozzens also drew, in that year, an American whaling ship entering New Bedford Harbor flying the private signal of her owner, William Potter (a white flag with a red diamond). A fine 1887 fishing boat, called *Heading for the High Seas*, has been catalogued.

Cozzens drew many versions of boats that were familiar in the New York waters. One of these is a sailing ship with Battery Weed in the background. Another is of a boat called a "sharpie." A sharpie was a long, narrow, flat-bottomed boat having a centerboard and one or two masts each rigged with a triangular sail. Cozzens did a pencil and wash version of one of these sharpies in 1888. *Sail and Paddle Magazine,* in the issue of March, 1889, showed a woodcut from an outline drawing of Cozzens' entitled, "George A. Warder's Canoe."

In 1890 Cozzens did a fine version of *Sailing for Bluefish,* showing a large boat in choppy water with two men trolling for bluefish from the stern while a third man holds the tiller. The scene is full of action with the Jersey shore and Sandy Hook lighthouse in the background. This watercolor was made into a print by Bradlee and Reardon in 1890.

In the July 5, 1890 issue of *Illustrated America,* there appeared an engraving by Kurtz of a Cozzens watercolor of General Paines' celebrated yacht, *Volunteer.* The Department of Naval Architecture at Massachusetts Institute of Technology has two pencil and wash drawings, circa 1890, of the steamer, *Niagara* and the steamer, *City of Paris.* Both are signed but undated.

On the Cruise, page 29 of a forty-eight page advertisement of *Rushon's Portable Boat, Canton Street, Lawrence, New York* dated March 15, 1890, shows a man reading while seated in his canoe which is protected by a canopy over it of tent-like appearance. It is signed in lower left and dated 1889.

Another Cozzens picture, *The Squadron of Evolution Under Sail* was used by *Harper's Weekly* in their August 2, 1890 issue.

In 1890 Cozzens was commissioned by O. T. Cotton to do some work for their trade cards. Lake George and San Francisco's Golden Gate Bridge were both completed in 1890. Two years later he did the *Statue of Liberty, Coney Island in Moonlight* and the three ships of Columbus for use on their trade cards.

In 1891, at the request of her owner, his good friend, Edwin Stevens of Hoboken, New Jersey, Cozzens did a watercolor of the yacht, *Petrol.* Stevens was pictured at the helm of his boat. This work is done in dark brown tones, very unusual coloring

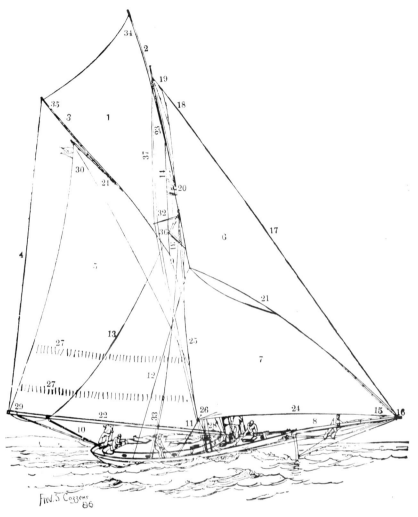

Fred. S. Cozzens
86

NAMES OF SPARS, RIGGING AND SAILS OF A SLOOP YACHT.

1. Club Topsail.	12. Jib Topsail Sheet.	25. Leach of Jib.
2. Club Topsail Sprit.	13. Topping Lift.	26. Clew of Jib.
3. Topsail Club	14. Gaff Topsail Clewed Down.	27. Reef Points.
4. Club Topsail Guy.	15. Tack of Jib.	28. Tack of Mainsail.
5. Mainsail.	16. Tack of Jib Topsail.	29. Clew of Mainsail.
6. Jib Topsail.	17. Luff of Jib Topsail.	30. Peak of Mainsail.
7. Jib (Forestaysail and Jib in one).	18. Head of Jib Topsail.	31. Throat of Mainsail.
	19. Jib Topsail Halliards.	32. Main Cross Trees.
8. Bowsprit.	20. Leach of Jib Topsail.	33. Masthead Runner and Tackle.
9. Club Topsail Tack Line.	21. Main Gaff.	34. Head of Club Topsail.
10. Mainsheet.	22. Main Boom.	35. Clew of Club Topsail.
11. Foresail or Forestaysail Sheet.	23. Main Topmast.	36. Tack of Club Topsail.
	24. Foot of Jib.	37. Topmast Shrouds.

for Cozzens to use. This picture is on display at Stevens Institute of Technology on their campus at Hoboken, New Jersey, once the home of the Stevens family.

During his lifetime, many authors used work by Cozzens to illustrate their nautical books. *The Illustrated Nautical Dictionary, Unabridged* by Captain Howard Patterson, copyright in 1891, was illustrated with line drawings by Cozzens.

Page 75   *Names of Spars and Rigging and Sails of Sloop Yacht,* 1886

Page 79   *Cutter Yacht Underway; Lowering Spinnaker Boom,* 1886

Page 81   *Cutter Yacht Underway Showing Spinnaker Set,* 1886

Page 85   *Yawl Yacht Hove-To,* 1886

Page 89   *Schooner Yacht Under Way Showing Balloon Jib Topsail,* 1886

Page 91   *Schooner Yacht Under Way Showing Squaresail Set,* 1886

Page 93   *Schooner Yacht Under Way, Showing All Plain (Working) Sail Set,* 1886

Page 94   *Schooner Yacht Under Way, Showing Mainsail Reefed and Foretop Mast Housed,* 1886

Page 123 *Side View Names of Spars, Rigging and Various Parts of Steam Yachts,* n.d.

These illustrations show the particular knowledge that Cozzens possessed of the various parts of both sailing and steam vessels as well as his impeccable draftsmanship.

Cozzens continued to busy himself doing many different versions of sailing ships in the harbor or Narrows area that had a universal appeal. He repeated these subjects many times.

In 1892, *Century Magazine* was one of the magazines that asked him to illustrate for them. His watercolors of the yachts, *Priscilla* and *Mischief*, both dated 1892, were used by *Century* in an article about yachts in the August, 1893 issue entitled, *Cup Defenders, Old and New.*

The Rhode Island Historical Society possesses a watercolor of racing boats done in 1892. This same year he also did a fine fog scene with two workboats entering fog banks near land and a lighthouse area. We can also find examples of beached sailboats and unidentified two-mast sailing vessels. Cozzens occupied his spare time, when he was not working directly on a commission or illustration order, to do watercolors of sailboats, dories and beach scenes.

In 1892 Cozzens did a study of the U.S.S. *Massachusetts*. The Museum of the City of New York has a watercolor of the Narrows that he did in 1892.

In the 1892 *Supplement of Illustrated America*, there appeared two lithographs which were taken from Cozzens' watercolors, dated 1887. *Now Then, Boys* shows men from a life-saving station, dressed in sou'westers, trying to launch their boat in very rough water. A foundering vessel can be seen in the distance. A companion print, *Hold Fast, Then*, was the second illustration. The same men are attempting to keep their boat upright as they bring ship-wrecked seamen ashore. The Coast Guard Station in New London has these two prints.

In another lithograph of this era, Captain Nathaniel Herreshoff can be seen coming out of the New London harbor in a catamarran. His red beard is very visible.

After the success of his yachting books and sets of prints, Cozzens embarked on a new venture that was to keep him busy until 1900. In 1892 he began a study, in detail, of American naval ships. Again, he collaborated with Lt. Kelley in illustrating several books about the United States Navy, many of which were issued in portfolio sets.

Although he had a close relationship with naval personnel during this period, nowhere could information be found that Cozzens had any contractual arrangement with the Navy for this work. The printing of the portfolio sets of naval pictures was purely a commercial venture attempting to capitalize on the surging interest in the New Navy and the Great White

Fleet. But the enormous amount of work entailed in these sets of naval ships and the exactitude of the work, points to the fact that Cozzens spent a great deal of time with the personnel of the Navy and had a close working relationship with a great many of them. The detailed study of the ships of the U.S. Navy that resulted has proven invaluable as a historical record of the fighting ships of that time.

The sixteen vessels of the Great White Fleet captured the imagination and interest of every American. In fourteen months, this Great White Fleet traveled 45,000 miles and visited six continents. Although its mission was partly to meet a Japanese threat, its pursuit was ostensibly peaceful. It was the most formidable armada ever to set forth on such a venture. The appearance of these sixteen ships, sailing in perfect formation, not yards apart, in a line three miles long, attracted the attention of the world as a show of strength. Many cities wished to welcome the fleet but their channels were too shallow to accommodate them. The armada of ships included the 4,500 ton *Chicago*, steam and sail; the 3,000 ton *Atlanta*, steam and sail; the 3,000 ton *Boston*, steam and sail; 1,500 ton *Dolphin*, steam and sail; the protected cruiser, *Charleston*; the protected cruiser, *Baltimore*; the second-class battleship, *Texas*; the warship, *Indiana*; the warship, *Massachusetts*; the battleships, *Oregon, Brooklyn, Vesuvius, Katahdin* and *Maine*, the armored cruiser, *New York*; and the pre-dreadnaught battleship, *Connecticut*. The ships were all painted white and presented a mighty picture. They came home on February 22, 1909 and were welcomed at Hampton Roads by Teddy Roosevelt, aboard the presidential yacht, *Mayflower*. Many Americans were familiar with these vessels since Cozzens had included them in his portfolio of prints in the United States Navy.

Cozzens and Lt. Kelley issued the first book with an accompanying set of chromolithographs in 1892. The title of the book was, *Our Navy, Its Growth and Achievements*. It was published by the American Publishing Company of Hartford, Connecticut in 1892 with watercolor sketches by Fred. S. Cozzens. A second edition of this book was published by the same publisher in 1897.

The set of chromolithographs, "Our Navy, Its Growth and Achievements," gave the title and names of ships listed on the back of each print. The print set was issued by Armstrong and Company of Boston. The twenty-four watercolor plates presented the most famous war vessels of the American Navy from the *Hornet* and the *Constitution* of the early days of the *Massachusetts* and the *Brooklyn* of the time of publication. The plates in the 1892 set are:

1 *Boston, Baltimore*
2 *Atlanta, Chicago, Yorktown, Boston*
3 *Charlestown, San Francisco*
4 *Richmond, New York, Cushing*
5 *Miantonomah, Newark*

6 *Kearsage, Constitution*
7 *Alarm, Philadelphia, Vesuvius*
8 *Machias, Massachusetts, Marblehead*
9 *Enterprise, Petrol, Vesuvius*
10 *Philadelphia, Petrel*
11 *Colorado, Hartford, Franklin, Powhaton*
12 *Bennington, Katahdin, Iowa*
13 Type of *Monadnock, Canonica* (type of), *Passaic, Ajax*, etc. *Naugatuck, New Ironsides, Nantucket*
14 *Detroit*
15 S.S. *New York, Vamose, New Hampshire, Dolphin*
16 *Dispatch, Atlanta, Yorktown*
17 *Portsmouth, Constellation, Bancroft, Saratoga*
18 *Cincinnati, Terror, Indiana*
19 *Concord, Stiletto, Columbia*
20 *Brooklyn* (new) and *Brooklyn* (old)
21 *Amphitrite, Puritan, Montgomery, Ericsson*
22 *Raleigh, Castine, Maine*
23 *Texas, Olympia, Minneapolis*
24 *Naval Review 1893*; Foreign Lines, American Lines

The plates in this set of prints were issued in a portfolio which cost $1.25 per set. Each set of prints depicts roughly seventy-five vessels shown with great technical competence showing sailing vessels, transitional, steam sailers and all steam vessels.

This popular set was reprinted by the American Publishing Company of Hartford, Connecticut in 1897 as "Our Navy." This 1897 printing contained twenty-four lithographs with title and outline sketch on verso but there are minor variations in the two sets. Items with "*" denote sail.

1 *Baltimore, Boston*
2 *Chicago, Boston, Atlanta, Yorktown**
3 *San Francisco, Charleston*
4 *New York, Cushing, Richmond*
5 *Miantonomah, Newark, Yorktown*
6 *Constitution, Kearsage, Macedonian**
7 *Alarm, Philadelphia, Vesuvius*
8 *Machias, Massachusetts, Marblehead*

9 *Enterprise, Pennsylvania, South Carolina, Hornet**
10 *Philadelphia, Petrol, Vesuvius*
11 *Pensacola, Hartford, Franklin, Powhaton*
12 *Bennington, Iowa, Katahdin*
13 *Monitor, Passaic, Monadnock, Keokuk, New Ironsides*
14 *Monterey, Detroit, Oregon*
15 *New Hampshire, Dolphin, Chicago, New York* (liner)
16 *Atlanta, Dispatch, Yorktown*
17 *Portsmouth, Constellation, Bancroft, Saratoga*
18 *Cincinnati, Terror, Indiana*
19 *Brooklyn* (new) and *Brooklyn* (old)
20 *Amphitrite, Puritan, Montgomery, Ericsson*
21 *Raleigh, Castine, Maine*
22 *Texas, Olympia, Minneapolis*

THE SANDY HOOK LIGHT-SHIP.—DRAWN BY F. S. COZZENS.

23 *Columbian Naval Review, 1893*; Foreign Lines, American Lines

24 *Concord, Stiletto, Columbia* passing the Statue of Liberty

The Franklin D. Roosevelt Library at Hyde Park, New York contains the original watercolor of the *Amphrite, Montgomery* and *Ericsson* which became Plate 21 of the series.

Cozzens issued another set of ships of the United States Navy. It was entitled, "Old Naval Prints," and was published by the American Publishing Company of Hartford, Connecticut. It was copyright 1892-94. There were twenty-four colored plates in the "Scarce and unusual collection of prints reproduced from the watercolors of Fred. S. Cozzens." The plates were supplemented by notes which in some cases fill in interesting, if

INTERVIEWING NEWFOUNDLAND FISHERMEN AS TO THE PRESENCE OF CRUISERS INSHORE.

not essential, information. The ships in each print are identified on the back of each print. There were seventy-five vessels depicted in the series which was also priced at $1.25 per set. The lithographing was done by Armstrong and Company of Boston.

Another set of U.S. Navy prints was issued by the National Military Publishing Company of New York in 1893-94. Armstrong and Company of Boston were the lithographers. This was listed as "a scarce and unusual collection of twenty-four prints in color depicting seventy-five ships; ships identifed on rear." Plate #24, the *Naval Review* print, was used on the cover of the box which held the set of prints.

These prints are technically invaluable as they depict the early white and buff pattern employed by the vessels of the New Navy early in the 1890s. Many of these steelsteamers are depicted under their auxiliary sailing rig as well, a feature of additional interest.

There has been a great deal of confusion about these sets of naval prints. One finds references to Cozzens' series of the Great White Fleet, The New Navy, American Warships in Color and American Warships at Sea, but there is no factual evidence to support any of these titles. The supposition is that the identification has been erroneous. At any rate, only four sets of naval prints have been found to date. These are:

1 "Our Navy, Its Growth and Achievement," American Publishing Co. Hartford, Ct 1892
2 "Our Navy, Its Growth and Achievement," Armstrong and Co. Boston, 1897
3 "Old Naval Prints," Armstrong and Co. Boston, Copyright 1892-94; American Publishing Co. Hartford, Ct.
4 "Old Naval Prints," National Military Publishing Company, New York, 1893

During the years from 1880 to 1890, when an important Cup race or trial run was to take place, the daily New York newspapers would charter the fastest tug in the harbor and stock it

with reporters and artists. It was their task to give the readers the feeling that they were also witnessing the race. Cozzens went on many of these trips. He drew the scenes where the trials took place, especially in the Narrows.

He drew many yachting pictures through the years for the *New York Herald*. Many of his grandchildren believe that he was the official yachting editor of the paper, specializing in yachting pictures. However, it is improbable that he was a permanent member of the *Herald* staff because he would have been required to make pictures of the minor yacht races during the year as well as of the notable ships entering or leaving the harbor, and Cozzens chose only to make pictures of the important races. This leads one to the conclusion that he was a free lance artist who drew what interested him and the *New York Herald* was one of his regular customers from 1880 to 1893. We have no indication that he ever wrote anything for the paper except the captions of his pictures.

Reading the old yachting sections of the *New York Herald* of those days, one notices that there are many yachting drawings in the paper that were not done by Cozzens. These drawings are unsigned so it is difficult to ascribe them to any specific artist. Cozzens was always allowed to sign his work, although it is instantly recognizable by the texture, shading of sails and seawater.

The year 1893 was a Cup race year and Cozzens was very busy. Lord Dunraven had sent over his new cutter, *Valkyrie II* as a challenge to the New York Yacht Club. A New York syndicate with Calvin Iselin at the head asked Nathaniel Herreshoff of Bristol, Rhode Island to build them a defender. The brothers, John and Nathaniel Herreshoff and their families were to become as important in ship design and ship building as the Stevens Family of Hoboken had been early in the 19th century. The new American defender was called *Vigilant*.

A Cozzens drawing appeared in the *New York Herald* of September 10, 1893. It is a line drawing, dated 1893, *The Gallant Vigilant Showing the Way Home...with Spinnakers Set, Crosses the*

Finish Line in Advance of the Jubilee. It is a fine piece, showing four yachts coming straight on. This race was the second of three races to decide the opponent of the British in the America's Cup race.

In the September 12th issue, there appeared two line drawings, *The Vigilant Nearing the Finish* and *The Vigilant and the Columbia at the Start.* Thus, the *Vigilant* is to defend the Cup. The September 24 issue showed a starboard side view of the *Valkyrie* with full spinnakers. In the October 6 issue, there was one Cozzens piece, *The Vigilant in the Doldrums.* On October 8, the *Herald* issued a large line drawing across the top third of a page, *Together the Vigilant and the Valkyrie Start Away.* The headline read, "*Vigilant* outfoots the *Valkyrie.*" There is a line drawing, *The Vigilant Finishes in Front,* showing the winner surrounded by steamships. There are puffs of smoke from some of the ships suggesting a cannon salute to the winner.

In the October 10th issue there are three line drawings that cover one third of the page; *Starting Away Together, The Valkyrie's First Tack* and *The Vigilant Rounding the First Mark.* The headline was *Vigilant* outpoints *Valkyrie.* On page 6 there are three line drawings; *At the Turning Point, Five Miles from the Finish,* and *Crossing the Line a Winner.*

In the October 12th issue, there is a small line drawing, *The Vigilant in the Lead.* The headline was, "*Vigilant* led but no Victory; But the Fickle Wind Fell With the Setting Sun But Not in Time to Finish the Race."

The October 14th issue of the *Herald* ran this headline, "America's Cup Stays in America. Accident to *Valkyrie* Permits the *Vigilant* to Win the Third and Deciding Contest For the Prize." A large line drawing, dated 1893, took up the top third of the page, *Rent in Valkyrie's Spinnaker;* "The challenger and defender were close together in the race for home when the British yacht sails gave way, sending her to the rear and ultimate defeat."

Cozzens' coverage of this race was seen by more people than

any other presentation of the contest, as the *New York Herald* at that time had the largest circulation in the world: 240,000 readers. He also did many versions of this race between the *Vigilant* and the *Valkyrie.*

The *Illustrated America Supplement*, issued in 1893, showed five Cozzens lithographs from his set, "Our Navy," which had been published in 1897. These were:

Plate 2- dated 1892 showing the *Atlanta, Chicago, Yorktown* and *Boston,* four modern steel sail and steam U.S. ships at sea.

Plate 6- showing the *Kearsage, Constitution,* a Cozzens lithograph of the past and present showing two wooden U.S. Navy ships. The *Kearsage* is a steam ship of 1860

Now Then Boys,
Collection of Arthur Baker

vintage while the *Constitution* is the famous War of 1812 sailing ship.

Plate 9- showing the *Enterprise, Pennsylvania, South Carolina* and *Hornet,* four wooden U.S. Navy ships of the War of 1812 period. The *Pennsylvania* and *South Carolina* have guns on three of the four decks. The others are smaller warships The *Enterprise* is firing a salute to the other vessels.

Plate 11- shows the *Colorado, Hartford, Franklin* and *Powhaton,* four sailing ships of the U.S. Navy of the Civil War period. The ships are evidently being attacked at sea as plumes of water are exploding near the ships.

Plate 17- showing the *Portsmouth, Costellation, Bancroft* and *Saratoga,* three sail and steam and one sailing ship. The *Bancroft* was a steel-sided ship. It is shown at sea in almost calm water.

Ahmed John Kenealy, yachting editor of *Outing Magazine* was another author who wrote on marine topics. He published *Yacht Races for the America's Cup: 1851-1893.* It was published by the New York Outing Company, Ltd. of New York and

Untitled,
Collection of Arthur Baker

London in 1894. This is an account of America's victory at Cowes in 1851 and subsequent contests for the trophy as well as the international history of the Breton's Reef and Cape May Cups and the Mission of Navahoe of 1893. Cozzens' work was used for thirty of the eight-seven illustrations. Unless otherwise noted, they are all signed and dated 1893.

Frontispiece: *Vigilant*; a photographic reproduction of an undated Cozzens watercolor.

This is an exciting picture; a yacht is shown coming straight toward the artist. Tugboats and a host of other craft are in the background

Page 142   Photocopy of a watercolor of the race between the *Vigilant*, owned by Morgan Iselin syndicate, and *Colonia*, owned by Rogers syndicate.

Page 144   Photocopy of a watercolor of the race between the *Jubilee*, the Paine Cup defender and the *Pilgrim*, owned by the Boston syndicate.

Opposite Page 173 is a photocopy of a watercolor of a race between the *Valkyrie, Satanita, Brittanic, H.H.H. Prince of Wales*

A Cozzens watercolor, *Raising the Halyard*, done in 1894, was sold at auction recently in New York City. In this same year he was again busy doing illustrations for *Outlook Magazine*. They used his sloop picture, *Corsair*, in the June 9, 1894 issue. In this year, he also did a watercolor of a catboat, the *Acorn*, showing her sails full of wind. The Peabody Museum at Salem has three pencil sketches of various ships, all dated 1895. Mystic Seaport Museum shows a yachting scene, dated 1895, of racing vessels. *The Book of the Fair*, issued in May, 1895 boasted of two Cozzens drawings for illustrations. One, *Full Moon*, is a night scene with a two-mast ship with davits, and the second shows a two-mast ship sailing out of the harbor. He did two pen and ink drawings to illustrate the *Official Illustrated Signal Program and Handbook of the International Yacht Races* in 1895. They both showed the rigging of a yacht and were dated 1895. He found time to do *Beacon Light off the Point at New Bedford*, and *Running In*, a starboard quarter view of a racing vessel and a sailing ship in full sail in this year.

A fine Cozzens watercolor of a sailing ship in full sail with the Quarantine Station on Staten Island in the background, is dated 1896. In the same year, he did *Going Out In the Skiff Through Surf* and *Sailboats Passing the Lighthouse*. Cozzens was also commissioned by the Iselin family to do a picture of a Cup defender yacht flying their signal. He went down to the Jersey shore to do a blue fishing beach scene with a dory and a sailboat in the background. Another watercolor, *Going Out*, is dated 1896, as is a picture of two sailboats off a sandy shore with two large rocks in the scene.

In 1895, a Long Island collector, Lawrence Lawrence, purchased a rescue scene by Cozzens. He was so pleased with it, that he commissioned Cozzens to do two more rescue and lifeboat paintings for him. They are dated 1897.

A fine watercolor, dated 1897, appeared on the market recently. It centered on seaweed-covered rocks with breakers in the foreground. Two schooner-rigged ships are in the far distance.

Cozzens did a great deal of work during the years 1884 to 1897. If one contemplates the number of marine prints that were made from his watercolors, it is easy to figure the tremendous number of watercolors and line drawings that he did during this period.

After the unfortunate dispute over the defeat of the *Valkyrie* in 1895, a succession of challenges were sent over to America by Sir Thomas Lipton. From the first *Shamrock* yacht in 1899 to *Shamrock* V in 1930, all the sportsman's efforts were defeated.

Miantonomah,
Collection of Arthur Baker

Sir Thomas Lipton, of the Royal Ulster Yacht Club of Belfast, Ireland, sent his first *Shamrock* across the Atlantic in 1899. He was of Irish descent and had started life as a grocery clerk. Although he came from a poor family, he became a successful tea merchant by sheer hard work and native ability and built a business that made him a fortune. In thirty-two years, from 1899 to 1930, he made five attempts to "lift the ayld mug" as he explained it. He was a good yachtsman and a good sportsman. Cozzens knew Sir Thomas personally and often sketched onboard his boats.

The first race between the *Columbia* and the *Shamrock* took place in 1899. The America's Cup races had by now evolved into a race between yachts built for this express purpose. No longer was the pleasure cruising yacht suitable because syndicates of wealthy men or rich individuals commissioned boats to be built that were light and speedy. Often, they were uncomfortable boats and many were wet boats. Cozzens commented on this fact in the *New York Times* interview in 1920.

Portsmouth,
Collection of Arthur Baker

William Fife built the first *Shamrock* for Lipton. She was constructed of maganese bronze with aluminum topsides, all tied together with stringers, strap and cross braces inside. Her racing mast, boom and gaff were of steel. She was 128 feet long, with 13,492 square feet of canvas. Her hull was flat and broad and she had a fin-like keel and a yawl rig.

J. Pierpont Morgan and C. Oliver Iselin asked Nathaniel Herreshoff to design the *Columbia* and she was built at their yards at Bristol, Rhode Island. She was 131 feet long and carried 13,135 square feet of sail. She was plated with manganese bronze below the water and steel above. The spars were of steel. The U. S. Government promised to lend a hand keeping the very large fleet of excursion boats away from the races at all times.

The first race took place on October 16, 1899, in a thin fog with a moderately easterly wind. It was a fifteen ESE mile run from Sandy Hook Lightship and return. The *Columbia* finished ten minutes and eleven seconds ahead of the *Shamrock*.

The next day, October 17, 1899, the fog had lifted. They were to sail a triangular course from Sandy Hook Lightship. *Shamrock*'s club topsail collapsed to leeward. The topmast snapped clean off just above the masthead and she was towed back.

October 20, 1899 began as a fine day with a brisk, northerly wind that whipped the tops off the tumbling seas. It was to be a leeward and windward course. *Shamrock* got a jump on the *Columbia* but the *Columbia* crossed the finish line an easy winner with six minutes to spare. Lipton was elected to honorary membership in the New York Yacht Club and he went back to England with the *Shamrock* in tow of the steam yacht, *Erin*.

For *Shamrock* II, Lipton went to George Watson, who had designed *Madge* and the *Thistle* and the two *Valkyries*. The light boat was plated with immadium. She was a flat boat with a deep, narrow fin. She was 137 feet long, 14,027 square feet of canvas.

Boston, Baltimore—Old Naval Prints, #1

Atlanta, Chicago, Yorktown, Boston—Old Naval Prints, #2

Charleston, San Francisco—Old Naval Prints, #3

Richmond, New York, Cushing—Old Naval Prints, #4

Miantonomah, Newark—Old Naval Prints, #5

Kearsage, Gonstitution—Old Naval Prints, #6

137

Alarm, Philadelphia, Vesuvius—Old Naval Prints, #7

Machias, Massachusetts, Castine—Old Naval Prints, #8

Enterprise, Pennsylvania, South Carolina, Hornet—Old Naval Prints, #9

Philadelphia, Petrel, Vesuvius—Old Naval Prints, #10

Colorado, Hartford, Franklin, Powhatan—Old Naval Prints, #11

Machias, Katahdin, Iowa—Old Naval Prints, #12

Monadnock, Canonicus, Passaic, Ajax, Naugatuck, Nantucket, New Ironsides—Old Naval Prints, #13

Detroit, Monterey, Oregon—Old Naval Prints, #14

New York, Vamose, New Hampshire, Dolphin—Old Naval Prints, #15

Dispatch, Atlanta, Yorktown—Old Naval Prints, #16

Portsmouth, Constellation, Bancroft, Saratoga—Old Naval Prints, #17

Cincinnati, Terror, Indiana—Old Naval Prints, #18

Concord, Stiletto, Columbia—Old Naval Prints, #19

Brooklyn (New), Brooklyn (Old)—Old Naval Prints, #20

The Herreshoff Yards were again asked to build a defender and they expected the result, named the *Constitution*, to be very fast. However, a new defender arose in a Boston boat, the *Independence*, owned by Thomas W. Lawson. Thus the yachting season opened with three big sloops in the field. During the season, the *Constitution* and the *Columbia* met in twenty-two races. It was demonstrated that the *Columbia* was the fastest and the easiest to handle and she was chosen to vie with *Shamrock* II, as Lipton had named his new boat.

For the first race of 1901, on September 28, there was a moderate breeze of eight to ten knots strength and a smooth sea. The course was fifteen miles to windward from Sandy Hook Lightship and return. The *Columbia* passed *Shamrock* on the way home and crossed the line thirty-five seconds ahead.

On October 3, the two yachts met off the Hook. There was a rattling breeze of twelve knots strength over a triangular course. *Columbia* started late but gained ground on the Irish boat and crossed the finish line one minute and eighteen seconds ahead.

The next day, October 4, the breeze was at ten knots at the start. The wind was off shore, the course was a leeward and windward one of thirty miles. They finished forty-one seconds apart, the *Shamrock* losing. It was the first time that there was no open water between the boats at the end of the sailing.

The 1903 series saw the end of the sacrifices made in yacht design and construction for the sake of speed. Evolving into a flat, screw-like racing shell, these boats were useless except for this one race.

Thomas Lipton brought another ninety-foot cutter across the Atlantic in 1903. The *Shamrock* III had been built by William Fife. She was beautifully modelled with excessively long ends. She was not as big as her predecessor, but was a narrow cutter built of nickel steel coated with white enamel. She was 134 feet long, with 14,154 square feet of canvas and was steered by a wheel instead of the customary tiller.

Amphitrite, Puritan, Ericsson, Montgomery—Old Naval Prints, #21

Raleigh, Castine, Maine—Old Naval Prints, #22

Texas, Olympia, Minneapolis—Old Naval Prints, #23

Foreign Line, Naval Review 1893, American Line—Old Naval Prints, #24

Herreshoff designed a ninety foot racing yacht for a syndicate of Cornelius Vanderbilt, William Rockefeller, Elbert H. Gary, Clement A. Griscom, James J. Hill, W. B. Leeds, Norman B. Ream, Henry Walters and P. A. B. Widener. The new boat was called *Reliance*. She was an extremely flat craft with a shallow body, long flat ends and a deep keel. She reverted back to the "skimming dishes" that had been so popular long ago. She spread 16,160 square feet of canvas. A steel spar was built with a wooden topmast telescoping inside. It was difficult to race without breaking the topmast. She was built of Tobin bronze and was 143 feet long.

On August 22, 1903, fifty-two years to a day after the first Cup race, there was a moderate wind coming from the New Jersey beaches and there was something of a sea on. The course was fifteen miles to windward and return. *Reliance* slid across the line eight minutes and fifty-six seconds ahead of the Lipton yacht.

The August 28 race was over the triangular course. The American boat went over first in a fresh wind. They finished six minutes and twenty seconds apart with the *Reliance* ahead.

On September 3, 1903, there was no wind and the sky was gray and misty. It was a fifteen mile beat to windward and return. Any man can make a boat go in a breeze, but the master is one who makes her move in light weather. The wind came out of the east and a big fog bank rolled in shutting out the boats from view. *Reliance* loomed out of the fog first. *Shamrock* got off her course in the fog and missed the lightship entirely. The series of 1903 was over. Lipton's failure to win the Cup was a great disappointment to him.

The fourth attempt to lift the Cup by Sir Lipton saw new rules for racing; three races out of five, alternating windward and leeward and triangularly, of thirty miles outside of Sandy Hook with a time limit of six hours.

But Lipton did not despair and came forward with a new *Shamrock* IV, designed by C. E. Nicholson. She was a long boat with flat ends of laminated wood constructed over steel frames. She was seventy-five feet on the water with 10,459 square feet of canvas.

Resolute was chosen to defend the Cup for the New York Yacht Club syndicate of Henry Walters, J. P. Morgan, Cornelius Vanderbilt, F. G. Bourne, George F. Baker, Jr. and Arthur Curtiss James. *Resolute* had been built at the Herreshoff yards.

On July 15, 1920, a light breeze wind was hardly strong enough to keep the sails filled. It was black in the southwest with indications of thunder squalls later on. During the race, squalls, with a deluge of rain, came on, but not much wind. This rain soaked the *Resolute*'s main sail and caused it to shrink. The extra strain proved too much for the halyards and they parted at the hoisting winch below decks. The *Resolute* was disabled and did not finish.

The second race was to be run on July 17th but the wind was too light and the race was called off. On July 29, the light balloon sail on the *Shamrock* was torn and a make-do sail was set. *Resolute* crossed ten minutes and five seconds behind *Shamrock IV*. *Shamrock IV* had now won two races and it looked as if the Cup might go back across the Atlantic.

The third race, on July 21, was a close one in a light wind. Both boats sailed the course in exactly the same time. There had been a nineteen second margin in favor of the *Resolute*.

On July 23, a thick fog burned away in a south, southwest breeze. *Resolute* finished three minutes and forty-one seconds before the green yacht, *Shamrock*. On July 27th, there was a light northwest wind. *Resolute* slid over the finish line ahead. She had won three races in a row after the challenger had won two. The Cup stayed in America!

The years 1897 to 1928 showed a diminution in Cozzens' output. Occasionally, a marine magazine would call upon him for a drawing, but commissions began to dwindle. The use of photographs rather than watercolors or line drawings for newspa-

Untitled
Collection of Arthur Baker

Untitled,
Collection of Arthur Baker

per illustrations accounted for a good deal of this dwindling of his work. Newspaper illustrations from 1876 to 1888 consisted of an occasional woodcut or map. About 1892, the papers began to use reduced facsimilies of pen and ink drawings from its illustrators rather than woodcuts. However, starting in 1893, occasional, crude direct photographs began to appear in the New York newspapers. They spelled the end of the use of drawings to illustrate news of sporting events. For instance, the *New York Herald* used only photographs for the coverage of the 1901 America's Cup races. In the September 26, 29 and October 1, and 5 stories, there were no drawings by Cozzens and few drawings in the paper at all. By 1901, photographic reproductions began to predominate. By 1920 there were no drawings at all. This spelled finis to a great part of Cozzens' work.

Ahmed John Kenealy wrote *Boat Sailing in Fair Weather and Foul* in 1896. His book, *Yachting Wrinkles*, published by the Outing Library of Sport in 1899, was illustrated by Cozzens' watercolors or pen and ink outline drawings. It was a practical and historical handbook of useful information for the racing and cruising yachtsman. Opposite page 13, *With Topmast Housed*, is a photocopy of a signed watercolor. This is a racing scene in rough water.

The following, unless otherwise noted, are photographs of pen and ink outline drawings:
Opposite Page 38 *America* 1851, *Maria* 1851
Opposite Page 49 The cutter, *Oriva*
Opposite Page 83 *Madge*
Page 85 *Vesta*
Page 133 The sloop, *Gracie*
Page 134 The schooner, *Sappho*

The following are photocopies of watercolors and are dated 1893:
Page 224 *Vigilant*
Page 243 *Valkyrie*

A splendid Cozzens picture, entitled, *Sunset on the Kill Van Kull*, was used in the October 27, 1898 issue of the *Staten Island*

News Illustrated. This is a large chromolithograph, engraved from a Cozzens watercolor by H. D. Turner. It shows a hazy, smoky view of the Kills, looking toward Newark with only slight detail of ships and shore. This edition was a special issue of the paper celebrating Staten Island becoming a part of the city of New York. This and three other chromolithographs by other artists were given in a special supplement of the newspaper. It is one of the most beautiful pictures ever to appear in a Staten Island newspaper.

Mystic Seaport Museum has a Cozzens watercolor of the U.S.S. *New York* in a starboard view with full steam that he did in 1898. A fine watercolor came to light recently of a sailing ship pulling away from a large two-masted ship with her sails down. It is dated 1898 and possesses a ghost-like effect. This same year he did many cod fishing scenes, men fishing or hauling nets into their dories and one that he entitled, *Open Seas.* The Staten Island Institute of Arts and Science has a watercolor, dated 1899, of a seacoast scene with beach, rocks and a far-distant sailboat. It may be a view of Prince's Bay, Staten Island with a large rock that he included in many of his pictures.

The March 11, 1899 issue of the *Staten Island News Illustrated* mentioned the fact that "Fred. S. Cozzens, the Staten Island artist, is making a picture of the fight at Manila de Santiago, a Spanish-American war picture." The Admiral's Office in the Naval Historical Foundation in Washington D.C. has two Cozzens watercolors representing famous Spanish-American War naval victories. One, at Manila Bay, entitled *Fleet Entering Manila Bay* and another at Santiago de Cuba, also dated 1899, entitled, *Battle of Santiago*, showing a large United States and Spanish fleet engaged in combat. These pictures, undoubtly, are the ones mentioned in the newspaper reference.

In the year 1900, Cozzens again busied himself with different versions of fishing boats aground with men on the beach, cod fishing scenes and desolate beach scenes. He also did, in 1900, the famous clippership, *Sweepstakes.* The New York Yacht Club is proud of a Cozzens watercolor, dated 1903, entitled, *Preparations for a Race*, showing the *Reliance* with the race-committee

Vesuvius, 1893,
Collection of Arthur Baker

Tug,
Collection of William Sullivan

boat and other yachts in blue water with dark markings on the crest of the waves. Cozzens filled the water with debris and barrels floating in the water.

In the fitting-out number of *Rudder Magazine* of March 1903, there appeared an article by A. Cary Smith, with text by William P. Stevens. The illustrations were by Cozzens. There were eleven half-pages of brown and white outline drawings of some of the yachts that Cozzens had drawn many times before; *Mischief*, *Valkyrie*, *Gorilla*, *Hesper*, *Iroquois*, *Intrepid*, *Ariel*, *Fortuna*, *Yampa* and *Elmira*. All of these drawings are signed "Fred. S. Cozzens, 1903" and one is signed "Fred. S. Cozzens after A. Cary Smith." It is obvious that there are many mistakes in the spelling of the names of the yachts but there is no mistake in the drawings. They are superb!

Raising the Halyard
Courtesy of Sotheby Parke Bernet Gallery

The March 1906 issue of *Rudder Magazine* contained an article entitled, "The Sandbaggers" by William E. Simmons with six tinted reproductions of drawings by Cozzens of this type of boat. Sandbaggers were developed from small, half-deck boats of the New York watermen. They were wide, shallow, centerboard craft designed to carry an enormous amount of sail by shifting ballast. They carried sandbags on their decks to keep from upsetting and the bags had to be shifted from one side to the other when she turned. Failure to do so fast enough ended in an upset. They had two rigs, cat and sloop, and could be raced under either rig on short notice.

Cozzens' drawings of the sandbaggers are small (6″x5″) and they are signed and dated 1903. They are entitled, *Pluck and Luck, Susie S., A Friendly Brush, Must Go, Mollie C.* and *Capsize*

Going Out in the Skiff through Surf
Courtesy of Sotheby Park Bernet Gallery

Staten Island at Dusk,
Collection of Arthur Baker

to Windward. The last one shows a boat on its side in the water, its sails and crew afloat. The ships were shown at the time of the annual Newburgh, New York, regatta.

The list of magazine illustrations must be considered as only a partial listing. Undoubtedly, there are many more than have escaped detection to date.

The Seawanhaka Corinthian Yacht Club has a Cozzens port stern view of the *Vigilant*, dated 1903, and a very beautiful port view of the private yacht of Arthur James Curtis, the *Aloha*, showing her black hull, dated 1903.

The Bicentennial Inventory of American paintings mentions a 1941 sales catalogue of a New York City auction gallery that

Beach Rescue,
Collection of Anita Jacobsen

cited a Cozzens watercolor of the brigantine, *Aloha,* that was dated 1904. The Peabody Museum of Salem has three pencil sketches, dated 1905 by Cozzens and a watercolor and gouache of the American sloop, *Pluck and Luck* that is dated 1905. Cozzens also did a small sailing vessel in a fog in debris-laden water with a four-masted ship looming up into view. He also did *Yachts of the Sea, A Whaler in Port,* and *Fishermen at Work,* all dated 1905. A New York City auction gallery sold a tug pulling a three-masted vessel from this year.

In 1907, Cozzens did a port side view of a sailing yacht with the private signal of Charles Adams. He also drew *Morning with a Sea Fog,* showing the West Bank Light. We find the stern view of a pilot vessel meeting a motor vessel that is dated 1907 and the usual sailboat and dory scenes.

The Seawanhaka Corinthian Yacht Club displays a Cozzens watercolor of a starboard view of the *Tamerlain* that he did in 1908, and a cod fishing scene from the same year. The New York Historical Society owns one entitled, *Cod Fishing on the Newfoundland Banks; Nantucket to Grand Bank,* that is dated 1908. An unusual Cozzens, also dated 1908, shows an early morning scene in which six men are unloading a surfboat and loading a donkey-drawn cart which stands on the wet sand. It is entitled, *Sea Fog.* He also did two versions of a distress scene with men in a dory with un upturned oar. There is a sailing vessel coming into view and the two men look expectantly toward it. Harper's *Early Painters and Engravers of Canada* mentions a Cozzens watercolor of cod fishing that is dated 1908. He started to do shore scenes which he called, *Enyole Beach,* which are desolate shore scenes with a large rock promontory on one side with a sandy beach and a sailing ship that is far distant. He also did in the year 1908, a bow view of a two-masted vessel in a deep trough and the stern view of an unidentified pilot vessel meeting a motor vessel.

The New York Historical Society owns a Cozzens watercolor, dated 1909, entitled, *A Quiet Night* with Tompkinsville on the right. Tompkinsville is a small village on Staten Island where Cozzens once lived. They also possess a small watercolor of the

Half Moon and the *Clermont* in the Hudson River that is dated 1909. In 1974, a version he called *South Beach* came on the market at public auction in New York City. South Beach is on the south shore of Staten Island. Cozzens drew it in 1907.

A scene, entitled *Castle Garden, New York Bay*, drawn by Cozzens in 1909, appeared recently on the market. Castle Garden is the old, circular stone building at the Battery in New York City. Originally, it had been a fort, later an amusement hall where Jenny Lind and others artists appeared and is at present (although not on the original site) an aquarium. It is interesting to note the emphasis on the nautical aspect of Cozzens' title for this picture. Calling it *Castle Garden, New York Bay*, he emphasized the New York Bay.

Cozzens drew versions of the whaling and cod fishing industries, but he also did small versions of the clam and oystering business. Clam digging was an important industry when the waters of New York Bay and surrounding areas were not polluted. He drew a charming watercolor, which he called *Tonging for Clams*, in 1909. Clam diggers went out from the beach in small boats at low tide and dug for clams with large wooden tongs which resemble a post hold digger with long handles. Cozzens also did a strong watercolor entitled, *Tarpon Fishing in Florida* in the same year.

An old stone pier that figured in many of his paintings was located at Rosebank, Staten Island. Rosebank is a little town that nestles close to the waters of the Narrows and this pier was a favorite sketching spot since there was always a lot of activity nearby. He drew one endearing version of this pier in 1910. He also did one he entitled, *No Wind*, showing boats in a calm with their sails hanging limply.

In the year 1910, Cozzens moved to Georgia with his daughter, Marie Simmons. One of his grandsons, Frederic Meylert, knew of at least one painting that emerged during his stay in Georgia. It was of a large stone mountain outside Atlanta. He did not return to the New York area until 1915. It was believed that Cozzens did not do any work during this five year period

Rounding the Lightship,
Collection of Anita Jacobsen

New York Yacht Club Schooner,
Collection of Arthur Baker

but we have evidence that he did with pieces dated 1911, 1912, 1913, 1914 and 1915. The Seawanhaka Corinthian Yacht Club has a starboard view of the *Avenger,* dated 1911. The Chesapeake Bay Yacht Club has two Cozzens watercolors, dated 1911. One is a square-rigged ship headed straight on with a freighter. The other shows a sailing vessel. Another 1910 piece shows two sailing ships and a tug. Of course, Cozzens could do any of these pieces from memory and did not need to be on the scene to do any of them.

During this period, Cozzens did a great many deserted beach scenes. His titles varied. In 1908 he called one *Enyole Beach.* It might be *Eny Ole Beach* or *No Man's Land*; they all stressed desolation and loneliness.

One beach scene that he did in 1912, used very bright coloring, a departure from his usual palette. In 1912, he also drew, *Red Beacon Near the Point* which still has the original label pasted on the back of the picture, showing the title he gave to the piece.

The Museum of the City of New York is showing a Cozzens watercolor of the *Chesapeake* and the *Shannon.* The Staten Island Institute of Arts and Science has a view that he called *The Breakers.* He entitled a superb watercolor, *Home from Cathay.* This shows a large merchant vessel surging home from a trip to the Orient. He also drew many square-rigged vessels in that same year, 1913.

In 1914, Cozzens did a set of three small pictures of beach scenes. An interesting note is their trick signature. He put his given name on the first picture, signed "S." on the second one and put his surname on the third.

The year 1915 produced at least one fine watercolor that is in the collection of the author. The Ambrose Lightship, now a part of the permanent collection of the South Street Seaport Museum on the New York City waterfront, is pictured with a superb white vessel. The Staten Island Historical Society has a watercolor, dated 1915, of a passenger liner off Fort Wadsworth, Staten Island. This picture was loaned to the exhi-

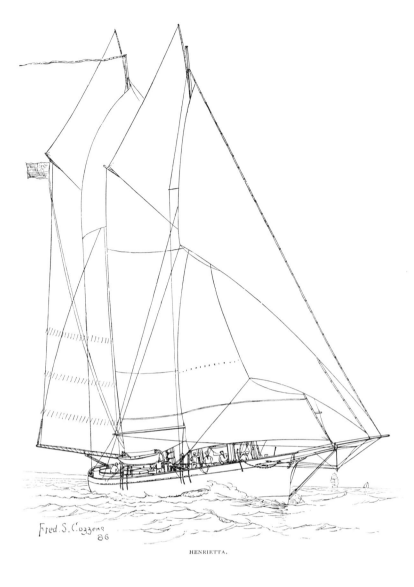

Fred. S. Cozzens
86

HENRIETTA.

bition of *Treasures of Staten Island* held by the Staten Island Institute of Arts and Science in September of 1952. A private collector in Massachusetts has a Cozzens watercolor of a Fall River Line steamer, the *Priscilla*, dated 1915. The Massachusetts Institute of Technology, Department of Naval Architecture, has a watercolor of the sloops *Resolute* and *Vanitie*, dated 1915, in a trial match off Sandy Hook held in 1914. This piece had formerly been in the collection of Captain Arthur A. Clark, author of *The Clipper Ship Era.*

In the year 1916, Cozzens did an interesting picture of a Dutch eel boat with four figures on board that is beached at the edge of a sandy shore. Nearby is a small dory with three figures in typical Dutch costumes. Cozzens inscribed it, "To Mrs. Ernest V. Hubbard, with compliments." Ernest V. Hubbard was one of his patrons. The Peabody Museum at Salem has a Cozzens watercolor of the schooner, *Sylvia*, which had been built in Scotland. Cozzens drew her in 1917. The Peabody Museum also has Cozzens' version of the New Bedford, an American whaling ship which he painted in the same year.

We know of at least one clipper ship that he painted in the year 1918. In 1919 he was commissioned by the Great Northern Railway Company to do some work which was used in their advertising. He painted the tea ship, *Oriental*, for them in 1919. In the *New York Times* article that was printed in 1926, Henry J. Brockmeyer mentioned this specific commission. A print of this watercolor was issued by the McGill Lithographic Company of Minneapolis, Minnesota. The *Oriental* was a famous clipper ship, the forerunner of the famous Oriental Train of the Great Northern Railway Company. Cozzens also drew the ship, *Columbia*, for the State Street Trust Company of Boston to be made into a calendar by this bank, as well as a beach scene that is owned by the Staten Island Institute of Arts and Science.

In 1920 we know that Fred. S. Cozzens paid his attorney, Frank Mebane, for legal work by painting him a watercolor of the Ambrose Lightship. It was during this year that Cozzens did three views of Indian life, a radical departure from his

Early Morning,
Collection of Arthur Baker

Sou'wester,
Collection of Arthur Baker

marine work. He also drew other scenes with the crew of an abandoned ship being rescued by the Coast Guard in boats launched off the beach. In 1921 Cozzens drew a view of an Eskimo village in Alaska. He also did the bluenose schooner, *John M. Emory,* that had been built in Elizabethport in 1919 by William W. Sullivan.

According to the American Watercolor Society exhibition notices, Cozzens exhibited his *Delawana Esperanta Running Under Her Lee* in the year 1921. In 1922 he drew the clipper, *Dreadnaught,* which sailed under the famous Captain Samuels.

Commissions in 1923 must have been scarce because only three watercolors dated in this year have been found. Two are of beach scenes with rocks and debris washed up on shore and another depicts a three-masted vessel in a becalmed sea. This, probably, means that they were both non-commissioned pieces.

The New York Historical Society has a Cozzens watercolor of a small, coastal schooner inscribed, "To My Old Sailor Friend, ex-Gov. Sulzer." It is dated 1924. The Museum of the City of New York has a watercolor that Cozzens did of the whaler, *Wanderer,* off New Bedford. He also did the ships, *Sweepstakes* and *Sovereign of the Seas,* as well as a ship flying the pennant, *T.B.A.,* and a British sailing vessel in the same year.

The ship, *Thames,* of New York, owned by the Quaker merchant and ship owner, Isaac Hicks, was drawn in 1925 by Cozzens as he envisioned her to have been in 1795, for his contemporary patron, Frederick Hicks.

In 1926 he drew the port side of a schooner sailing vessel flying the New York Yacht Club pennant with a motor boat flying the Atlantic Yacht Club burgee. The Mariners Museum at Newport News has a large pencil sketch of the vessel, *Staghound,* done in 1926.

In the Narrows,
Collection of William Sullivan

In the book, *Old Ship Prints*, published in London in 1927 by John Lane for the Bodley Head Limited, the author, A. Kemble Chatterton, used one black and white reproduction of a Cozzens watercolor of the 1876 America's Cup race showing four yachts, two steamships and a small boat. This had been made into a chromolithograph in 1884.

In 1927 Cozzens drew a scene at Westhampton Beach on Long Island that is currently in the collection of the New York Historical Society.

In 1928, the year in which he died, Cozzens did a fine watercolor of his favorite rock jetty with four men in sou'westers with storm signals flying from the mast. There is a dory moored at the jetty and the rough green water is shown with some ships in the distance. Members of his family insist that this is the final piece of his long career.

Many artists lose their strength and virility as they grow old but not Cozzens. He seemed to age gracefully and never lost his deft touch as he matured.

In 1919, Henry Collins Brown edited the 1918-1919 *Valentine's Manual of Old New York*; volume three, New Series, 1919. He dedicated this volume to the merchants and mariners of old New York. This volume is illustrated with many black and white illustrations as well as eleven ship pictures in color. No credit is given in the picture title but the familiar Cozzens signature in red lettering can easily be seen in the lower left corner of seven of these beautiful ship pictures. The illustrations that he did show great strength and mastery of the art, although he was in his seventies when he drew them. He relished this type of task. He enjoyed drawing the old tea trade ships and clippers. The pictures of the trading ships that he turned out for this assignment show his talent in an extraordinary manner. A picture of the ship, *Charles M. Marshall*, was painted by Antonio Jacobsen. The other three ship pictures are uncredited.

The ship, *Challenge*, (1851) was drawn by Cozzens in 1918. It appeared in volume three. She was a fully rigged square sail tea ship, a famous China-trading ship, owned by N. L. and G. Griswold, that had been built by Webb of New York. Commanded by Captain Waterman, another of the famous sailors and a man of remarkable ability, she was later engaged in the California trade and made her voyages in 108 days in the 1850s. Captain Waterman founded the town of Fairfield in California where he died in 1884. The *Challenge* was a beautiful ship and enjoyed a great reputation and brought much profit to her owners.

Cozzens' rendition of the *Challenge* is a superb watercolor of the kind that he liked to draw best. She was pictured at sea in pale, green water with little foam. She was a three-masted ship with square sails on each mast. Her hull was black.

Cozzens also painted the *New Hampshire* in 1918 for *Valentine's Manual*, volume three. She was a clipper ship used as a Liverpool packet in the 1850s by the State Line, contemporaneous with the Black Ball Line and others of the 1830s and 1840s. She was a beautiful ship and for a long time, one of the noted square-rigged beauties of South Street where she docked, later to be put in the California and Australia trade. She belonged to a line whose ships were named after states.

Cozzens pictured her sailing to the right in New York Harbor. Castle William and sailing craft can be seen in the background. She is a stunning ship with three masts, spaced far apart, and four square sails. She had a black hull and a red stripe. She rode at anchor in placid blue-green water. A rowboat with three men is in the left foreground.

Cozzens also painted the *William H. Macy* in 1918 for volume three. She was a China tea ship; one of the early traders and a distinguished member of the group which created the era known as the "Roaring Forties." She was a staunch, trim-looking ship, as well known in Liverpool and the Orient as she was in New York. William H. Macy, her owner, was a representative of the high grade of men who built and sailed the merchant ships of old New York.

Battle of Santiago Bay,
Courtesy Office of the Admiral,
Washington Naval Yard

Fleet Entering Mobile Bay,
Courtesy Office of the Admiral,
Washington Naval Yard

Cozzens' picture showed the great strength of the ship and of the sea as well. The *William H. Macy* is sailing from left to right. She was a three-masted ship with six square sails and a black hull, pictured in blue water at sea with white highlight.

Cozzens pictured the ship, *Andrew Jackson*, in volume three. She was a famous, early California clipper that made the run to San Francisco in 89 days. At the close of her brilliant career, she had four consecutive passages averaging 98$^1/_2$ days. The splendid career of the American clipper came to an end as a result of the Civil War.

The captain of the *Andrew Jackson*, John W. Williams, received much attention for his record runs. A picture of this beautiful ship was used by the Maritime Exchange on its letterhead for many years.

Cozzens pictured the *Andrew Jackson* in a dignified, serene picture of the beautiful, three-masted vessel in a blue-green running sea. She was a large sailing merchant ship, built in 1855. She was considered a sharp, medium clipper. She sailed in the picture from right to left.

Cozzens portrayed the *Young America* (1853) in 1918. She was one of the most beautiful clippers ever built by William H. Webb of New York. She rounded Cape Horn more than fifty times. In 1888 she foundered with all hands while on a voyage from Philadelphia to a foreign port. This was one of the most famous vessels owned by A. A. Low and Brothers, who were, perhaps, the leading merchants of New York.

The picture of *Young America* shows a glorious, three-masted clipper with all sails up, proceeding from right to left in green, foam-crested water. She was a ship of great beauty; a clipper of the 1850s, with five square sails.

In *Valentine's Manual of Old New York*, volume six, published in 1922, Cozzens is given credit for his picture which was used as the frontispiece. Signed in red in the lower left, it pictures the Hudson River Canal boats at anchor at their docks along West

Street in New York City. This interesting scene shows six canal boats and a Hudson River sloop. There are advertising signs on the sails of the sailing ships. "New York, Elmira and Corning Lines" and other signs advertising the lines for shipping to Elmira in covered barges. The scene is colorful with red brick buildings on the banks of West Street, dull red trim on the canal boats and green water. There is a forest of spars and masts in the background. People are busy on the canal boats and on the shore.

On page 274 of *Valentine's Manual of Old New York*, 1927, there appeared a black and white picture of Cozzens' entitled *Grain Ships Awaiting Cargo at Gowanus Creek*. Eight three- or four-mast schooners are shown tied up with sails reefed. The ever-present Cozzens skiff with two or three men is included in the foreground. The viewer looks out at the scene from the shore. There are a great many logs floating in the water. The piece is signed lower left but undated. In 1880 Cozzens had used this theme in the April 10th edition of *Harper's Weekly* with his line drawing of *Grain Ships Awaiting Cargo at Gowanus Creek*.

SCHOONER "MADELEINE."

Aloha,
Collection of Arthur Baker

Codfishing on the Newfoundland Banks,
Courtesy of New York Historical Society

Cozzens' picture of the U.S.S. *George Washington*, dated 1919, appeared in the fourth volume of the *Manual*, 1920. She was shown leaving New York harbor on December 2, 1918 for the Peace Conference at Paris with President Wilson on board. The grey U.S. ship sails from right to left, past the Statue of Liberty in the harbor. Camouflaged ships and harbor craft can be seen. A biplane is in the sky. The sea is a placid green.

Another Cozzens ship picture, dated 1919, was of the *Samuel Russell* (1847), a famous flyer in the China trade. She was a beautiful vessel with plenty of light canvas for moderate weather but heavily sparred and every inch a clipper. She had been built by Brown and Bell. She presented a beautiful picture and Cozzens pictured her with her canvas up in front of Castle William on Governors Island with the Narrows and shore in the background. The sea is calm but choppy with no waves. The water is grey-green. The black hull of the *Samuel Russel* contrasts with the grey sky.

Another illustration in *Valentine's Manual* was of the *N. B. Palmer* (1850), painted in 1919. The *N. B. Palmer* was one of Jacob Westervelt's crack creations and was commanded by Captain Charles P. Low. Cozzens pictured this handsome three-masted, square-rigged ship in a serene painting of blue-grey water. She had three widely spaced masts. It is a calm scene with many other sailing craft and a dory in the foreground.

In a picture dated 1919 and signed in red in the lower left, Cozzens portrayed the *Houquah*, 1844, as she appeared entering Hong Kong harbor. The *Houquah* was one of the famous ships in the China trade. Commanded by Captain Nathaniel B. Palmer, she had been named in honor of Houquah, a well-known merchant of Canton who was much respected by the English and American residents in China for his integrity, kindness and business ability.

The *Houquah* was a three-masted, fully-rigged ship and Cozzens showed her sailing to the right in rough, blue water with white foam. A Chinese junk is shown in the far background.

Cozzens' picture of the U.S.S. *Aloha* was done in 1919. It is signed in red in the lower left. The *Aloha* was the private yacht of Commodore Arthur Curtis James who gave it to the government for service during World War I. He put the yacht at the disposal of the Third Naval District in 1917 and it was designated as S.P. No. 317 and assigned as flagship of Rear Admiral C. McR. Winslow, U.S.N. She is shown sailing right to left in rough, grey-green water with deep swells, a grey steam yacht with three masts. Another steamship is at left and black smoke can be seen.

Cozzens' picture of Lt. Vincent Astor's yacht, the U.S.S. *Noma*, on duty on the high seas, is dated 1919 and is signed in red in the lower left. The *Noma* was on full duty in European waters under Admiral Simms. She escorted the *City of Savanna* to sea, attacked submarines, carried wounded men, escorted the steamer, *Carolyn*, searched for the U.S.S. *Rehobeth* from which an SOS had been received, attacked the enemy, and picked up a convoy of five American transports. Cozzens pictured the grey steam yacht in heavy, light-green water with white caps.

In the 1919 *Valentine's Manual of Old New York*, Cozzens also portrayed the *Corsair*, the steam yacht of J. P. Morgan, given to the government for service in the war during 1917-1918. She was very active as part of the U.S. Naval Fleet in European water under Admiral Simms. She sailed with the First Expeditionary Forces for France escorting vessels and operating against enemy submarines. Cozzens' watercolor, signed in red in lower left and dated 1919, showed a long, grey steam yacht belching black smoke and making way, in rough water, from left to right. Cozzens' water in this scene was light green with a great deal of foam.

The end of the clipper ship era and the dawning of the age of photography had a great impact on Cozzens' career. In the 1870s and 1880s it was necessary to have an artist go out to the scene to sketch and return to the office to have his drawing reproduced in the newspapers. Today it is possible to send a

Sea Fog,
Collection of Arthur Baker

Becalmed Sailing Ship,
Collection of Arthur Baker

photo into a news room via wire photo service in a few minutes. In the days when Cozzens was working, however, there was no way to speed pictures around the world. It had to be done laboriously by hand and the artist who could quickly capture the thrill of action was in greater demand. About 1890 the art of chromolithography was superceded by photography. Although it has many advantages, photography will never take the place of the artist who drew his lithographic and chromolithographic drawings and prints. A moving boat becomes static in a photograph but a capable draftsman can overcome all of these difficulties and bring the viewer into his perception of the scene. However, photography has the advantage of speed and low price and thus it became a severe rival to the artist and his lithographic process, ending the demand for the illustrator and bringing to an end a great deal of Cozzens' commissions. As the age of sail came to an end, so did the age of marine painting.

Frederic Schiller Cozzens died in St. Vincent's Hospital on Staten Island on August 29, 1928 at the age of eighty-two years and ten months. His address at this time was 32 Howard Court, in Livingston, a small town of Staten Island. He suffered from carcinoma of the esophagus and although he had been ill for a year and a half, he continued to paint until ten weeks before he died. He was buried on Friday, September 3, 1928 at Fairview Cemetery on Victory Blvd. from the Episcopal Church of the Ascension which was located at that time on Richmond Terrace in Port Richmond, Staten Island. And so came the end of an illustrious career!

There were many inaccuracies in the glowing obituary notices accorded to him, such as the wrong birth date, but the important element was the respect all of the newspapers gave to his art.

Cozzens' forte was the faithful recording of an era in our maritime history. Most people associate him only with yachting and racing but his drawing encompassed all type of watercraft. He drew not only the beauty of the racing yacht but the entire U.S. Navy, as well as the merchant ships and individually owned craft of all kinds.

Even after his death, many books on boating have been illustrated with his paintings. He is one of the marine illustrators mentioned in the book, *Early American Book Illustrators and Wood Engravers, 1670-1870* by Sinclair Hamilton, published in 1968.

In 1929, the Yale University Press put out a fifteen volume set "Pageant of America Series," *A Pictorial History of the United States*. In volume fifteen, *Annals of American Sport*, a splendid Cozzens watercolor is used, *The Maria outsails the America*, from that never-to-be forgotten Cup race of 1851. John Allen Krout wrote in the section entitled, "Yachting and Aquatics," in this series, "Fred. S. Cozzens was an artist who specialized in marine paintings and acquired a reputation as a draftsman of boats. His work shows all types of English and American watercraft in use in the last century."

This watercolor of the *Maria* outsailing the *America* was also used in Winfield, Thompson and Lawson's, *The Lawson History of the America's Cup*, published in Boston in 1902. In the centerfold of the yachting and aquatic section of the *Annals of American Sport*, another Cozzens drawing appeared. It is the *Atalanta*, drawn in 1883. The *Atalanta* was owned by George J. Gould and was more powerful than the *Namouna*, owned by James Gordon Bennett. Both were long, narrow, express steam craft with light, beautifully built hulls that were constructed in the Herreshoff yards.

Although photographs are used for the bulk of the illustrations in the book, *America's Cup Races* by Herbert L. Stone, Wm., H. Taylor and Wm. W. Robinson, four Cozzens line drawings were used for illustrations when the book was published in 1958:
Page 11   *America*
Page 31   *Magic* (under sail)
Page 51   *Madeleine*
Page 62   *Mischief*

The June, 1944 issue of *Rudder Magazine* contained an article entitled, "Marine Pictures," by L. Francis Herreshoff. Number

Lobsterman in Dory,
Collection of Arthur Baker

Spanish Galleon,
Collection of William Sullivan

11 of the thirteen illustrations was listed as a color lithograph by Fred. S. Cozzens. It is a small reproduction showing a number of ships. The original title is not given and the signature and date are not supplied. Mr. Herreshoff verified that Cozzens had illustrated some of his earlier writing.

The McMillan Book of Boating by William N. Wallace, published in 1972, has an illustration of the *America* rounding the turning mark and leading in a New York Yacht Club race. Shown are the *Maria, Una* and *Ray*. It is signed in red in the lower left and dated 1884. Another Cozzens painting was *For the Challenge*, 1881. A. Cary Smith designed a compromise sloop called *Mischief*, which won handily against Britain's *Atalanta*. This drawing, signed in red in the lower left is dated indistinctly. A Fred. Cozzens print shows the Hudson River scene of 1883. Jay Gould's yacht, *Atalanta*, passes the *Stranger* on the left and a cargo ship can be seen in the rear. A launch puffs down stream and the Palisades are in the background. There are three small line drawings of Cozzens' work used on pages 26 and 27.

When Horace P. Beck wrote an article entitled, "A Maritime Heritage" in the January issue of *American Neptune*, he mentioned Cozzens in a long list of better known ship painters.

A Cozzens woodcut was used for illustration in *The Pictorial History of American Yachting; Yachts of the Atlantic Yacht Club*.

In 1971 Durham House Inc., of Stamford, Connecticut, reproduced a series of Cozzens' racing pictures entitled, *A Portfolio of Great American Yachts. Selected From a Limited Edition Illustrated by Fred. S. Cozzens in 1887*. The portfolio, limited to 500 sets, contained an essay on the history of yachting by Bill Robinson, editor of *Yachting Magazine*. There are eight black and white 11"x14" line drawings with an explanatory text describing the boat and her place in the race. All of the drawings were originally produced in *Yachts and Yachting* published by Cassell in 1887. They include the *Sappho, Henrietta, Magic, Mischief, Una, Madeleine* and *America*. All are dated 1887.

Cozzens did many watercolors that were not a part of a set or series. There are many versions of the *Columbia-Shamrock* race of October 20, 1899 as well as the October 3, 1901 version of that race.

Although we have a record of all of his work that is now in museums and yacht clubs and have endeavored to keep track of the work that has surfaced for sale in the past twenty years, there is no mention here of his vast volume of work for wealthy clients who hung the pieces in their homes or boats. Cozzens never kept a list of the work that he did. These commissioned watercolors were probably a major part of his output. A post-publication checklist will be continued in the hope that some indication of these works that have never been sold or recorded may be made. There are also many watercolors that are undated. A complete list of his work will be found in the catalogue raisonné.

Staten Island is a small island in New York Harbor, only thirteen miles by seven miles. The south shore faces the Narrows and looks out to the Atlantic Ocean. The north shore faces the Kill Van Kull. The people of Staten Island have always been attracted to the water. They supported a large number of yacht and athletic clubs with boat-houses right at the water's edge. Cozzens did a great deal of his art work on Staten Island.

After the New York Yacht Club was organized aboard the yacht, *Gimcrack*, in 1844, a boathouse was built on a picnic area called Elysian Fields on the Stevens' family estate in Hoboken, New Jersey. The first boathouse was used until 1868 when the New York Yacht Club left it for another clubhouse located on Staten Island. The new clubhouse was located at Clifton within sight of the Narrows between Abbott Street and Andrease Street near the foot of Hylan Boulevard. The building was a gracious, Victorian structure, known as the Brandt House, originally a private residence, built in 1846, with a fine three acre lawn. A print of the clubhouse grounds appeared in the *Harper's Weekly* of July 4, 1868, showing the clubhouse and spacious grounds. The water in front of the property was dotted with sailing vessels, steam yachts and row

Fred. S. Cozzens.
86

"CLYTIE."

Paddlewheel Passing Hong Kong,
Collection of Morton S. Vose

Untitled (Large Sailing Ship),
Collection of William Sullivan

boats. The property swept up from a bluff at the edge of the beach. A pier ran out into the water for the use of the members of the club, and the water directly in front of the clubhouse was usually filled with the boats of members and their guests. Cozzens did not live on Staten Island at this time but often came to the area to sketch and draw.

Situated high on the bluffs of Staten Island overlooking the Narrows, Fort Wadsworth has always strategically controlled the waters of New York Harbor. It is the oldest continuously manned position in the United States. The Dutch first built a fort there in 1636; the English enlarged it and the State of New York increased its importance during the War of 1812. Three forts were built on the cliff overlooking the water, but New York State allowed these forts to fall into disuse. The property was purchased by the Federal Government in 1836, reactivated in 1847 and rearmed during the Civil War. Battery Weed, completed in 1861 had implacements for more than 200 guns. Fort Richmond was renamed Fort Wadsworth to honor Brigadier General James S. Wadsworth who was killed in 1864. The entire area eventually became known as Fort Wadsworth. The New York Yacht Club clubhouse is within walking distance of the fort. Cozzens frequented the clubhouse and often sketched on the grounds of the fort. A relative of his lived on the grounds of the fort and gave him access to come and go whenever he pleased. He often sat and sketched the activity in the harbor from this area.

Clifton is an old Staten Island town right on the Narrows. For a time it took the name of Vanderbilt's Ferry Landing after Commodore Vanderbilt started a ferry from the foot of Vanderbilt Avenue. There was a large stone pier or dock here that is depicted in many of Cozzens' pictures, as well as a large rock near the dock on which the shad fishermen dried their nets.

The Staten Island Athletic Club, formed in 1877, had a yachting department and built a boat house on the north shore of Staten Island in the town of New Brighton in 1879. In 1885 new grounds were acquired and the club moved to the old Campbell Mansion on the Cove of the North Shore of Staten

Island where a boat house was built on the water's edge. The Cove is the indentation of the shore near the old Cruzer Pelton House. The Athletic Club had a decennial celebration on the club grounds on Labor Day, September 5, 1887. The commemorative booklet put out on this occasion contained woodcuts of the boathouse and a woodcut from a pen and ink drawing of the great American yacht, *Volunteer*, drawn by Cozzens. He drew a picture of the Staten Island Athletic club-house in 1926. In this pleasant but undistinguished picture, the Staten Island shore is visible in the background.

There were many athletic and boating clubs on the north shore of Staten Island at the time when Cozzens was sketching. There were rowing drills and a different kind of water activity than the yachting races and trial matches that took place on the south shore of Staten Island. There were many water events taking place every day which Cozzens sketched. Old Staten Island residents remember him sketching with his folding easel and paintbox at many of these places. His favorite haunt on Staten Island, in addition to the grounds of Fort Wadsworth, was at the old ferry dock at the railroad crossing at Clifton, where he could see all the vessels coming in or leaving the harbor. He would set up his easel and his folding camp chair near the old stone dock and start to work. In later years he sketched at Cedar Grove, farther south along the shore and at Lemon Creek in Prince's Bay.

He made innumerable sketches of a group of rocks jutting out of the water on the south shore of Staten Island. These rocks are remnants of the Ice Age, some 30,000 years ago, when the Wisconsin Glacier created a trough-like lake filled with melt water. The glacier was plugged at the south end by a moraine or dam made of the rocks that the glacier had pushed before it. As the glacier melt-off continued, the ocean rose and breached the moraine. The rocks that Cozzens depicted so often are remnants of this moraine. At times he showed the rocks bare; sometimes he covered them with seaweed. Breakers were usually in the foreground and a square-rigged ship might be sailing in the far-distance. Cozzens could dash off one of these rock

scenes from memory and did so often. Some of this work is banal and monotonous, but occasionally one emerged that is superb. Cozzens kept a small boat in the Fresh Kills Creek behind historic St. Andrew's Church in Richmondtown, the county seat. From here, he could row to any spot he desired on the shore.

Cozzens sketched by himself and was never known to have collaborated with any artist in his work. Cozzens not only did boat pictures but many shoreline scenes of rocky coasts and sandy beaches too. He walked the beach and found numerous occasions to sketch the craft that frequented New York Harbor. Many people associate him only with the important international Cup races but his work included sloops, schooners, ice boats, cutters, catboats, pilotboats, yawls, rescue boats, dories, canoes, catamarans, workboats and rowboats. He worked not only on Staten Island and in the New York area but up and down the New England and New Jersey coasts as well. The craft in his works are shown in the waters of New York Bay, Cape May, Sandy Hook, the Hudson River, New London, New Bedford, Nantucket, Boston Bay and Marblehead. He had a vast knowledge of all kinds of boats and their specific rigging and scorned the artists who made mistakes in this national touch. When he was working during the great yachting races, he was often invited on many of the private racing boats. L. Francis Herreshoff remembered that Cozzens was a frequent guest on many of the racing sailboats of the 1880s or on the judge's boat where he sketched right at the scene.

Although he was often an observer at important yachting events, Cozzens rarely left the harbor area and never crossed the Atlantic. In spite of the fact that he drew many European-type ships, such as a Dutch eel boat or Scotch and English fifes, he never traveled to Europe. There are some Oriental watercolors that he did without any travel experience in the Orient. It is known that he traveled around the New England seacoast sketching the seascapes and dunes. Recently, some watercolors came on the market that Cozzens had used to pay for rent on a cottage on Cape Cod. He also spent a few weeks on Long Island and did some sketches of its shore and

Liner Aground in Fog,
Collection of Arthur Baker

Trolling for Bluefish,
Collection of Anita Jacobsen

ships. He frequented many of the yachting and boating clubs to obtain commissions although he was not a member of any of them.

Very late in his life he did not go out to sketch, working only in his room. At an advanced age, his daily routine was to read the *New York Times* right after breakfast, and then go up to his room to work at his easel. He painted every day. Painting was his only occupation, but he always considered it to be his hobby. He worked very slowly, producing an average of one painting a week in his later years. In his prime he turned out two or three a week. There is a great deal of painstaking work in a watercolor, especially when one uses the techniques of washes and transparent handling that Cozzens excelled at. After he completed a few paintings, he would pack them and take them to New York City to sell them.

Cozzens usually gave titles to his works. They were unique and usually were in nautical terms such as *Black Squall* or *Before the Wind*. He usually wrote the name of the painting in pencil. This information is often covered by the mat and many not be known until the painting is rematted. Many of the Cozzens watercolors had a sticker on the back of the picture with his title to the picture. Often these stickers would come off, losing his original title for ever.

The earliest Frederic S. Cozzens signature of which there is any record was in his application to Rensellaer Polytechnic Institute on September 14, 1864. Here he wrote his full name, Frederic Schiller Cozzens, Jr. It is interesting that he used Jr., although his name was not identical to his father's, Frederic Swartwout Cozzens. However, in the eighteen-hundreds, his father was a well-known writer and humorist and the son may not have wanted any mistake about his identity.

When Cozzens signed his art work, he usually printed his name with a different capital "F" and capital "S" than in his signature of 1864.

Cozzens usually signed his work Fred. S. Cozzens, not spelling out his full name. Neither the author-father or the artist-son used a "k" at the end of their first name. The application to Rensellaer shows Frederic with no "k." When Frederic Schiller's grandson, Frederic Meylert, was in primary school, his grandfather reprimanded him for spelling his first name with a "k." "You know how to spell it properly!" he said.

In his latest signatures, the script capital "S" became a printed "S." His painting signatures are in red, green or grey and at times he used a combination of colors.

In his book, *American Yachts, Their Clubs and Races*, which he published in 1884 with Lt. Kelley, he signed his plates with an interesting monogram which intertwined a large "C" with an "F" interlaced with an "S."

Goodspeed's *This Month* mentioned that on at least one occasion, Cozzens signed himself as "Sparrowgrass Jr." but no other reference to this fact or verification has ever been found. *Sparrowgrass Papers* was a famous book written by his father. In a note that he wrote to his patron, Frederick Hicks, late in his life in 1925, Cozzens used an unusual printed "F" with an elongated tail going to the left. He usually accompanied his signature in the corner of his work with the date year. His signature is unique, clear, precise and readable, as he wanted it to be.

There is little evidence of the fees that Cozzens charged for his work. His grandchildren claimed that the fees varied and that he charged whatever the traffic would bear. Like Antonio Jacobsen, he believed himself to be a good businessman. Indeed, they were both good businessmen because their painting realized an income that was sufficient to support their families without any other means of support. We do know that Cozzens' work that appeared in exhibitions was priced between $75 and $200. In 1881 he priced two watercolors at $60 each. In 1916 he asked $50 for the watercolor *Ideal Head*.

There is no evidence that Cozzens ever had an agent. Although he had a large circle of friends in the yachting world who gave him commissions for pictures of their boats, Cozzens

Noma,
Collection of Arthur Baker

Tug,
Collection of Arthur Baker

had the responsibility of caring for the needs of his large family alone. It is difficult to imagine the far-reaching effects that this financial drain had on his work. When his grandchildren were asked why their grandfather never had a one-man show, they replied, "He could not afford to accumulate enough work for that kind of show. He had to sell paintings every week in order to pay his bills." This responsibility hung like a millstone round his neck and prevented him from ever traveling far from home. There was never any extra money for indulgences of this sort.

A proud man, Cozzens might not have accepted help from anyone although it might have provided momentary help from everyday monetary necessity.

Cozzens' financial success as an artist is difficult to estimate today. He succeeded in commanding sufficient patronage and commissions to yield him a modest livelihood. His painting income was sufficient to provide for a large family until his death. When his grandson, Frederic Meylert, was asked if his grandfather was considered financially successful in his day, he replied, "He was considered, in his day, to be one of the leading watercolorists of all time. He had a large family to support, so he might not have been considered successful from a monetary angle, but I believe that he was successful from an artistic point of view. He never received any 'big money' for his work because he could not hold out for a better price." Meylert believed that Cozzens had a regular clientele in the financial society of New York City. He would paint all week, wrap up the work on Saturday, depart for New York and come home with the money.

When Cozzens was working there were relatively few channels through which an artist could reach the public. He could send examples of his work to a regular art exhibit or to a fair or industrial show. Cozzens took advantage of many methods to sell his paintings. He went to his patrons, wealthy clients and galleries. He received commissions from private people as well as companies. He illustrated books, magazines and newspapers. His work was made into print sets. Department stores sold reproductions of his work.

One of the commercial companies from which he received orders was Clark Cotton. Clark's O.N.T. Spool Crochet Cotton issued trade cards or advertising cards at the turn of the century. They were very popular items, collected and usually mounted in Victorian scrapbooks or albums. The 7½" x 5¼" cards came in gold, pink and tans. Signed and dated 1890, one depicts Lake George, another San Francisco's Golden Gate (long before the bridge of that name). He also sold Clark pictures of the Statue of Liberty in New York Harbor, the three ships of Columbus and one entitled *Moonlight, Coney Island*.

Some of Cozzens' work was used as calendar art. The State Street Trust Company of Boston used a fine example of Cozzens' work in their calendars, years ago. The scene was of the ship *Columbia* at anchor, trading with the Indians shortly after entering the river to which Captain Grey gave the name of his ship in 1792.

Cozzens did some work that would not fall into the marine category. In an article that appeared in the magazine *Antiques* in 1933, E. A. Wright and J. A. McDevitt list Cozzens as a New York City artist who made covers for sheet music before 1870. Three unusual Cozzens views of Indian life, signed and dated 1920, came on the market in 1969.

Almost every collector of his work treasures a foreign scene such as an oriental junk or a Dutch eel boat. One collector has a romantic, Italian-type painting that would never be taken for a Cozzens piece.

During his lifetime, he produced book, magazine and newspaper illustrations, sheet music covers and trade cards using shore or water scenes, ship portraits and harbor views as well as racing and sailing event scenes.

Cozzens' work was never awarded a prize. According to a strong family tradition his work was entered in the Columbian World's Fair in 1895 and supposedly won a gold medal. However, the family insists that the publishing house kept the

Three Men in a Dory,
Collection of William Sullivan

Beached Boat,
Collection of William Sullivan

medal and never gave it to him. Some of his grandchildren thought it was a picture of the U.S. Navy ships which took first prize. Others thought it was one of his yachting series. However, a search of all the literature and official catalogues of the Exposition, fail to reveal any mention of Cozzens either as a contestant or winner of any medal. Nothing was ever found to substantiate the fact that he won a medal in this competition.

Information about the art exhibitions in which Cozzens' work appeared is sketchy. A few bits of data were gleaned from old exhibition catalogues and must in no way be considered complete. From these notices, we are able to learn some of the details of the location of his studios, the prices he was asking for his work at that time and the popularity and degree of success attained.

Appleton's Cyclopedia of American Biography, published in 1888, states that Cozzens had exhibited his watercolor sketches in New York, Boston and Philadelphia. They add that he is particularly successful with fog effects and surf boat subjects. To date, no other mention has been found that he exhibited in Boston or Philadelphia.

Although he was not a member of the National Academy of Design, whenever Cozzens entered a painting in one of their exhibitions, his work was hung "on the line," which was the highest compliment he could receive. This meant that the work was displayed at eye level during a showing, the coveted place for art work to be shown to best advantage.

The American Watercolor Society allowed works by non-members to be exhibited at its exhibitions. From their catalogues we find a twenty-five year period, from 1895 to 1920, in which Cozzens did not exhibit there at all. In 1880 he exhibited *Winter Down the Bay* and *Morning Off the Isle of Shoals* in their spring exhibit. The Art Division of the New York Public Library in New York City has a small engraving of Cozzens', cut from the 1880 catalogue. It shows five fishing craft and one large sailing ship. The sun is rising as men are hauling a net in the foreground.

In the 1881 annual exhibition of the National Academy of Design, Cozzens exhibited two of his watercolors, *Return of the Whaler, New Bedford* and *Blue Fishing, Great Point, New Bedford*. Each was priced at $60. His name does not appear on any other exhibition lists from the Academy.

The Brooklyn Art Association held a show in March, 1881 in which Cozzens exhibited two of his paintings; *Now then, Bill*, and *Making a Harbor*, both priced at $150. This is the first found mention of *Now then, Bill*. Apparently it was not sold in the Brooklyn Art Association exhibition because we find it entered in the fourteenth annual exhibition of the American Watercolor Society priced at $100.

In this exhibition, held from December 1 to December 21, 1881 there were 803 works by 226 artists displayed. In the North Room, *Making a Harbor* was priced by Cozzens at $150. In the Northwest Room, his *Dreamy* was exhibited with a price of $125. *Now then, Bill*, later made into a print, was hung in the corridor.

Koehler's *U.S. Art Directory and Year Book, 1882-1884*, lists Fred. S. Cozzens of 176 Broadway, New York, in the 15th American Watercolor Society annual exhibition, held from January 30 to February 25, 1882. In the North Gallery he showed *A Fair Wind*, priced at $200. In the next annual exhibition of that organization, held from January 29 to February 25, 1883, Cozzens was represented in the corridor with *A Free Wind, New York Bay*, priced at $175. Koehler further listed the 17th annual exhibition, held from February 4 to March 1, 1884 and in which Cozzens showed some of his work, although no mention was made of what this work was.

In the exhibition catalogue of the Art Institute of Chicago, *A Collection of Painting in Watercolor of American Artists, In the Fog* by Cozzens, lent by Gustave H. Buck of Brooklyn, was listed.

In the Fifth Avenue Art Gallery exhibition held on November 26, 1915, a sale of 205 paintings from the estate of Ermina J. Proal and E. A. Raymond, the catalogue lists a Cozzens work,

Two Work Boats,
Collection of Arthur Baker

Cynthia Ann,
Collection of Arthur Baker

#82, *Ideal Head*, a 26″ x 19″ watercolor, for sale at $50. *Ideal Head* was listed as an oil painting but this may have been a cataloguing error.

The American Watercolor Society of 1083 Fifth Avenue, lists Fred. S. Cozzens of Mundy Avenue, Staten Island, as an exhibitor in their 54th annual exhibition in 1921 with a painting of a ship, *Delawana Esperanta Running from Under Her Lee*, which he priced at $100.

In April of 1926, the State Island Institute of Arts and Science held an exhibition of paintings and sculpture by Staten Island artists. Cozzens was one of twenty-eight artists who were represented. He entered two pieces, *Field Trip of the New Mexico* and *In Harbor*. The *Bulletin* of 1926 makes no mention of the dates of either piece.

A reproduction of Cozzens' watercolor, *Lifeboat with Figures* or *Action by the Navy* was exhibited in the Lyman Allen Museum in New Haven, Connecticut from March 4 to April 15, 1943. As #5 in the catalogue, it shows seven men trying to free their lifeboat from the sand where it has become mired.

The Staten Island Institute of Arts and Science held an exhibit from September 7 to December 15, 1952. *Treasures of Staten Island*, a show of paintings and art objects from the homes of Staten Islanders. The Staten Island Historical Society lent a watercolor entitled, *Ocean Liner in the Narrows*, done in 1915.

The Wilmington Society of Fine Arts held a maritime exhibition in the Delaware Art Center Building in 1955 that featured 19th-century steam and sail ships. Catalog entry #24 is *The White Fleet*, three lithographs by Cozzens done in 1892–3 illustrating the transition from sail to steam. This is the only reference that has been found of the set *The White Fleet*, possibly another name for one of his sets of naval pictures.

The Montclair Art Museum of New Jersey held an exhibition in 1973 of the *Piscatorial Pictorials of America*. Their catalogue listed a Cozzens watercolor, *Surf Casting Along the Jersey Coast*, dated 1885. The catalogue mentions Cozzens as known mainly for his seascapes and American yachting subjects.

A special exhibition of the work of Frederic Cozzens was featured by the Penobscot Maritime Museum of Searsport, Maine in July of 1976. The exhibition included twenty-four watercolors, eight chromolithographs, seven pencil sketches and fourteen prints, as well as a copy of his book, *American Yachts, Their Clubs and Races*. The watercolors exhibited were:

Barque, New Bedford, 1917
Barque, Andrew Hicks, 1925
Two vessels in Heavy Seas, 1902
Egypt, Running a Gale, 1883
Beach Scene, Two Boatmen in Dory, 1910
Lobsterman Standing in Dory in Quiet Water, 1906
Beaching a Fishing Boat, 1908
Hand Lining for Cod, 1898
Lost Fishermen, 1908
Two Fishing Schooners, 1904
Schooner, Steam Vessel Meeting Rough, Foggy Sea, 1903
Beached Coastal Schooner, 1904
Schooners, Clifford N. Carver and Inez N. Carver
Fully Rigged Ship, 1925
Unidentified Ship Awaiting Pilot, 1925
Ship Passing Pilot Boat, 1910
When the Cynthia Ann Came Ashore in '14, 1914
Constitution and Java, 1926
Serapis and Bonhomme Richard, 1923
Constitution and Guerriere, 1925
Brig, Alert, 1925
Mayflower, 1925
Pirate Ship, 1925
Launching of the Surf Boat, 1888

A great deal of Cozzens' work was commissioned by specific people. Unfortunately we have the records of only a few of these commissions. We know of two paintings that he did for the home of Cuthbert Mills, a resident in the Fort Wadsworth area of Staten Island. Another was of Mr. Mill's private chapel

Schooner and Steam Vessel in Fog,
Collection of Arthur Baker

Old Galleon,
Collection of William Sullivan

WRECKERS AT WORK ON THE SUNKEN STEAMER "IBERIA."—Drawn by F. S. Cozzens.

and old Fort Wadsworth. Mention has been made previously of Cozzens' watercolor of the clippership, *Columbia*, commissioned by the Great Northern Railway Company. A special celebration was planned for the centennial of the original trip the *Columbia* made around the Cape of Good Hope for a rendezvous with the first transcontinental railroad. The train and the boat met in California. Mr. Judd, the president of the railroad company at that time, sent Cozzens a handsome parchment invitation to the ceremonies but Cozzens did not accept. He felt that he was too old to make the long trip from New York to California, but he was not too old to make a splendid picture of the *Columbia* for the company to reproduce into lithographs which were given as souvenirs to the customers of the railroad.

W. C. Hubbard, secretary of the Cotton Exchange in New York City was also a patron. Cozzens did a number of paintings for him including a large picture of a Spanish galleon with decorated sails. Cozzens personally inscribed one of his Dutch eelboat scenes to Mrs. Hubbard.

The article by Brockmeyer, that appeared in the *New York Times* in June, 1926, reported that Cozzens had painted a series of racing pictures for members of the New York Yacht Club in 1926. That same year he was also commissioned by the Great Northern Railroad to paint a picture of the tea ship, *Oriental*.

One of Cozzens' patrons during the last quarter of the 19th century was the late Hon. Frederick C. Hicks, representative in the Congress from the First District of New York. Before his death in 1925, Hicks had individually commissioned Cozzens to paint more than thirty-five watercolors over a period of years.

A note from Cozzens to Hicks has been preserved by the later's son, Frederic S. Hicks, in which Cozzens mentions that he had sent six pictures by express to his office. The note was dated August 1, 1925 and was sent from Mundy Avenue, Staten Island, three years before his death.

Long Island Sharpie,
Collection of Arthur Baker

Hand Lining for Cod,
Collection of Arthur Baker

Mr. Hicks assembled one of the largest and most comprehensive and diverse collections known. It was Hicks who decided upon the individual subjects to be painted. One, in particular, was the whaler, *Andrew Hicks*, named for a paternal ancestor. Another subject was the ship, *Thames*, of New York, owned by the Quaker merchant and ship owner, Issac Hicks, done in 1925 as Cozzens envisioned her to have looked in 1795.

In the collection there are two watercolors of the famous *Gimcrack*, on whose deck the New York Yacht Club was organized while she lay at anchor off the Battery on July 30, 1844. The collection includes Cozzens' version of such ships as Hudson's *Half Moon*, the *Mayflower* and the old *Constitution*.

Hicks was especially anxious to have a picture of Adrian Block's *Onrust*, a Dutch word meaning restless. In the history of the Dutch Colony of New Amsterdam, there is mention of a yacht or boat, built for pleasure, named *Onrust*, that was built in Manhattan in 1614. It is claimed to be the first decked vessel built in America. Adrian Block's *Quest* is also pictured in the collection. The three ships of Columbus, the *Pinta*, *Nina* and *Santa Maria* are easily recognizable. In 1924, the year before Hicks' death, another old whaler, the *Wanderer* of New Bedford and the whaler, *Charles W. Morgan*, were painted for Hicks by Cozzens. He also painted a Spanish galleon of the 16th century, an 18th century Royal George and a mystery ship. The Battle of Lake Erie was represented in his rendition of Perry's flagship, *Niagara*. He painted the American privateer of the War of 1812, the burning of the frigate *Philadelphia* at Tripoli in 1804 and the *Chesapeake* and the *Shannon* in 1813.

Cozzens used photographs as well as his imagination when he painted long gone ships. There are two tea-ships in Hicks' collection, the British clippers, *Thermopylae* and the *Snark*. The American clippers, *Fanny B. Palmer* and the *Flying Cloud*, as well as the immortal yacht, *America*, round out the collection. Cozzens also painted the famous yacht races between the *Puritan* and the *Genesta* in 1885, the *Sappho* and the *Livonia* in 1871, the *Magic* and the *Cambria* in 1870, the *Mischief* and the *Atalanta*, the *Vigilant* and the *Valkyrie*, the last race between the *Resolute* and the *Shamrock*, and the *Madeleine* and the *Countess of Dufferin* for Hicks.

Before his death in 1973, L. Francis Herreshoff corresponded with this author concerning Frederic Cozzens and his place in maritime art history. He and his father, Nathaniel Herreshoff, both considered Cozzens to be the most accurate portrait painter of individual American yachts. Mr. Herreshoff mentioned that he possessed six Cozzens watercolors commissioned by Captain Arthur Hamilton Clark, who was supposedly preparing a book about Cozzens. A search of the Clark maritime collection, however, revealed no evidence of any research on Cozzens in his papers.

In the late 1920s, Lewis M. Thompson of 24 Stone Street, New York City, wrote a few words about Cozzens mentioning some patrons. "It is believed that many more pictures of yachts have been painted by this artist than any other man now living. Nearly every prominent yachtsman of a generation ago had specimens of his work. The Great Northern Railroad has several pictures by him. He is about to paint a series of historical naval pictures for Franklin Delano Roosevelt. The artist, Fred. S. Cozzens took many medals here and abroad and never failed to sell his work when it was on display. Some of his former and present patrons are: J. P. Morgan, Cornelius Vanderbilt and his son, Captain Donald McKay, son of the builder of the *Flying Cloud*, Latham Fish, W. C. Hubbard, George Flint, William Thomas, Lloyd Phoenix, Robert Maxwell, Com. Benedict, John Aspinwall, George Phynchon, Anson Phelps, Poultney Bigelow, Arthur Curtis James, Frank C. Munson, James C. Colgate, Dudley Olcott, Ogden Mills, Henry Morgan, C. N. Carver, Howard C. Smith, Henry D. Campbell and Captain Arthur H. Clark, author of *The Clipper Ship Era*."

Thompson was of the opinion that Clark had bought between thirty and forty of the artist's best pictures, afterwards acquired by the Massachusetts Institute of Technology. However, MIT did not acquire these paintings and their location at this time is not known. It is evident that the important financial men of this era, as well as the yachting enthusiasts, commissioned Cozzens to paint for them.

It must be remembered that this list of patrons can only be a partial listing and is in no way complete.

Cozzens was always careful to use a high quality paper for his work. This has been partially responsible for the good condition of many of them eighty or one hundred years later. There has been some fading and a tendency to light streaking if they were exposed to direct sunlight, but on the whole they have stood the test of time without much deterioration.

The roughness of the paper he chose created a grainy, textural effect. Whether he used rough, medium or smooth paper, he allowed the texture to speak; it whispers with subtle washes, flows with his soft lines, crackles with sparkle, or it becomes an imaginary world with his muted monotones.

The art world was pulsating with new thoughts and directions at the time of Cozzens' development into an artist. If one attempts to seek the artistic influences evident in his work, one immediately thinks of Turner, who possibly more than any other artist showed us the romantic view of nature. Turner was a forerunner of Impressionism, using color and movement to stir up the emotions or suggest a feeling. His paintings of ships are characterized by mists of flaming color, and Cozzens also used color often to evoke a mood or feeling.

Luminism was a landscape style that developed in the middle of the 19th century in which the study of light is critical. Luminist painting concentrated on capturing air, light and weather effects. They tried to portray water and light in delicately realistic, yet poetic ways by means of infinitely careful gradations of tones and by the most exact study of the placement of objects within the picture. Hudson River School artists such as Kensett, Sanford, Gifford and Fitz Hugh Lane produced Luminism. Martin Johnson Heade concerned himself more with the fleeting effects of mists and sudden thunderstorms, with clouds and atmosphere rather than with light itself.

Cozzens was working at this time in the area and could not help being influenced by all of these attempts. His work abounds in the fleeting effects of squalls, sudden storms and effects of light at specific times.

Impressionism differed radically from Luminism. The former, developing in France, was involved in an awareness of light perceived only as constantly changing sensations. Form is perceived as light, reflected from a surface, while shadows are merely light of a lower intensity. The Impressionists were fascinated with color, especially the color of changing seasons, the times of day and the effects of light playing on the landscape.

All these diverse forces were felt in American art. After the Civil War, a new spirit, a reflection of the mood of the people,

Dutch Eel Boat,
Collection of Anita Jacobsen

THE LAUNCH OF THE IRON CLIPPER-SHIP "T. F. OAKES."—From a Sketch by F. Cozzens.

invaded American art. The work of Thomas Birch, who worked in the Philadelphia and Delaware areas, began to emphasize a sense of air, of sunshine and open spaces. He preferred to work in pale tones with pink and silver effects in contrast to the warm golden tones favored by traditional artists. Birch worked in watercolors and did harbor scenes that emphasized the constant battle between ships and the sea. James Hamilton, who succeeded Birch, was a painter of the sea whose work began to take on a romantic, imaginative quality. John J. Enneking became famous for his Impressionistic autumn sunsets and misty woodland scenes.

In retrospect, it is easy to say that Cozzens became eclectic and took whatever he thought might improve his own output. One finds examples of his work with an Impressionistic feeling in them, evidence of his preoccupation with the effects of light on his subjects. His painting, at times, is pure mood, with misty, rosy or more sober overtones, but no matter from what school he borrowed, he remained strictly within his own sphere, narrowing his observation of the world to one interest: marine painting. He did all of his work in this field. Cozzens belonged to no school, following the traditional way of painting. He matured and perfected his art at a time when a new light had entered the art world. No longer were all paintings turned out in brown tones. Artists were searching to record nature as they saw her.

Cozzens matured in a small, tightly knit group of marine artists who frequented the eastern coastline and particularly the New York Harbor area. Robert Salmon, 1775–1844 and Fitz Hugh Lane, 1804–1865, preceded him. Some of his contemporaries were James Bard, 1815–1856, Antonio Jacobsen, 1850–1921, Fred Pansing, William Stubbs, active circa 1885, James Buttersworth, 1817–1894, Winslow Homer, 1836–1910, Thomas Eakins, 1884–1916 and Alfred Bricker, 1837–1908.

A few of these professional painters of marine scenes were artists of high caliber whose contribution to art in general and to marine art in particular was considerable. The early men contented themselves with formal, traditional artistic conventions. The later artists, competent enough to record the constant changes of the sea, interested themselves in the changing effects as seen in the play of light and shadow. They used the open sea as a symbol of the mystery of life itself. The sea is as mysterious as life and death and has no concern for the men and boats who come and go over it and leave no trace of their activity. Every sailor believes that all ships have souls. Only a few marine artists were able to picture the breath and life of the sea and ships.

Although Cozzens was primarily self-taught, his innate skill with brush and watercolors enabled him to paint skillfully. He was described early in his career as "a developing young artist, skillful and honest, using no tricks of the brush to exploit his cleverness." This description of his working techniques applied throughout his long career. An extremely competent draftsman, he brought much more to his art than technical skill. Cozzens' concern was not merely to make an exact likeness of the boat in the scene but to catch the spirit of the scene. His ability to capture the fleeting, evanescent quality of atmosphere helped to produce paintings of strong yet delicate beauty.

His paintings are deceptively simple, never cluttered with extraneous detail. They are composed simply and show a balance of light and dark masses. The horizon is often placed one third of the way up the paper. His backgrounds are usually unimportant, showing a building, or a lightly sketched lighthouse to give a vertical element. His shoreline was often nondescript, the sea and land at times blending into one another.

Cozzens liked to paint from a low vantage point, such as a small boat looking up at the scene or on the shore looking out into the water. The eye is carried back into the painting through the use of the line of a sail or a distant sailboat. As a rule, he placed a small dory in the foreground to give balance.

Cozzens had the rare ability to capture the spontaneity of a moment showing the beauty of sunlight, mist or fog, as well as

Untitled,
Collection of Arthur Baker

the danger and excitement of sailing. His mastery of different watercolor techniques enabled him to tell us of the varying effects of light, such as strong or early daylight or reflected light. He was often able to convey a mood in his work such as loneliness, by a lone figure in a boat heading nowhere. His was a rare talent. He was a proficient artist who received many commissions for illustration work, yet was able to produce fine art from which he achieved great acclaim.

The foremost characteristics are the pale tones he used in his work, especially the greys, greens and blues that he used in depicting water. Although Cozzens first sketched in pencil and did some pen and ink outline drawings, he was primarily a watercolorist. He used opaque and transparent tempera paints. Although he had available a color range of more than forty tints, he repeatedly used severely restricted range of colors and tone values in his work. Cozzens was aware of the fact that colors on a bright day flatten out and tend to become hues of one color. Yet, with this self-imposed limitation, he never achieved a pale or anemic effect. His watercolors, due to their delicate coloring and lack of any brilliant local color, have been likened to a shell. These soft, pale colors created a quiet, gentle quality in his work.

Cozzens' use of indistinct forms and pale, luminous colors shows his capacity to convey an awareness and sensitivity to mundane things. He worked his fog scenes in dull and muted colors with indistinct outlines of forms, using soft blues and greens to create a feeling of mystery. The viewer feels enveloped in fog so thick that it is difficult to see where the sail ends and the fog begins. One can almost hear the creak of oarlocks as one views the outline of a dory looming up out of the fog.

Cozzens was more interested in the interaction of light in the sky and water than he was in making an exact picture of the boat in the water. One notices his fascination with the effects of light, color and atmosphere, and the fluidity of watercolor is eminently suitable for the expression of evanescent atmospheric effects. A bright day done by Cozzens sparkles with his keen strokes. The time of day and the atmosphere that he recorded are instantly recognizable.

Cozzens was concerned with visual impression. He displayed unusual versatility in the composition of his works. In his early works, one seldom finds two like pictures carrying out the same scheme of action. His background and experiences created a highly personal style and a penetrating way of organizing his work. Cozzens' favorite format was to have a ship in view, squarely in the center of the picture. Another favorite idea was a ship pulling away from view, offering a full view of the stern with every sail pulling in a cloud of canvas. At times his space seems to move up rather than back, giving great depth to the pieces.

Cozzens' technique depended upon transparent handling. He built up the desired translucent effect that he wanted with transparent washes. Shading, as on the sails, was accomplished with successive coats of watercolors, shading the portion of the sail to achieve the effect desired. Cozzens' use of several tones of similar color is noticeable, especially on his sails.

Another of Cozzens' most characteristic features is his rendition of sea water. Even when he concentrated on the quiet aspects of the sea, one is always aware of the tremendous power of the water. Cozzens's understanding of the power, strength and moods of the ocean is reflected in his work. One senses Man's helplessness and smallness in comparision to moving sea water. Some of his seascapes record the wildness of a storm that dashed waves against a gallant ship. Whether his water is vigorous or calm, it is always believable. The water in his work has a translucence indicating great depth of ocean. It has been said that the water in his work seems to change according to the light in which it is seen; at times the picture seems to be of deep, green water, while under different light conditions, the water takes on a pale, ghost-like quality. He achieved great success in his subtle interpretation of still, shallow water.

Watercolor is, perhaps, the most suggestive medium to convey a sense of water receding from a beach. Cozzens' paintings show waves sucking on a beach, or waves that lap endlessly on the shore. Cozzens know how the surf moved and he visualized the constant motion in one split second. His mastery of

Liner in the Narrows,
Courtesy of the Staten Island Historical Society

various watercolor techniques enabled him to express many of the facets of moving sea water. Cozzens' water may be deep green, calm blue, luminous grey or choppy blue-green with white caps. He delighted in painting waves pounding up on a beach. His use of reflection showing the slight movement that is ever-present on the surface of sea water lent balance to the composition. When he was once complimented on his sea water, and asked how he made his beautiful water he replied, "Why!, just like anyone else!"

Cozzens' skies are always well drawn but usually without minute detail. Some of his skies are blinding with hot sunshine or luminous with storm. Others show dramatic clouds from which light filters with a magical brilliance. He did not, as a rule, use gulls or other birds in his sky. In many of his pieces, the wind is high, the sea is rough and the sky is full of clouds. A rolling sea, choppy waves and a dramatic formation of clouds were favorite Cozzens elements. He worked in watercolor paints and the only white in his work was the paper he worked on.

Cozzens' work is easy to distinguish, when one sees his simple, harmonious arrangements, pale colorings, indistinct forms, his play of light and his transparent handling. His water is truly identifiable and his nautical accuracy is unquestioned.

Cozzens' ability to communicate his feelings through the watercolors is self-evident. He told of the tranquility of a calm, bright day, of a good ship's struggle to keep herself erect against wind, cold and water. He told of the violence of the elements, the inherent force of ocean water and the spirited, colorful ships that faced those forces. In spite of his pale, shell-like colorings, his watercolors achieved amazing power. No one excelled him at portraying the yachting or racing scene. There is always the tacit understanding of the relationship of his boats to the water in which they sailed. Collectors of his work speak in glowing terms of his ability to capture in watercolors the dampness of ocean air or the blinding light of sun shining on wet canvas.

However, Cozzens' real talent transcended the ships and seas that he painted. His stress was upon ideas; the verve of a good ship rounding the buoy, the straining of every man in her crew to get the best from the boat. He could convey the dull monotony of a calm or the challenge of danger on the water. The greatness of his work lies in the simple truths that he was able to portray; he told of the heat of the sun; of the wetness of water and the loneliness of the human soul. You may share with him the joy of being out on the water, of taking part in the hundreds of tasks aboard a boat. He never consciously tried to awaken his fellow men to anything except his own love affair with the sea. He was drawn early in life to the sea and it evoked a powerful response from him. This response is his legacy to the world, crystallized out of his own experiences and dreams.

During Frederic S. Cozzens' lifetime, his unique ability to draw marine pictures made him the darling of the marine world, although the art world ignored him. Upon hearing the name Cozzens, one immediately thought of rolling seas or billowing canvas. Unfortunately, as his reputation did not extend beyond the marine world, his name did not appear in many of the art directories or books on American painters of his day.

Although many people believe Cozzens to have been an experienced yachtsman, he never owned a racing boat and did not sail. This did not prevent him from coming to the yachting and boating scene well prepared. His pictures depict naval architecture with a direct and precise understanding and attention to detail.

Fred. Cozzens contributed to the popularity of yachting not only among the wealthy, who owned boats, but also with the general public who followed, vicariously, every aspect of the national and international races by means of his drawings. Through his pictures, Cozzens was able to tell them of the greatness of the sea and the beauty of sail in an incomparable way.

He drew every aspect of life on the water. Not only did he know every detail of each schooner, sloop or cutter, but he could convey the atmosphere, and excitement as well as the dangers, thrill or gloom at the end of a race. He popularized boating and brought it to the attention of much more than the wealthy, leisure class. Cozzens captured the attention and interest of common people who quickly became interested in his interpretations of the thrills, the dangers and the joys of pleasure boating.

After his death in 1928, his fame fell into oblivion. Although little has been written about him since then, collectors still seek out his work. These collectors have been quietly acquiring every Cozzens watercolor and lithograph that appears on the market. As a result of this interest, most of his work is now in the hands of private collectors rather than in museums or art galleries.

His emergence as a highly successful master dates back only a few decades but his position is now firmly established. It has been said that Cozzens is an artist who was as estimable in his work as he was obscure in his personality. He has emerged from the shows of obscurity as one of the most talented marine artists of his time. The variety and quality of his oeuvre has entranced the collectors. More than fifty years after his death, his work is now attracting the attention it has long deserved. Years after he painted them, his watercolors still seem to be alive and within their richness of pale coloring, Cozzens' watercolors will mark his name as one of the finest marine watercolorists of America.

Catalogue Raisonné

Classification Method

I Marine-ship; Pleasure
  1 Named vessel
    A Yacht
      a Specific vessel, time event
      b Specific place
      c Unidentified event
      d Unidentified place
    B Other
    C Canoe
  2 Unnamed vessels
    A Yacht
    B Other

II Marine-ship; Commercial
  1 Named vessel
    A Fishing
    B Whaler
    C Dory
    D Collier
    E Barge
    F Sailing ship
    G S.S. Line
    H Passenger ship
    I British Navy
    J Ferry
    K Lightship
    L Tug
    M Grain ship
    N Paddlewheel
  2 Unnamed vessel
    A Fishing
    B Whaler
    C Dory
    D Collier
    E Barge
    F Sailing ship
    G S.S. Line
    H Passenger ship
    I British Navy
    J Ferry
    K Lightship
    L Tug
    M Grain ship
    N Paddlewheel

III Marine-ship; United States Navy
  1 Named vessel
  2 Unnamed vessel

IV Marine-ship; Disaster, Rescue
  1 Named vessel
  2 Unnamed vessel

V Marine-scene
  1 Named vessel
    A Coastal shoreline
    B Beach
    C Harbor scene
    D River
    E Lake
    F Lighthouse or channel marker
    G Rocks
    H Open water
    I Atmospheric or seasonal
    J Marsh
    K Bay
  2 Unnamed vessel
    A Coastal shoreline
    B Beach
    C Harbor scene
    D River
    E Lake
    F Lighthouse or channel marker
    G Rocks
    H Open water
    I Atmospheric or seasonal
    J Marsh
    K Bay

VI Landscape

VII Data unknown

The notation "Location unknown" in the catalogue means that the location of Cozzens' original work is unknown. We may have a copy of *Harper's Weekly* showing his work, but we do not know the location of Cozzen's original work for the issue.

Many auction galleries and art dealers generously supplied us with information about the Cozzens work they had handled through the years, but did not divulge the names of the buyers of each piece. Therefore, these items were labeled "Location unknown."

1864-1867: Character sketches, street scenes; Pencil, pen, ink; 6.1x4cm. to 20x12.5cm. Rensselaer Polytechnic Institute; VI 1
1870: Pen, ink drawings; Illustration: *Punchinello*, Vol. 1, April 2—September 24, 1870 and Vol. 2 Oct. 2—Dec. 24 1870; Location unknown VII 2
1870: *The First Attempt of the British to Recover the America's Cup*; Pen, ink drawing; Illustration: *Harper's Weekly*, August 1870; Location unknown I 1 A a 3
1870: *The Finish off Staten Island*; Watercolor; *Old Sales Bulletin*, of Old Print Shop; Location unknown I 1 A a 4
1870: *Magic and Cambria*; Watercolor; Museum of the City of New York; I 1 A a 5
1871: *Sappho and Livonia*; Watercolor; Museum of the City of New York; I 1 A a 6
1873: *Shore at Fairhaven, Mass. Looking Across to New Bedford and Fort Phoenix*; 21.5x28cm.; Private collection; V 2 C b 7
1875 *Stern View of One-Mast Vessel Offshore; Debris in Water*; Watercolor; 16.5x18cm.; Private collection; V 2 A c d 8
1875: *Annual Regatta of the New York Yacht Club*; Pen, ink drawing made into woodcut; Illustration: *Daily Graphic*, June 19, 1875; Location unknown I 1 A a b 9
1875: *Annual Regatta of the New York Yacht Club, Ah! We'll Catch Them!*; Pen, ink drawing made into woodcut; Illustration: *Daily Graphic*, June 19, 1875; Location unknown I 2 A a b 10
1875: *Annual Regatta of the New York Yacht Club, Go it! Young 'Un's!*; Pen, ink drawing made into woodcut; Illustration: *Daily Graphic*, June 19, 1875; Location unknown I 2 A a b 11
1875: *Annual Regatta of the New York Yacht Club, She's Charming! See Her Come Up!*; Pen, ink drawing made into woodcut; Illustration: *Daily Graphic*, June 19, 1875; Location unknown I 1 A a b 12
1875: *Annual Regatta of the New York Yacht Club, Madcap nearing the Climax*; Pen, ink drawing made into woodcut; Illustration: *Daily Graphic*, June 19, 1975; Location unknown I 1 A a b 13
1875: *Annual Regatta of the New York Yacht Club, Madcap Rounding the Mark*; Pen, ink drawing made into woodcut; Illustration: *Daily Graphic*, June 19, 1875; Location unknown I 1 A a b 14
1875: Annual Regatta of the New York Yacht Club, Rounding the Lightship; Pen, ink drawing made into woodcut; Illustration: *Daily Graphic*, June 19, 1985; Location unknown I 1 A a b 15
1875: *Annual Regatta of the New York Yacht Club, Not a Visionary Jib* (refering to the yacht, *Vision*); Pen, ink drawing made into woodcut; Illustration: *Daily Graphic*, June 19, 1875; Location unknown I 1 A b 16
1875: *Annual Regatta of the New York Yacht Club, Rounding the First Spit*; Pen, ink drawing made into woodcut; Illustration: *Daily Graphic*, June 19, 1875; Location unknown I 1 A a b 17
1875: *Annual Regatta of the New York Yacht Club, Neck and Neck*; Pen, ink drawing made into woodcut; Illustration: *Daily Graphic*, June 19, 1875; Location unknown I 1 A a b 18
1875: *Annual Regatta of the New York Yacht Club, Home Again*; Showing a yacht with sails down in a calm sea; Pen, ink drawing made into a woodcut; Illustration: *Daily Graphic*, June 19, 1875; Location unknown I 1 A a b 19
1875: *City of New Bedford; A Young Whaler*; Pen, ink drawing; Illustration: *Daily Graphic*, 11/2/75; Location unknown II 2 B b 20
1875: *City of New Bedford; Old Whaler; Boy Whaled on his Backside by his Mother*; Pen, ink drawing made into woodcut; Illustration: *Daily Graphic*, 11/2/75; Location unknown V 2 C a b 21
1875: *City of New Bedford; Epizootic over the River; Ox-Drawn Fire Engine*; Pen, ink drawing; Illustration: *Daily Graphic*, 11/2/75; Location unknown VI 22
1875: *City of New Bedford; Hove Down, Calking and Sheathing; Whaler on her Side*; Pen, ink drawing; Illustration: *Daily Graphic, 11/2/75*; Location unknown II 2 B b 23
1875: *City of New Bedford; Two Piers with Six or Seven Whaling Ships*; Pen, ink drawing; Illustration: *Daily Graphic*, 11/2/72; Location unknown II 2 B b 24
1875: *City of New Bedford; Wamsutta Mills*; Illustration: *Daily Graphic*, 11/2/72; Location unknown VI 25
1875: *City of New Bedford; Just Arrived; Full Cargo*; Pen, ink drawing; Illustration: *Daily Graphic*, 11/2/75; Location unknown II 2 B b 26
1875: *City of New Bedford; Down the River, View of New Bedford*; Pen, ink drawing; Illustration: *Daily Graphic*, 11/2/75; Location unknown V2D c d 27
1875: *City of New Bedford; City Hall and the Library of New Bedford*; Pen, ink drawing; Illustration: *Daily Graphic*, 11/2/75; Location unknown VI 28
1875: *The New Clubhouse of the New York Yacht Club in Stapleton, Staten Island*; Pen, ink drawing; Illustration: *Daily Graphic*, May 1, 1875; Location unknown V 2 A a b 29
1876: *Madeline and Countess of Dufferin*; Watercolor; Museum of the City of New York; I 1 A a 30
1878: *Ships in New York Harbor*; Watercolor; 30.5x45.5cm.; Private Collection; V 2 C b 31
1878: *Sailing Vessel Wrecked in Storm*; Woodcut made from a watercolor; 20x25.5cm.; Location unknown IV 2 c d 32
1878: *Side Wheel Vessel Wrecked in Storm*; Woodcut made from watercolor; 20x25.5cm.; Location unknown IV a d 33
1878: *Arctic Search for the Schooner, Eothen*; Pen, ink drawing; Illustration: *Harper's Weekly*, June 29, 1878; Location unknown II 1 F a b 34
1879: *River Tow*; Wash and opaque; 21.5x33.5cm.; New York Historical Society; II 2 E c d 35
1879: *Sandy Hook Lightship*; Pen, ink drawing; Illustration: *Harper's Weekly*, September 27, 1879; Location unknown II 1 k b 36
1879: *City of Tokyo Steaming up the San Francisco Bay with General Grant*; Pen, ink drawing; Illustration: *Harper's Weekly*, October 25, 1879; Location unknown V 1 a 37
1879: *Buoy Station at Quarantine Landing, Staten Island*; Pen, ink drawing; Illustration: *Harper's Weekly*, September 27, 1879; Location unknown V 2 A b 38
1879: *Steam Paddle-Wheel in Ice Flow*; Watercolor; 25.5x33 cm.; Auction catalogue of A. Weschler; Location unknown II 2 N c d 39
1879: *Explosion Aboard the Bark, Amalfi, off Staten Island, May 20, 1879*; Pen, ink drawing; Illustration: *Leslie's Magazine*, June 7, 1879; Location unknown V I C a 40
1879: *Quarantine Station: Water Area in Front of the Quarantine Area with Many Ships Awaiting Clearance*; Pen, ink drawing; Illustration: *Harper's Weekly*, September 4, 1879; Location unknown V 2 C a b 41
1879: *Quarantine Station; Swinbourn Island After the Hospital Buildings had Been Erected*; Pen, ink drawing; Illustration: *Harper's Weekly*, September 4, 1879; Location unknown V 2 C a b 42
1879: *Quarantine Station; Floating Hospital Ship that was Used from 1859 to 1863*; Pen, ink drawing; Illustration: *Harper's Weekly*, September 4, 1879; Location unknown V 2 C a b 43
1879: *Quarantine Station; Doctor's Gig Being Rowed Out to Sailing Vessel Anchored in the Narrows*; Pen, ink drawing; Illustration: *Harper's Weekly*, September 4, 1879; Location unknown V 2 C a b 44
1879: *Tugboat*; Private Collector; II 2 J 45
Early 1880's *The Yachts, Wenonah and Muriel Racing Under the Signal of James Stillman*; Watercolor; Private Collector; I 1 A a 46
1880: *Ocean Steam Yacht, Anthracite*; Pen, ink drawing; Illustration: *Harper's Weekly*, July 31, 1880; Location unknown I 1 A a 47
1880: *Ship Collision off Newfoundland*; Mentioned in book, *Early Painters and Engravers of Canada*, by Harper J. Russell; Location unknown IV 2 a 48
1880: *Lighthouse at Robbins Reef with Sailing Vessel and Men in Dory*; Watercolor; Private Collector; V 2 F b 49
1880: *Steam Yacht, Corsair, Owned by J. C. Osborn*; Watercolor; Illustration: *Harper's Weekly*, August 7, 1880; Location unknown I 1 A a 50
1880: *Early Sailing Ship*; Private Collector; II 2 F c d 51
1880: *Running from the Sunken Meadows*; Pen, ink drawing; Illustration: *Harper's Weekly*, July 17, 1880; Location unknown VII 52
1880: *Grain Ships Laid up in Gowanus Creek Waiting for Cargoes*; Pen, ink drawing; Illustration: *Harper's Weekly*, April 10, 1880; Location unknown II 2 G b c 53
1880: Large center picture of a set of six from the yacht, *Nettie*; Marine scenes; Watercolor; New York Yacht Clubhouse; I 1 A a 54
1880: Smaller companion of set of six from the yacht, *Nettie*; Racing scene; Watercolor; New York Yacht Clubhouse; I 1 A a 55
1880: Smaller companion of set of six from the yacht, *Nettie*; Racing scene; Watercolor; New York Yacht Clubhouse; I 1 A a 56
1880: Second large center picture of set of six from the yacht, *Nettie*; Panoramic view of New York City and harbor showing Castle William, Brooklyn Bridge from bow of yacht; Watercolor; New York Yacht Clubhouse; I 1 A a 57
1880: Smaller companion marine of set of six from yacht, *Nettie*; Winter scene; Watercolor; New York Yacht Clubhouse; I 1 A a 58
1880: Smaller companion marine of set of six from yacht, *Nettie*; Moonlight yachting scene; Watercolor; New York Yacht Clubhouse; I 1 A a 59
1880: *Bluefishing, Great Point, New Bedford*; Watercolor; Record f National Academy of Design Exhibition in 1881; Location unknown II 2 A a b 60
1880: *Five Fishing Craft with One Large Sailing Ship*; Woodcut made from watercolor; Record of American Watercolor Society, 1880 Exhibition; Location unknown II 2 A c d 61
1880: *Morning off the Isle of Shoals*; 68.5x25.5cm; Watercolor; Record of American Watercolor Society 1880 Exhibition; Location unknown I 2 A b 62
1880: *Winter Down the Bay*; Watercolor; Record of American Watercolor Society 1880 Exhibition; Location unknown V 2 K c d 63
1880: *Cleopatra's Needle*; Ship *Dessoug*; Pen, ink drawing; Illustration: *Harper's Weekly*, Sept. 8, 1880; Location unknown II 1 A G a b 64
1880: *Cleopatra's Needle*; Removal of Monolith from hold; Pen, ink drawing; Illustration: *Harper's Weekly*, Sept 8, 1880; Location unknown V 1 C a b 65
1880: *Cleopatra's Needle*; Obelisk in hold of Dessoug; Pen, ink drawing; Illustration: *Harper's Weekly*, Sept 8, 1880; Location unknown II 1 A G a b 66
1880: *Cleopatra's Needle*; Copper Crows or anchors which secure obelisk to its base; Pen, ink drawing; Illustration: *Harper's Weekly*, Sept. 8, 1880; Location unknown V 1 C a b 67
1880: *Cleopatra's Needle*; Lateral view of base of obelisk; Pen, ink drawing; Illustration: *Harper's Weekly*, Sept. 8, 1880 Location unknown VI 1 68
1880: *Cleopatra's Needle*; Anchorage of Obelisk to its base; Pen, ink drawing; Illustration: *Harper's Weekly*, Sept. 8, 1880; Location unknown VI 1 69
1880: *Cleopatra's Needle*; Obelisk being towed up the bay; Pen, ink drawing; Illustration: *Harper's Weekly*, Sept. 8, 1880; Location unknown II 1 E a b 70
1881: *Race Between the Madge and the Schemer; The First Match*; Pen, ink drawing; Illustration: *Harper's Weekly*, October 8, 1881; Location unknown I 1 A a 71
1881: *Race Between the Madge and the Schemer*; Pen, ink drawing; Illustration: *Harper's Weekly*, October 8, 1881; Location unknown I 1 A a 72
1881: *Race Between the Madge and the Schemer*; Pen, ink drawing; Illustration: *Harper's Weekly*, October 8, 1881; Location unknown I 1 A a 73
1881: *Ideal Head* (listed as oil painting); Record of American Watercolor Society 1881 Exhibition; Location unknown VII 74
1881: *Now Then, Boys*; Watercolor made into chromolithograph; Watercolor exhibited at American Watercolor Society, 1881 Exhibition, and at Brooklyn Art Exhibit in 1881; Location unknown IV 2 c d 75
1881: *Return of the Whaler*; Watercolor; Record of the National Academy of Design, 1881 Exhibition; Location unknown II 1 B a b 76
1881: *Obelisk in Central Park*; Pen, ink drawing; Illustration: *Harper's Weekly*, February 12, 1881; Location unknown VI 77
1881: *Dreamy*; Watercolor; Record of American Watercolor Society, 1881 Exhibition, Location unknown VII 78
1881: *Making a Harbor*; Watercolor; Record of American Watercolor Society, 1881 Exhibition, and Record of Brooklyn Art Association, 1881 Exhibition; Location unknown VII 79
1881: *America's Cup Races Off Newport*; Watercolor; Made into chromolithograph; 47.7x81cm. Sold at Sloan Auction Galleries, 2/19/78; I 2 A b 80
1881: *Ice Yachting on the Hudson*; Pen, ink drawing; Illustration: *Harper's Weekly*, February 19, 1881; Location unknown I 2 A a b 81

1881: *Ice Yachting on the Hudson; Air Hole;* Pen, ink drawing; Illustration: *Harper's Weekly,* February 19, 1881; Location unknown I 2 A a b 82
1881: *Ice Yachting on the Hudson; Rearing;* Pen, ink drawing; Illustration: *Harper's Weekly,* February 19, 1881; Location unknown I 2 A a b 83
1881: *Puritan and Genesta;* Watercolor; September 14, 1881; Museum of the City of New York; I 1 A c d 84
1882: *Old Whaler Hove Down for Repairs;* Pen, ink drawing; Illustration: *Harper's Weekly,* December 9, 1882; Mentioned in *Adventures of America 1857-1900* by John A. Kouenhoven; Location unknown II 2 B a 85
1882: *Sailing Vessels and Dory;* Watercolor; 19.5x26.5cm.; Private collection; I 2 A c d 86
1882: *Hauling in the Catch;* Watercolor; 19x25.5cm.; Sold at Parke Bernet Galleries auction #2977 1970; BIAP Survey; Location unknown II 2 A c d 87
1882: *Girl Sitting on Stranded Boat;* Pencil sketch on back of sheet of music; July 20, 1882; 28x21.5cm.; State University of New York; V 2 B c 88
1882: *A Fair Wind;* Watercolor; Record of the American Watercolor Society, 1882 Exhibition; Location unknown VII 89
1883: *A Free Wind;* Record of the American Watercolor Society, 1883 Exhibition; Location unknown VII 90
1883: *Two Steam Yachts;* Watercolor made into chromolithograph; Penobscot Marine Museum; Exhibited in F. S. Cozzens Exhibition at Penobscot Marine Museum, 1976; I 2 A a c d 91
1883: *Sandbagger Racing Sloops;* Made into lithograph; Penobscot Marine Museum; Exhibited in F. S. Cozzens Exhibition at Penobscot Marine Museum, 1976; I 2 A a c d 92
1883: *Sailboat Race From San Francisco to Hawaii in 1883;* Watercolor; 35x51cm.; Smithsonian Inventory of Paintings BIAP Survey; Restricted; Location Unknown I 2 A a b 93
1883: *Launching of the Iron Clipper, T. F. Oakes;* Pen, ink drawing; Illustration: *Harper's Weekly,* October 6, 1883; Location unknown II 1 F a b 94
1883: *Sailing Vessel Near Lightship;* Watercolor Royal Vancouver Yacht Club; I 2 A b c 95
1883: *Atalanta;* Pen, ink drawing; Illustration: Centerfold in *Annals of American Sport;* Location unknown I 1 A a 96
1883: *Yacht Race;* Watercolor; 35.5x26.5cm.; Auction catalogue from Parke Bernet Auction Galleries, Sale #568, 1944; BIAP Survey; Location unknown I 2 A c d 97
1883: *British Steamer, Egypt, Running a Gale;* Watercolor; Peabody Museum; Exhibited in F. S. Cozzens Exhibition at Penobscot Marine Museum Exhibition, 1976; II 1 G c 98
1883: *Admiral Pauling With his Staff Reviewing the U.S. Fleet at Oyster Bay;* Watercolor; 49.5x75.7cm.; Franklin Delano Roosevelt Library; Smithsonian Institute Inventory of Paintings BIAP Survey; III 2 a 99
1883: *Racing Sloops Rounding the Mark;* Watercolor, made into chromolithograph; Exhibited at F. S. Cozzens exhibition at Penobscot Marine Museum Exhibition, 1976; I 2 A c d 100
1883: *Yachts Rounding the Mark;* Watercolor, made into lithograph; Exhibited at F. S. Cozzens Exhibition at Penobscot Marine Museum, 1976; I 2 A b 101
1883: *Racing Schooner Yacht;* Watercolor; Penobscot Marine Museum; Exhibited at F. S. Cozzens Exhibition in Penobscot Marine Museum, 1976; I 2 A c d 102
1883: *First America's Cup Race on August 8, 1870;* Watercolor; Illustration: *New York Times,* May 16, 1926; Location unknown I 1 A a b 103
1883: *Cup Race; Broadside View of Yachts Racing with Sailors Climbing the Rigging;* Watercolor; 40.5x51 cm. Private collection; I 2 A c d 104
1883: *Iron Collier, Frostberg;* Process print; Newport Historical Society; II 1 D c d 105
1883/4: Plate 1: *The Early Racers; Maria, America, Una, Ray;* Watercolor; Illustration: *American Yachts, Their Clubs and Races;* Made into lithograph; Location unknown I 1 A a 106
1883/4: Plate 2: *Sandy Hook to the Needles, 1866; Henrietta, Fleetwing, Vesta;* Watercolor; Illustration: *American Yachts, Their Clubs and Races;* Made into lithograph; Location unknown I 1 A a b 107
1883/4: Plate 3: *An Old Rendezvous, New London; Jessie, Valkyr, St. Mary's;* Watercolor; Illustration: *American Yachts, Their Clubs and Races;* Made into lithograph Location unknown I 1 A a b 108
1883/4: Plate 4: *Off Brenton's Reef; Ileen, Wenonah, Oriva;* Watercolor; Illustration: *American Yachts, Their Clubs and Races;* Made into lithograph; Location unknown I 1 A a b 109
1883/4: Plate 5: *Rounding the Lightship; Fanny, Gracie, Rover;* Watercolor; Illustration: *American Yachts, Their Clubs and Races;* Made into lithograph; Location unknown I 1 A a b 110
1883/4: Plate 6: *The Finish off Staten Island, 1870; Cambria, Dauntless, America, Idler, Magic (late Madgie);* Watercolor; Illustration: *American Yachts, Their Clubs and Races;* Made into lithograph; Location unknown I 1 A a b 111
1883/4: Plate 7: *In the Narrows; A Black Squall; Dora, Rambler, Wanderer;* Watercolor; Illustration: *American Yachts, Their Clubs and Races;* Made into lithograph; Location unknown I 1 A a b 112
1883/4: Plate 8: *Running Out, New Bedford: Peerless, Ruth, Metric, Roslyn;* Watercolor; Illustration: *American Yachts, Their Clubs and Races;* Made into lithograph; Location unknown I 1 A a b 113
1883/4: Plate 9: *Off Soundings; A Smoky Sou'Wester; Bedouin, Intrepid, Namouna;* Watercolor; Illustration: *American Yachts, Their Clubs and Races;* Made into lithograph; Location unknown I 1 A a b 114
1883/4: Plate 10: *Robbins Reef, Sunset; Albertina, (late Susie S.), Lady Emma, (late W. R. Brown), Valiant, Lita;* Watercolor; Illustration: *American Yachts, Their Clubs and Races;* Made into lithograph; Location unknown I 1 A a b 115
1883/4: Plate 11: *Around the Cape; Marblehead; Hera, Fearless, Adrienne, Gitana, Mona, Shadow, Fannie;* Watercolor; Illustration: *American Yachts, Their Clubs and Races;* Made into lithograph; Location unknown I 1 A a b 116
1883/4: Plate 12: *Over the Cape May Course, 1873; Sharp Shooter, Negus, Reindeer, Dreadnaught, Enchantress, Clio;* Watercolor; Illustration: *American Yachts, Their Clubs and Races;* Made into lithograph; Location unknown I 1 A a b 117
1883/4: Plate 13: *By Sou'West Spit; Roamer, Crocodile, Clytie, Grayling, Fanita;* Watercolor; Illustration: *American Yachts, Their Clubs and Races;* Made into lithograph; Location unknown I 1 A a b 118
1883/4: Plate 14: *Moonlight on Nantucket Shoals; Ibis, Tidal Wave, Estelle, Sagitta, Aeolus;* Watercolor; Illustration: *American Yachts, Their Clubs and Races;* Made into lithograph; Location unknown I 1 A a 119
1883/4: Plate 15: *Lying To Off George's Bank; Norseman, Atalanta;* Watercolor; Illustration: *American Yachts, Their Clubs and Races;* Made into lithograph; Location unknown *I 1 A a b 120*
1883/4: Plate 16: A Stern Chase and a Long One, 1876; Countess of Dufferin (now Countess), America, Grant, Madeline; Watercolor; Illustration: *American Yachts, Their Clubs and Races;* Made into lithograph; Location unknown I 1 A a 121
1883/4: Plate 17: *A Breezy Day Outside; Columbia, Sappho, Palmer;* Watercolor; Illustration: *American Yachts, Their Clubs and Races;* Made into lithograph; Location unknown I 1 A a b 122
1883/4: Plate 18: *Crossing the Line, New York Bay; Coming, Montauk, Comet, Kelpie;* Watercolor; Illustration: *American Yachts, Their Clubs and Races;* Made into lithograph; Location unknown I 1 A a b 123
1883/4: Plate 19: *Minot's Ledge Light; Tempest, Viva, Fortuna, White Cap;* Watercolor; Illustration: *American Yachts, Their Clubs and Races;* Made into lithograph; Location unknown I 1 A a b 124
1883/4: Plate 20: *For the America's Cup; The Start, 1881; Atalanta, Mischief;* Watercolor; Illustration: *American Yachts, Their Clubs and Races;* Made into lithograph; Location unknown I 1 A a b 125
1883/4: Plate 21: *A Misty Morning; Drifting; Utowana, Nokomis (late Nettie), Crusader, Hildegard;* Watercolor; Illustration: *American Yachts, Their Clubs and Races;* Made into lithograph; Location unknown I 1 A a b 126
1883/4: Plate 22: *In Down East Waters, Boston Bay; Syren, Beetle, Countess, Halcyon, Phantom, Adelita, Sappho;* Watercolor; Illustration: *American Yachts, Their Clubs and Races;* Made into lithograph; Location unknown I 1 A a b 127
1883/4: Plate 23: *Before the Wind, Newport, 1883; Social (late Cornelia), Vixen, Arrow, Permelia (late One Hundred), Maggie;* Watercolor; Illustration: *American Yachts, Their Clubs and Races;* Made into lithograph; Location unknown I 1 A a b 128
1883/4: Plate 24: *Under the Palisades; Stranger, Rover, Atalanta;* Watercolor; Illustration: *American Yachts, Their Clubs and Races;* Made into lithograph; Location unknown I 1 A a b 129
1884: Plate 25: *Ice Boating on the Hudson; Avalanche, Gypsie, Icicle, Haze, Whiff, Echo;* Watercolor; Illustration: *American Yachts, Their Clubs and Races;* Made into lithograph; Location unknown I 1 A a b 130
1884: Plate 26: *Signal Chart; Yolande in vignette;* Watercolor; Illustration: *American Yachts, Their Clubs and Races;* Made into lithograph; Location unknown I 1 A a b 131
1884: Plate 27: *For the America's Cup, Near the Finish; Puritan, Genesta;* Watercolor; Illustration: *American Yachts, Their Clubs and Races;* Made into lithograph; Location unknown I 1 A a b 132
1885: *Surf Casting Along the Jersey Shore;* Watercolor; Exhibited at Montclair Art Museum Exhibition in 1973; Private Collector; V A b 133
1885: *Two Racing Sloops;* Chromolithograph; Exhibited at Penobscot Marine Museum, F. S. Cozzens Exhibition in 1976; I 2 A c d 134
1885: *Two Sailing Vessels;* 56x71 cm.; Watercolor; Private collection; II 2 F c d 135
1885: *Port Quarter View of Sailing Vessel with Two Men in Stern; Man Rowing Dory in Foreground; Evening Sky;* Watercolor; 25.5x35.5 cm.; Private collection; II 2 F c d 136
1885: *Beach Scene with Five Men and Two Dories on Shore; Foundering Vessel Offshore;* Watercolor; 35.5x56 cm.; Private Collection; IV 2 C d 137
1885: *Large Sailing Ship Near Buoy;* Watercolor; 56x71 cm.; Provident National Bank; II 2 F c 138
c. 1885/6: *Cup Defender;* Watercolor; New York Yacht Club; I 2 A c d 139
1885: *Sailing Ship in Storm;* Watercolor; 20x42 cm.; Private Collection; IV 2 c d 140
1886: *Mayflower and Galatea Contest;* Watercolor; 33x38 cm.; Illustration: Frontispiece, *Yachts and Yachting;* Location unknown I 1 A a 141
1886: *International Race, 1885; Puritan and Genesta;* Watercolor; Illustration: *Typical American Yachts;* Location unknown I 1 A a 142
1886: *Yacht Off Marblehead with Topmast Housed ;* Woodcut made from pen, ink drawing; Illustration: *Harper's Weekly,* September 4, 1886; Staten Island Institute of Arts and Science; I 1 A a b 143
1886: *Fishermen Putting Out to Sea;* 47.7x72 cm.; Sotheby, Parke Bernet Galleries, Sale #3823 #71 1975; Location unknown II 1 A c d 144
1886: *Coming In;* Watercolor; 21.5x36.7 cm.; Sold at Kennedy Galleries; Location unknown V 2 C c d 145
1886: *Side Wheeler, Banshee Running the Blockade Off Galveston in 1865;* Watercolor; New York Yacht Club; II 1 N a b 146
1886: *Rescue Boat;* Watercolor; Sold at Sotheby, Parke Bernet Galleries; IV 2 c d 147
1886: *Names of Spars and Rigging of Sails of Sloop Yacht;* Pen, ink drawing; Illustration: *Patterson's Illustrated-Nautical Dictionary,* p. 75; Location unknown I 2 A e 148
1886: *Cutter Yacht Underway Lowering Spinnaker Boom;* Pen, ink drawing; Illustration: *Patterson's Illustrated Nautical Dictionary,* p. 79; Location unknown I 2 A e 149
1886: *Yawl Yacht Hove to;* Pen, ink drawing; Illustration: *Patterson's Illustrated Nautical Dictionary,* p. 85; Location unknown I 2 A e 150
1886: *Cutter Yacht Unerway,* showing spinnaker set; Pen, ink drawing; Illustration: *Patterson's Illustrated Nautical Dictionary,* p. 81; Location unknown I 2 A e 151
1886: *Schooner Yacht Underway,* showing balloon jib topsail; Pen, ink drawing; Illustration: *Patterson's Illustrated Nautical Dictionary,* p. 89 Location unknown I 2 A e 152
1886: *Schooner Yacht Underway,* showing square sails set; Pen, ink drawing; Illustration: *Patterson's Illustrated Nautical Dictionary,* p. 91; Location unknown I 2 A e 153
1886: *Schooner Yacht Underway,* showing all plain (working) sails set; Pen, ink drawing; Illustration: *Patterson's Illustrated Nautical Dictionary,* p. 93; Location unknown I 2 A e 154
1886: *Schooner Yacht Underway,* showing mainsail reefed, foretop mast housed; Pen, ink drawing; Illustration: *Patterson's Illustrated Nautical Dictionary,* p. 94; Location unknown I 2 A e 155
1886: *Side view;* Names of spars, rigging and various parts of steam yacht; Pen, ink drawing; Illustration: *Patterson's Illustrated Nautical Dictionary,* p. 123; Location unknown I 2 A e 156
1886: Fourteen Outline Drawings of Yachts; Pen, ink drawings; Illustration: *Outing Magazine,* April 1886 to illustrate an article on yachting by Edward S. Joffrey. Illustrations later used in *Yachts and Yachting;* Location unknown I 1 A a 157
1886: Eighteen Outline Drawings of Yachts; Pen, ink drawings; Illustration: *Outing Magazine;* May 1886 to illustrate an article on American yachting by C. J. C. McAlister; Illustrations later used in *Yachts and Yachting;* Location unknown I 1 A a 158

1886: Thirteen Outline drawings; Pen, ink drawings; Illustration: *Outing Magazine*, June 1886 to illustrate an article on yachting by R. F. Coffin; Illustrations later used in *Yachts and Yachting*; Location unknown I 1 A a 159

1886: Eleven Outline Drawings; Pen, ink drawings; Illustration: *Outing Magazine*, July 1886, to illustrate Part II of "History of American Yachts", Illustrations later used in *Yachts and Yachting*; Location unknown I 1 A a 160

1886: Ten Outline Drawings; Pen, ink drawings; Illustration: *Outing Magazine*, August 1886, to illustrate Part III of, "American Yachting"; Illustrations later used in *Yachts and Yachting*; Location unknown I 1 A a 161

1886: Seven Outline Drawings; Pen, ink drawings; Illustration: *Outing Magazine*, September 1886, to illustrate Part IV of "American Yachting"; Illustrations later used in *Yachts and Yachting*; Location unknown I 1 A a 162

1886: Six Outline Drawings; Pen, ink drawings; Illustration: *Outing Magazine*, October 1886, to illustrate Part V of "History of American Yachting"; Illustrations later used in *Yachts and Yachting*; Location unknown I 1 A a 163

1886: Four Outline Drawings; Pen, ink drawings; Illustration: *Outing Magazine*, November 1886, to illustrate Part VI of the "History of American Yachting"; Illustrations later used in *Yachts and Yachting*; Location unknown I 1 A a 164

1886: *Yacht, Adrienne*; Pen, ink outline drawings; Illustration: *Yachts and Yachting*, p. 66; Location unknown I 1 A a 165

1886: *Yacht, Aida*; Pen, ink outline drawing; Illustration: *Yachts and Yachting*, p. 131; Location unknown I 1 A a 166

1886: *Yacht, Alpha*; Pen, ink outline drawing; Illustration: *Yachts and Yachting*, p. 23; Location unknown I 1 A a 167

1886: *Yacht, America*; Pen, ink outline drawing; Illustration: *Yachts and Yachting*, p. 22; Location unknown I 1 A a 168

1886: *Yacht, Atalanta*; Pen, ink outline drawing; Illustration: *Yachts and Yachting*, p. 119; Location unknown I 1 A a 169

1886: *Yacht, Athlon*; Pen, ink outline drawing; Illustration: *Yachts and Yachting*, p. 74; Location unknown I 1 A a 170

1886: *Yacht, Atlantic*; Pen, ink outline drawing; Illustration: *Yachts and Yachting*, p. 93; Location unknown I 1 A a 171

1886: *Yacht, Bedouin*; Pen, ink outline drawing; Illustration: *Yachts and Yachting*, p. 87; Location unknown I 1 A a 172

1886: *Yacht, Bianca*; Pen, ink outline drawing; Illustration: *Yachts and Yachting*, p. 44; Location unknown I 1 A a 173

1886: *Yacht, Buttercup*; Pen, ink outline drawing; Illustration: *Yachts and Yachting*, p. 153; Location unknown I 1 A a 174

1886: *Yacht, Camilla*; Pen, ink outline drawing; Illustration: *Yachts and Yachting*, p. 117; Location unknown I 1 A a 175

1886: *Yacht, Carlotta*; Pen, ink outline drawing; Illustration: *Yachts and Yachting*, p. 147; Location unknown I 1 A a 176

1886: *Yacht, Clytie*; Pen, ink outline drawing; Illustration: *Yachts and Yachting*, p. 61; Location unknown I 1 A a 177

1886: *Yacht, Comet*; Pen, ink outline drawing; Illustration: *Yachts and Yachting*, p. 34; Location unknown I 1 A a 178

1886: *Yacht, Constance*; Pen, ink outline drawing; Illustration: *Yachts and Yachting*, p. 149; Location unknown I 1 A a 179

1886: *Yacht, Corsair*; Pen, ink outline drawing; Illustration: *Yachts and Yachting*, p. 116; Location unknown I 1 A a 180

1886: *Yacht, Crocodile*; Pen, ink outline drawing; Illustration: *Yachts and Yachting*, p. 78; Location unknown I 1 A a 181

1886: *Yacht, Cygnet*; Pen, ink outline drawing; Illustration: *Yachts and Yachting*, p. 11; Location unknown I 1 A a 182

1886: *Yacht, Dawn*; Pen, ink outline drawing; Illustration: *Yachts and Yachting*, p. 148; Location unknown I 1 A a 183

1886: Diagram of Yacht; Pen, ink outline drawing; Illustration: *Yachts and Yachting*, p. 105; Location unknown I 1 A a 184

1886: *Yacht, Diane*; Pen, ink outline drawing; Illustration: *Yachts and Yachting*, p. 152; Location unknown I 1 A a 185

1886: *Yacht, Dreadnaught*; Pen, ink outline drawing; Illustration: *Yachts and Yachting*, p. 33; Location unknown I 1 A a 186

1886: *Yacht, Egeria*; Pen, ink outline drawing; Illustration: *Yachts and Yachting*, p. 156; Location unknown I 1 A a 187

1886: *Yacht, Electra*; Pen, ink outline drawing; Illustration: *Yachts and Yachting*, p. 122; Location unknown I 1 A a 188

1886: *Yacht, Enchantress*; Pen, ink outline drawing; Illustration: *Yachts and Yachting*, p. 40; Location unknown I 1 A a 189

1886: *Yacht, Estelle*; Pen, ink outline drawing; Illustration: *Yachts and Yachting*, p. 60; Location unknown I 1 A a 190

1886: *Yacht, Fanita*; Pen, ink outline drawing; Illustration: *Yachts and Yachting*, p. 67; Location unknown I 1 A a 191

1886: *Sloop, Fanny*; Pen, ink outline drawing; Illustration: *Yachts and Yachting*, p. 47; Location unknown I 1 A a 192

1886: *Yacht, Fanny (Boston)*; Pen, ink outline drawing; Illustration: *Yachts and Yachting*, p. 51; Location unknown I 1 A a 193

1886: *Yacht, Fleetwing*; Pen, ink outline drawing; Illustration: *Yachts and Yachting*, p. 27; Location unknown I 1 A a 194

1886: *Yachts, Fortune, Boston*; Pen, ink outline drawing; Illustration: *Yachts and Yachting*, p. 63; Location unknown I 1 A a 195

1886: *Yacht, Frolic*; Pen, ink outline drawing; Illustration: *Yachts and Yachting*, p. 53; Location unknown I 1 A a 196

1886: *Yacht, Galatea*; Pen, ink outline drawing; Illustration: *Yachts and Yachting*, p. 106; Location unknown I 1 A a 197

1886: *Yacht, Galatea*; Pen, ink outline drawing; Illustration: *Yachts and Yachting*, p. 141; Location unknown I 1 A a 198

1886: *Yacht, Gertrude*; Pen, ink outline drawing; Illustration: *Yachts and Yachting*, p. 158; Location unknown I 1 A a 199

1886: *Yacht, Gimcrack*; Pen, ink outline drawing; Illustration: *Yachts and Yachting*, p. 15; Location unknown I 1 A a 200

1886: *Yacht, Gitana*; Pen, ink outline drawing; Illustration: *Yachts and Yachting*, p. 82; Location unknown I 1 A a 201

1886: *Yacht, Gracie*; Pen, ink outline drawing; Illustration: *Yachts and Yachting*, p. 39; Location unknown I 1 A a 202

1886: *Yacht, Grayling*; Pen, ink outline drawing; Illustration: *Yachts and Yachting*, p. 62; Location unknown I 1 A a 203

1886: *Yachts, Halcyon, Boston*; Pen, ink outline drawing; Illustration: *Yachts and Yachting*, p. 32; Location unknown I 1 A a 204

1886: *Yacht, Henrietta*; Pen, ink outline drawing; Illustration: *Yachts and Yachting*, p. 32; Location unknown I 1 A a 205

1886: *Yacht, Hope*; Pen, ink outline drawing; Illustration: *Yachts and Yachting*, p. 56; Location unknown I 1 A a 206

1886: *Yacht, Hornet*; Pen, ink outline drawing; Illustration: *Yachts and Yachting*, p. 17; Location unknown I 1 A a 207

1886: *Yacht, Intrepid*; Pen, ink outline drawing; Illustration: *Yachts and Yachting*, p. 55; Location unknown I 1 A a 208

1886: *Yacht, Ione*; Pen, ink outline drawing; Illustration: *Yachts and Yachting*, p. 151; Location unknown I 1 A a 209

1886: *Yacht, Irex*; Pen, ink outline drawing; Illustration: *Yachts and Yachting*, p. 143; Location unknown I 1 A a 210

1886: *Yacht, Isis*; Pen, ink outline drawing; Illustration: *Yachts and Yachting*, p. 59; Location unknown I 1 A a 211

1886: *Yacht, Julia*; Pen, ink outline drawing; Illustration: *Yachts and Yachting*, p. 19; Location unknown I 1 A a 212

1886: *Yacht, La Coquille*; Pen, ink outline drawing; Illustration: *Yachts and Yachting*, p. 14; Location unknown I 1 A a 213

1886: *Yacht, Lorna*; Pen, ink outline drawing; Illustration: *Yachts and Yachting*, p. 158; Location unknown I 1 A a 214

1886: *Yacht, Lucky*; Pen, ink outline drawing; Illustration: *Yachts and Yachting*, p. 25; Location unknown I 1 A a 215

1886: *Yacht, Madeline*; Pen, ink outline drawing; Illustration: *Yachts and Yachting*, p. 28; Location unknown I 1 A a 216

1886: *Yacht, Madge*; Pen, ink outline drawing; Illustration: *Yachts and Yachting*, p. 75; Location unknown I 1 A a 217

1886: *Yacht, Maggie*; Pen, ink outline drawing; Illustration: *Yachts and Yachting*, p. 88; Location unknown I 1 A a 218

1886: *Yacht, Magic*; Pen, ink outline drawing; Illustration: *Yachts and Yachting*, p. 48; Location unknown I 1 A a 219

1886: *Yacht, Maria*; Pen, ink outline drawing; Illustration: *Yachts and Yachting*, p. 18; Location unknown I 1 A a 220

1886: *Yacht, Maria (as Schooner, Maud)* Pen, ink outline drawing; Illustration: *Yachts and Yachting*, p. 38; Location unknown I 1 A a 221

1886: *Yacht, Marjorie*; Pen, ink outline drawing; Illustration: *Yachts and Yachting*, p. 150; Location unknown I 1 A a 222

1886: *Yacht, Maud*; Pen, ink outline drawing; Illustration: *Yachts and Yachting*, p. 38; Location unknown I 1 A a 223

1886: *Yacht, Mayflower*; Pen, ink outline drawing; Illustration: *Yachts and Yachting*, p. 107; Location unknown I 1 A a 224

1886: *Yacht, Miranda*; Pen, ink outline drawing; Illustration: *Yachts and Yachting*, p. 144; Location unknown I 1 A a 225

1886: *Yacht, Mischief*; Pen, ink outline drawing; Illustration: *Yachts and Yachting*, p. 69; Location unknown I 1 A a 226

1886: *Yacht, Mist*; Pen, ink outline drawing; Illustration: *Yachts and Yachting*, p. 16; Location unknown I 1 A a 227

1886: *Yacht, Montauk*; Pen, ink outline drawing; Illustration: *Yachts and Yachting*, p. 70; Location unknown I 1 A a 228

1886: *Yacht, Nooya*; Pen, ink outline drawing; Illustration: *Yachts and Yachting*, p. 126; Location unknown I 1 A a 229

1886: *Yacht, Nourmahal*; Pen, ink outline drawing; Illustration: *Yachts and Yachting*, p. 135; Location unknown I 1 A a 230

1886: *Yacht, Oriental*; Pen, ink outline drawing; Illustration: *Yachts and Yachting*, p. 131; Location unknown I 1 A a 231

1886: *Yacht, Oriva*; Pen, ink outline drawing; Illustration: *Yachts and Yachting*, p. 92; Location unknown I 1 A a 232

1886: *Yacht, Palmer*; Pen, ink outline drawing; Illustration: *Yachts and Yachting*, p. 52; Location unknown I 1 A a 233

1886: *Yacht, pastime*; Pen, ink outline drawing; Illustration: *Yachts and Yachting*, p. 120; Location unknown I 1 A a 234

1886: *Yacht, Polynia with Stiletto*; Pen, ink outline drawing; Illustration: *Yachts and Yachting*, p. 133; Location unknown I 1 A a 235

1886: *Yacht, Priscilla*; Pen, ink outline drawing; Illustration: *Yachts and Yachting*, p. 95; Location unknown I 1 A a 236

1886: *Yacht, Promise*; Pen, ink outline drawing; Illustration: *Yachts and Yachting*, p. 128; Location unknown I 1 A a 237

1886: *Yacht, Queen Mab*; Pen, ink outline drawing; Illustration: *Yachts and Yachting*, p. 145; Location unknown I 1 A a 238

1886: *Yacht, Radha*; Pen, ink outline drawing; Illustration: *Yachts and Yachting*, p. 133; Location unknown I 1 A a 239

1886: *Yacht, Ray*; Pen, ink outline drawing; Illustration: *Yachts and Yachting*, p. 24; Location unknown I 1 A a 240

1886: *Yacht, Rebecca*; Pen, ink outline drawing; Illustration: *Yachts and Yachting*, p. 30; Location unknown I 1 A a 241

1886: *Yacht, Sappho*; Pen, ink outline drawing; Illustration: *Yachts and Yachting*, p. 31; Location unknown I 1 A a 242

1886: *Yacht, Samoena*; Pen, ink outline drawing; Illustration: *Yachts and Yachting*, p. 155; Location unknown I 1 A a 243

1886: *Yacht, Sentinel*; Pen, ink outline drawing; Illustration: *Yachts and Yachting*, p. 121; Location unknown I 1 A a 244

1886: *Yacht, Spray*; Pen, ink outline drawing; Illustration: *Yachts and Yachting*, p. 13; Location unknown I 1 A a 245

1886: *Yacht, Shadow*; Pen, ink outline drawing; Illustration: *Yachts and Yachting*, p. 76; Location unknown I 1 A a 246

1886: *Yacht, Stranger*; Pen, ink outline drawing; Illustration: *Yachts and Yachting*, p. 91; Location unknown I 1 A a 248

1886: *Yacht, Sunbeam*; Pen, ink outline drawing; Illustration: *Yachts and Yachting*, p. 129; Location unknown I 1 A a 249

1886: *Yacht, Sybil*; Pen, ink outline drawing; Illustration: *Yachts and Yachting*, p. 12; Location unknown I 1 A a 250

1886: *Yacht, Tara*; Pen, ink outline drawing; Illustration: *Yachts and Yachting*, p. 154; Location unknown I 1 A a 251

1886: *Yacht, Thetis*; Pen, ink outline drawing; Illustration: *Yachts and Yachting*, p. 54; Location unknown I 1 A a 252

1886: *Yacht, Uledia*; Pen, ink outline drawing; Illustration: *Yachts and Yachting*, p. 146; Location unknown I 1 A a 253

1886: *Yacht, Una*; Pen, ink outline drawing; Illustration: *Yachts and Yachting*, p. 21; Location unknown I 1 A a 254

1886: *Yacht, Vesta*; Pen, ink outline drawing; Illustration: *Yachts and Yachting*, p. 36; Location unknown I 1 A a 255

1886: *Yacht, Viking*; Pen, ink outline drawing; Illustration: *Yachts and Yachting*, p. 125; Location unknown I 1 A a 256

1886: *Yacht, Vixen*; Pen, ink outline drawing; Illustration: *Yachts and Yachting*, p. 35; Location unknown I 1 A a 257

1886: *Yacht, Wanderer*; Pen, ink outline drawing; Illustration: *Yachts and Yachting*, p. 37; Location unknown I 1 A a 258

1886: *Yacht, Water Witch*; Pen, ink outline drawing; Illustration: *Yachts and Yachting*, p. 157; Location unknown I 1 A a 259

1886: *Yacht, Whisper*; Pen, ink outline drawing; Illustration: *Yachts and Yachting*, p. 135; Location unknown I 1 A a 260

1886: *Yacht, White Wing*; Pen, ink outline drawing; Illustration: *Yachts and Yachting*, p. 45; Location unknown I 1 A a 261

1886: *Yacht, Zoe*; Pen, ink outline drawing; Illustration: *Yachts and Yachting*, p. 80; Location unknown I 1 A a 262

1887: *Homeward Bound*; Disabled two-mast vessel being towed to port; Watercolor; 34.2x52 cm.; Sold by R. W. Skinner Auction Gallery, 5/11/78; Location unknown IV 2 c d 263

1887: *Fishing Boat Heading for the High Seas*; Watercolor; 25.5x35.5 cm.l Sold by Kennedy Galleries; II 2 A c d 264

1887: *American yacht, Volunteer*; Watercolor made into woodcut; Illustration: Staten Island Athletic Club Grounds Decennial Celebration, September 5, 1887; Location Unknown I 1 A a 265

1887: *Golden Gate, San Francisco*; Watercolor, made into ilthograph; Size of lithograph 20x25.5 cm.; Location of watercolor unknown II 2 F c d 266

1887: *Coal Barge Going Upstream Past Staten Island Light*; Watercolor; Private collection II 2 E a b 267

1887: *Harbor Scene*; Watercolor; 36.2x51.5 cm.; BIAP Survey; Private Collection V 2 C c d 268

1887: *American Whaling Ship Entering the Harbor of New Bedford*; House signal is red diamond on a white flag of William Potter of Dartmouth Mass.; Watercolor 47.7x75 cm.; Old Print Shop catalogue; Location unknown; II 1 B a b 269

1887: *Start of the Dauntless-Coronet Race Across the Atlantic Ocean*; Watercolor; Illustration: *Harper's Weekly*, March 19, 1887; Location unknown I 1 A a b 270

1887: *Collision of the Celtic and Brittanic*; Pen, ink drawing; Illustration: *Harper's Weekly*, May 28, 1887; Location unknown IV 1 A a 271

1887: *Flyers of the Atlantic Yacht Club*; Ink drawing; Illustration: *Harper's Weekly*, July 30, 1887; Location unknown I 2 A a b 272

1887: *Interviewing Newfoundland Fishermen as to the Presence of Cruisers Inshore*; Pen, ink drawing; Illustration: *Harper's Weekly*, August 13, 1887; Location unknown II 2 A a b 273

1887: *Ice Yacht*; Pen, ink drawing; Illustration: *Outing Magazine*; February, 1887; Illustration of article on ice yachts in mid-winter, by C.L. Norton; Location unknown I 2 A c d 274

1887: *Ice Yacht*; Pen, ink drawing; Illustration: *Outing Magazine*, February, 1887; Illustration of an article on ice yacht in mid-winter, by C.L. Norton; Location unknown I 2 A c d 275

1887: *Ice Yacht*; Pen, ink drawing; Illustration: *Outing Magazine*, February, 1887; Illustration of an article on ice yachts in mid-winter, by C.L. Norton; Location unknown I 2 A c d 276

1887: *Rescue Scene*; Watercolor, etching, 36.7 x 53 cm; by W. Wellstood; Locations unknown IV 2 c d 277

1887: *Two-Mast Sailing Vessel Breaking Apart with Life-Saving Service Boat Taking on a Woman and Baby*; Watercolor, made into etching; 35.5 x 56 cm; Private collection; Location of watercolor unknown IV 2 c d 278

1887: *Now then, Boys!*; Watercolor, made into chromolithograph; Illustration: *Illustrated America*, issue of 1892; U.S. Coast Guard in New London has chromolithograph; Location of watercolor unknown IV 2 c d 279

1887: *Hold Fast Then!*; Watercolor, made into chromolithograph; Illustration: *Illustrated America*, issue of 1892; U.S. Coast Guard in New London has chromolithograph; Location of watercolor is unknown IV 2 c d 280

1887: *International Yacht Race, 1887; Volunteer and Thistle; Just After the Start, the First Day*; Watercolor, made into lithograph; 53 x 35.5 cm; by Armstrong and Co. Boston; Printed by Riverside Press; Cambridge; Published by C.L. Jones, 1888; Location of watercolor unknown; Lithograph at Mariner's Museum, at Newport News, Va.; I 1 A a b 281

1887: Full page of illustrations of the Annual Meet of the American Canoe Association; Pen, ink drawings; Illustration: *Harper's Weekly*, September 10, 1887; Location unknown VII 282

1888: *Launching of the Surfboat*; Watercolor; Penobscot Marine Museum; In Exhibition of works of F.S. Cozzens held by Penobscot Marine Museum in 1976; IV 2 c d 283

1888: *Launching of the Surfboat*; Watercolor; 49.5 x 30.5 cm; Private collection; IV 2 c d 284

1888: *Yacht, Henrietta*; Watercolor; 58.5 x 82 cm; Provident National Bank; I 1 A a 285

1888: *Long Island Sharpie*; Pencil, wash; 25.5 x 38 cm; Private collection; I 2 A a c d 286

1888: *Wreckers at Work on the Sunken Steamer, Iberia*; Pen, ink drawing; Illustration: *Harper's Weekly*, December 8, 1888; Location unknown II 1 G a b 287

1888: *Three Men in Large Dory*; Watercolor; Private collection; II 2 A c d 288

1889: *Three Men in a Dory*; Watercolor; Private collection; II 2 C c d 289

1889: *Steam Vessel With Sailing Vessel in Background*; Watercolor; Private collection II 2 G c 290

1889: *Sailing Vessel with Tug Towing It*; Watercolor; 43 x 56 cm; Providence National Bank; I 2 A c d 291

1889: *Commerce on the Great Lakes*; Pen, ink drawing; Illustration: *Harper's Weekly*, April 13, 1889 Supplement; Location unknown II 2 b c 292

1889: *Tarpoon Fishing in Florida*; Watercolor made into chromolithograph; Mentioned in catalogue of Old Print Shop, June 1955 issue; Location of watercolor unknown; Chromolithograph; Private collection; I 2 A c d 293

1889: *George A. Warder's Canoe*; Pen, ink drawing; Woodcut; Illustration: *Sail and Paddle Magazine*, March 1889; Location unknown I 1 A a 294

1889: *On the Cruise; Rushon's Portable Boat*; Pen, ink drawing; Woodcut; Illustration: commercial art; Location unknown I 1 A a 295

1889: *Evolution of the Ferryboat*; Pen, ink drawing; Illustration: *Harper's Weekly*, January 5, 1889 Supplement; Location unknown II 2 J c d 296

1889: *In the Narrows*; A two-mast sailing vessel and other craft, with Staten Island in the background; Watercolor; Private collection; II 2 F c d 297

1889: *Ocean Steamers, City of New York*; Pen, ink drawing; Illustration: *Harper's Weekly*, March 30, 1889; Location unknown II 2 G b c d 297.9

1890: *Fishermen in a Boat With Lobster Pots*; Watercolor; BIAP Survey; Private collection; II 2 A a 298

c1890: *Steamer, City of Paris, Inman Lines*; Pencil wash drawing; Hart Nautical Museum; II 1 G a 299

c1890: *Steamer, Niagara*; U.S. Steam and Sail frigate; Pencil wash drawing; Hart Nautical Museum; III 1 C 300

1890: *Lake George*; Watercolor; Illustration: Advertisement for O.N.T. Cotton; Location unknown V E 301

1890: *San Francisco, Golden Gate*; Watercolor; Illustration: Advertisement for O.N.T. Cotton Location unknown V C a b 302

1890: *General Paine's Yacht, Volunteer*; Watercolor; Engraving made by Kurtz; Illustration: *Illustrated America*, July 5, 1890; Location unknown I 1 A a 303

1890: *The Squadron of Evolution Under Sail*; Pen, ink drawing; Illustration. *Harper's Weekly*, August 2 1890; Location unknown VII 304

1890: *Sailing for Bluefish*; Watercolor made into chromolithograph; Location of watercolor unknown; Chromolithograph in collection of the author; I 2 A a c 305

1891: *Petrel With her Owner, Col. Edwin A. Stevens, At the Helm*; Watercolor; Stevens Institute of Technology; I 1 A a 306

1891: *Landing Surf Boat Off Seabright, New Jersey*; Illustration: Advertisement for O.N.T. Cotton; Location unknown V 307

1891: *Yacht Race*; Watercolor; 36.7 x 39.5 cm; Kennedy Gallery; Location unknown I 2 A c d 308

1891: *Port Quarter View of Single-Mast Workboat*; Watercolor; 25.5 x 38 cm; Private collection; II 1 A c d 309

1892: *Beached Sailboat*; Watercolor; 47 x 53.2 cm; Private collection I 2 A c d 310

1892: *Two Workboats (stern view) Entering Fog Bank With Land, Lighthouse*; Watercolor; 25.5 x 56 cm; Private collection; II 2 A a d 311

1892: *Racing Boats*; Watercolor; 34.2 x 52.6 cm; Rhode Island Historical Society; I 2 A c d 312

1892: *Marine Scene*; 32.5 x 52.6 cm; Sotheby Parke Bernet Galleries Sale #2262, 1964; Location unknown VII 313

1892: *Unidentified Two-Mast Sailing Vessel*; Watercolor; 25.5 x 35.5 cm; Goodspeeds 1956 catalogue; Location unknown II 2 F c 314

1892: *View of the Narrows: Southeast*; Watercolor; 52.2 x 38 cm; Museum of the City of New York; V 2 C a b 315

1892: *U.S.S. Massachusetts*; 45.5 x 73.6 cm; Sotheby Parke Bernet Galleries Sale #2202, 1963; Location unknown III 1 a 316

1892: *Coney Island in Moonlight*; Watercolor; Illustration: Advertisement for O.N.T. Cotton; Location unknown V 2 A a 317

1892: *Three ships of Columbus, Pinta, Nina, Santa Maria*; Watercolor; Illustration: Advertisement for O.N.T. Cotton; Location unknown II 1 F a 318

1892: *Statue of Liberty*; Watercolor; Illustration: Advertisement for O.N.T. Cotton; Location unknown V 2 C a 319

1892: *Yacht, Priscilla*; Pen, ink drawing; Illustration: *Century Magazine*, August 1893, in an article, "Cup Defenders"; Location unknown I 1 A a 320
1892: *Yacht, Mischief*; Pen, ink drawing; Illustration: *Century Magazine*, August 1893; Location unknown I 1 A a 321
1892: *Nathaniel Herreshoff Coming Out of New London Harbor in a Catamarran*; Watercolor, chromolithograph; Location of watercolor unknown; Chromolithograph in private collection; I 2 A a 322
1892: *The Constitution Escaping From the British Squadron*; Pen, ink drawing; Illustration: *Our Navy, Its Growth and Achievements*, Part I, p. 27; Location unknown III 2 c d 323
1892: *Naval Equipment and Dress, Old Style*; Pen, ink drawing; Illustration: *Our Navy, Its Growth and Achievements*; Part I, p. 27; Location unknown III 2 cd 324
1892: *Captain O'Brien Capturing the Margaretta*; Pen, ink drawing; Illustration: *Our Navy, Its Growth and Achievements*, Part I, p. 29; Location unknown III 2 cd 325
1892: *Old Style Twelve Pounder*; Pen, ink drawing; Illustration: *Our Navy, Its Growth and Achievements*, Part I, p. 29; Location unknown III 2 c d 326
1892: *First Flags*; Pen, ink drawing; Illustration: *Our Navy, Its Growth and Achievements*, Part I, p. 37; Location unknown III 2 c d 327
1892: *Galleys Attacking the Phoenix and Rose*; Pen, ink drawing; Illustration: *Our Navy, Its Growth and Achievements*, Part I, p. 38; Location unknown III 1 a b 328
1892: *The Hornet and Penguin*; Pen, ink drawing; Illustration: *Our Navy, Its Growth and Achievements*, Part I, p. 39; Location unknown III 1 329
1892: *Belaying Pin*; Pen, ink drawing; Illustration: *Our Navy, Its Growth and Achievements*, Part I, p. 39; Location unknown III 2 c d 330
1892: *The Raleigh Surprising the English Fleet*; Pen, ink drawing; Illustration: *Our Navy, Its Growth and Achievements*, Part I, p. 46; Location unknown III 1 a b 331
1892: *The Chesapeake and Leopard*; Pen, ink drawing; Illustration: *Our Navy, Its Growth and Achievements*, Part I, p. 47; Location unknown III 1 c d 332
1892: *Uniform, Old Style*; Pen, ink drawing; Illustration: *Our Navy, Its Growth and Achievements*, Part I, p. 47; Location unknown III 2 c d 333
1892: *Captain Decatur*; Pen, ink drawing; Illustration: *Our Navy Its Growth and Achievements*; Part I, p. 52; Location unknown III 2 c d 334
1892: *Bonhomme Richard and Serapis*; Pen, ink drawing; Illustration: *Our Navy, Its Growth and Achievements*, Part I, p. 53; Location unknown III 1 a b 335
1892: *Life Preserver*; Pen, ink drawing; Illustration: *Our Navy, Its Growth and Achievements*; Part I, p. 53; Location unknown III 2 c d 336
1892: *Carronades*; Pen, ink drawing; Illustration: *Our Navy, Its Growth and Achievements*; Part I, p. 61; Location unknown III 2 c d 337
1892: *Capture of the Philadelphia*; Pen, ink drawing; Illustration: *Our Navy, Its Growth and Achievements*; Part I, p. 65; Location unknown III 1 a b 338
1892: *Capstan*; Pen, ink drawing; Illustration: *Our Navy, Its Growth and Achievements*, Part I, p. 65; Location unknown III 2 c d 339
1892: *Mosquito Squadron*; Pen, ink drawing; Illustration: *Our Navy, Its Growth and Achievements*; Part I, p. 72; Location unknown III a b 340
1892: *Constitution and Guerriere*; Pen, ink drawing; Illustration: *Our Navy, Its Growth and Achievements*; Part I, p. 73; Location unknown III 1 a b 341
1892: *Marlinspikes*; Pen, ink drawing; Illustration: *Our Navy, Its Growth and Achievements*; Part I, p. 73; Location unknown III 2 c d 342
1892: *Gun Captured From the Boxer, 1813*; Pen, ink drawing; Illustration: *Our Navy, Its Growth and Achievements*; Part I, p. 88; Location unknown III 1 b 343
1892: *The Enterprise and Boxer*; Pen, ink drawing; Illustration: *Our Navy, Its Growth and Achievements*; Part I, p. 89; Location unknown III 1 a b 344
1892: *Anchor, Old Style*; Pen, ink drawing; Illustration: *Our Navy, Its Growth and Achievements*; Part I, p. 89; Location unknown III 2 c d 345
1892: *Engagement on Lake Champlain, Plan of*; Pen, ink drawing; Illustration: *Our Navy, Its Growth and Achievements*; Part I, p. 98; Location unknown III 1 a b 346
1892: *Ship and Boats, 1598*; Pen, ink drawing; Illustration: *Our Navy, Its Growth and Achievements*; Part I, p. 114; Location unknown III 2 c d 347
1892: *Ship of the Line and Tender*; Pen, ink drawing; Illustration: *Our Navy, Its Growth and Achievements*; Part I, p. 115; Location unknown III 2 c d 348
1892: *The Frigate Congress*; Pen, ink drawing; Illustration: *Our Navy, Its Growth and Achievements*; Part I, p. 125; Location unknown III 1 c d 349
1892: *Anchor; Old Style*; Pen, ink drawing; Illustration: *Our Navy, Its Growth and Achievements*; Part I, p. 125; Location unknown III 2 c d 350
1892: *Ships Advance and Rescue*; Pen, ink drawing; Illustration: *Our Navy, Its Growth and Achievements*; Part I, p. 137; Location unknown III 1 c d 351
1892: *Chain Shot*; Pen, ink drawing; Illustration: *Our Navy, Its Growth and Achievements*; Part I, p. 137; Location unknown III 2 c d 352
1892: *A Denizen of Rotten Row*; Pen, ink drawing; Illustration: *Our Navy, Its Growth and Achievements*; Part I, p. 141; Location unknown III 2 c d 353
1892: *The Hartford at Mobile*; By permission of Wadsworth Library; Pen, ink drawing; Illustration: *Our Navy, Its Growth and Achievements*; Part I, p. 142; Location unknown III 1 a b 354
1892: *The Kearsage Sinking the Alabama*; Pen, ink drawing; Illustration: *Our Navy, Its Growth and Achievements*; Part I, p. 143; Location unknown III 1 a b 355
1892: *Fort Sumper*; Pen, ink drawing; Illustration: *Our Navy, Its Growth and Achievements*; Part I, p. 143; Location unknown III 2 a b 356
1892: *Naval Parade, October 11, 1892*; Pen, ink drawing; Illustration: *Our Navy, Its Growth and Achievements*; Part I, p. 172; Location unknown III 1 a b 357
1892: *Flags of the Naval Review*; Pen, ink drawing; Illustration: *Our Navy, Its Growth and Achievements*; Part I, p. 173; Location unknown III 2 a b 358
1892: *Signal Flag*; Pen, ink drawing; Illustration: *Our Navy, Its Growth and Achievements*; Part I, p. 173; Location unknown III 2 c d 359
1892: *The Vesuvius, Naval Equipment and Dress, Modern*; Pen, ink drawing; Illustration: *Our Navy, Its Growth and Achievements*; Part I, p. 1; Location unknown III 1 c d 360
1892: *Army and Navy Building, Washington, D.C.*; Pen, ink drawing; Illustration: *Our Navy, Its Growth and Achievements*; Part II, p. 1; Location unknown III 2 a b 361
1892: *Bugler*; Pen, ink drawing; Illustration: *Our Navy, Its Growth and Achievements*; Part II, p. 1; Location unknown III c d 362
1892: *A Conning Tower*; Pen, ink drawing; Illustration: *Our Navy, Its Growth and Achievements*; Part II, p. 15; Location unknown III 2 c d 363
1892: *Howell Torpedo*; Pen, ink drawing; Illustration: *Our Navy, Its Growth and Achievements*; Part II, p. 15; Location unknown III 2 c d 364
1892: *Howell Torpedo*; Pen, ink drawing; Illustration: *Our Navy, Its Growth and Achievements*; Part II, p. 33; Location unknown III 2 c d 365
1892: *Tuck's Submarine Torpedo Boat*; Pen, ink drawing; Illustration: *Our Navy, Its Growth and Achievements*; Part II, p. 33; Location unknown III 2 c d 366
1892: *Oars*; Pen, ink drawing; Illustration: *Our Navy, Its Growth and Achievements*; Part II, p. 33; Location unknown III 2 c s 367
1892: *Outside Steam Steering Wheel*; Pen, ink drawing; Illustration: *Our Navy, Its Growth and Achievements*; Part II, p. 35; Location unknown III 2 c d 368
1892: *Launching Boat in an Emergency*; Pen, ink drawing; Illustration: *Our Navy, Its Growth and Achievements*; Part II, p. 36; Location unknown III 2 c d 369
1892: *Figurehead of the Yorktown*; Pen, ink drawing; Illustration: *Our Navy, Its Growth and Achievements*; Part II, p. 37; Location unknown III 1 c d 370
1892: *Davit*; Pen, ink drawing; Illustration: *Our Navy, Its Growth and Achievements*; Part II, p. 37; Location unknown III 2 c d 371
1892: *Sims-Edison Torpedo*; Pen, ink drawing; Illustration: *Our Navy, Its Growth and Achievements*; Part II, p. 40; Location unknown III 2 c d 372
1892: *A Visiting Admiral*; Pen, ink drawing; Illustration: *Our Navy, Its Growth and Achievements*; Part II, p. 41; Location unknown III 2 c d 373
1892: *Anchor, Modern*; Pen, ink drawing; Illustration: *Our Navy, Its Growth and Achievements*; Part II, p. 41; Location unknown III 2 c d 374
1892: *Hotchkiss Gun*; Pen, ink drawing; Illustration: *Our Navy, Its Growth and Achievements*; Part II, p. 43; Location unknown III 2 c d 375
1892: *Ship in Drydock*; Pen, ink drawing; Illustration: *Our Navy, Its Growth and Achievements*; Part II, p. 45; Location unknown III 2 c d 376
1892: *Anchor, Modern*; Pen, ink drawing; Illustration: *Our Navy, Its Growth and Achievements*; Part II, p. 45; Location unknown III 2 c d 377
1892: *The Stiletto*; Pen, ink drawing; Illustration: *Our Navy, Its Growth and Achievements*; Part II, p. 45; Location unknown III 1 c d 378
1892: *The Cushing*; Pen, ink drawing; Illustration: *Our Navy, Its Growth and Achievements*; Part II, p. 45; Location unknown III 2 c d 379
1892: *The New Ironsides*; Pen, ink drawing; Illustration: *Our Navy, Its Growth and Achievements*; Part II, p. 48; Location unknown III 1 c d 380
1892: *The Passaic, Monitor*; Pen, ink drawing; Illustration: *Our Navy, Its Growth and Achievements*; Part II, p. 48; Location unknown III 1 c d 381
1892: *Turret of the Miantonomoh*; Pen, ink drawing; Illustration: *Our Navy, Its Growth and Achievements*; Part II, p. 49; Location unknown III 1 a b 382
1892: *Furling Sail*; Pen, ink drawing; Illustration: *Our Navy, Its Growth and Achievements*; Part II, p. 53; Location unknown III 2 c d 383
1892: *Capstan Bars*; Pen, ink drawing; Illustration: *Our Navy, Its Growth and Achievements*; Part II, p. 53; Location unknown III 2 c d 384
1892: *The Yantic and Thetis*; Pen, ink drawing; Illustration: *Our Navy, Its Growth and Achievements*; Part II, p. 56; Location unknown III 1 c d 385
1892: *The Destroyer*; Pen, ink drawing; Illustration: *Our Navy, Its Growth and Achievements*; Part II, p. 57; Location unknown III 1 c d 386
1892: *The Alarm*; Pen, ink drawing; Illustration: *Our Navy, Its Growth and Achievements*; Part II, p. 57; Location unknown III 1 c d 387
1892: *Firing Eight Inch gun*; Pen, ink drawing; Illustration: *Our Navy, Its Growth and Achievements*; Part II, p. 60; Location unknown III 2 c d 388
1892: *The Keokuk*; Pen, ink drawing; Illustration: *Our Navy, Its Growth and Achievements*; Part II, p. 61; Location unknown III 1 c d 389
1892: *A Pennant*; Pen, ink drawing; Illustration: *Our Navy, Its Growth and Achievements*; Part II, p. 61; Location unknown III 2 c d 390
1892: *Steam Launch*; Pen, ink drawing; Illustration: *Our Navy, Its Growth and Achievements*; Part II, p. 64; Location unknown III 2 c d 391
1892: *The Great Harry*; Pen, ink drawing; Illustration: *Our Navy, Its Growth and Achievements*; Part II, p. 65; Location unknown III 2 c d 392
1892: *Ship's Yawl*; Pen, ink drawing; Illustration: *Our Navy, Its Growth and Achievements*; Part II, p. 65; Location unknown III 2 c d 393
1892: *A Whistling Buoy*; Pen, ink drawing; Illustration: *Our Navy, Its Growth and Achievements*; Part II, p. 69; Location unknown III 2 c d 394
1892: *River Gunboat, Mortar and Tender, 1862*; Pen, ink drawing; Illustration: *Our Navy, Its Growth and Achievements*; Part II, p. 70; Location unknown III 2 c d 395
1892: *Dynamite Gun*; Pen, ink drawing; Illustration: *Our Navy, Its Growth and Achievements*; Part II, p. 71; Location unknown III 2 c d 396
1892: *Fulton, the First*; Pen, ink drawing; Illustration: *Our Navy, Its Growth and Achievements*; Part II, p. 75; Location unknown III 2 c d 397
1892: *The Friendly Light*; Pen, ink drawing; Illustration: *Our Navy, Its Growth and Achievements*; Part II, p. 75; Location unknown III 2 c d 398
1892: *The Enterprise and Ranger*; Pen, ink drawing; Illustration: *Our Navy, Its Growth and Achievements*; Part II, p. 80; Location unknown III 1 c d 399

1892: *Rapid Fire Ammunition*; Pen, ink drawing; Illustration: *Our Navy, Its Growth and Achievements*; Part II, p. 81; Location unknown III 2 c d 400

1892: *The Novgorod, Russian Ironclad*; Pen, ink drawing; Illustration: *Our Navy, Its Growth and Achievements*; Part II, p. 81; Location unknown III 1 c d 401

1892: *The Original Monitor*; Pen, ink drawing; Illustration: *Our Navy, Its Growth and Achievements*; Part II, p. 87; Location unknown III 1 c d 402

1892: *Taking a Smoke*; Pen, ink drawing; Illustration: *Our Navy, Its Growth and Achievements*; Part II, p. 87; Location unknown III 2 c d 403

1892: *The Bow of the Monterey Under Full Speed*; Pen, ink drawing; Illustration: *Our Navy, Its Growth and Achievements*; Part II, p. 91; Location unknown III 1 a b 404

1892: *Swab and Cartridges*; Pen, ink drawing; Illustration: *Our Navy, Its Growth and Achievements*; Part II, p. 91; Location unknown III 2 c d 405

1892: *Halstead's Whale*; Pen, ink drawing; Illustration: *Our Navy, Its Growth and Achievements*; Part II, p. 95; Location unknown III 1 a b 406

1892: *Landing, Naval Reserve Drill*; Pen, ink drawing; Illustration: *Our Navy, Its Growth and Achievements*; Part II, p. 96; Location unknown III 1 c d 407

1892: *Deck of the New Hampshire, Armory and Naval Militia*; Pen, ink drawing; Illustration: *Our Navy, Its Growth and Achievements*; Part II, p. 97; Location unknown III 1 c d 408

1892: *Sighting the Hotchkiss Gun*; Pen, ink drawing; Illustration: *Our Navy, Its Growth and Achievements*; Part II, p. 97; Location unknown III 2 c d 409

1892: *Guns, Old Style*; Pen, ink drawing; Illustration: *Our Navy, Its Growth and Achievements*; Part II, p. 105; Location unknown III 2 c d 410

1892: *Gun of the 15th Century*; Pen, ink drawing; Illustration: *Our Navy, Its Growth and Achievements*; Part II, p. 105; Location unknown III 2 c d 411

1892: *Small Boat Drill*; Pen, ink drawing; Illustration: *Our Navy, Its Growth and Achievements*; Part II, p. 105; Location unknown III 2 c d 412

1892: *Galleys of 1812*; Pen, ink drawing; Illustration: *Our Navy, Its Growth and Achievements*; Part II, p. 111; Location unknown III 2 c d 413

1892: *Surf Boats, 1847*; Pen, ink drawing; Illustration: *Our Navy, Its Growth and Achievements*; Part II, p. 111; Location unknown III 2 c d 414

1892: *Comparative Size of Guns*; Pen, ink drawing; Illustration: *Our Navy, Its Growth and Achievements*; Part II, p. 115; Location unknown III 2 c d 415

1892: *Cutlass Drill*; Pen, ink drawing; Illustration: *Our Navy, Its Growth and Achievements*; Part II, p. 115; Location unknown III 2 c d 416

1892: *Torpedo Launch*; Pen, ink drawing; Illustration: *Our Navy, Its Growth and Achievements*; Part II, p. 122; Location unknown III 2 c d 417

1892: *Stern of Columbia*; Pen, ink drawing; Illustration: *Our Navy, Its Growth and Achievements*; Part II, p. 123; Location unknown III 1 c d 418

1892: *Lookout*; Pen, ink drawing; Illustration: *Our Navy, Its Growth and Achievements*; Part II, p. 123; Location unknown III 2 c d 419

1892: *Modern Gun, Shield, and Implements*; Pen, ink drawing; Illustration: *Our Navy, Its Growth and Achievements*; Part II, p. 128; Location unknown III 2 c d 420

1892: *In the Boiler Room*; Pen, ink drawing; Illustration: *Our Navy, Its Growth and Achievements*; Part II, p. 129; Location unknown III 2 c d 421

1892: *Small Arms Drill*; Pen, ink drawing; Illustration: *Our Navy, Its Growth and Achievements*; Part II, p. 129; Location unknown III 2 c d 422

1892: *Ram of Puritan*; Pen, ink drawing; Illustration: *Our Navy, Its Growth and Achievements*; Part II, p. 135; Location unknown III 1 c d 423

1892: *Off Duty*; Pen, ink drawing; Illustration: *Our Navy, Its Growth and Achievements*; Part II, p. 135; Location unknown III 2 c d 424

1892: *Fore-deck of the Maine*; Pen, ink drawing; Illustration: *Our Navy, Its Growth and Achievements*; Part II, p. 140; Location unknown III 1 c d 425

1892 *Military Tops, Past and Present*; Pen, ink drawing; Illustration: *Our Navy, Its Growth and Achievements*, Part II, p. 140; Location unknown III 2 c d 426

1892 *A Drummer*; Pen, ink drawing; Illustration: *Our Navy, Its Growth and Achievements*, Part II, p. 141; Location unknown III 2 c d 427

1892 *The Minneapolis on Her Trial Trip*; Pen, ink drawing; Illustration: *Our Navy, Its Growth and Achievements*, Part II, p. 147; Location unknown III 1 a b 428

1892 *Signaling*; Pen, ink drawing; Illustration: *Our Navy, Its Growth and Achievements*, Part II, p. 147; Location unknown III 2 c d 429

1893 *Frontispiece*, Watercolor; Illustration: *Our Navy, Its Growth and Achievements*; Made into chromolithograph; Watercolor in private collection III 430

1893 Plate 1: *Baltimore, Boston*; Watercolor; Illustration: *Our Navy, Its Growth and Achievements*; Part II, opposite p. 32; Made into chromolithographic set; Location of watercolor unknown III 1 a 431

1893 Plate 2: *Atlanta, Chicago, Yorktown, Boston*; Watercolor; Illustration: *Our Navy, Its Growth and Achievements*, Part II, p. 36; Made into chromolithographic set; Location of watercolor unknown III 1 a 432

1893 Plate 3: *Charleston, San Francisco*; Watercolor; Illustration: *Our Navy, Its Growth and Achievements*, Part II, opposite p. 40; Made into chromolithographic set; Location of watercolor unknown III 1 A 433

1893 Plate 4: *Richmond, New York, Cushing*; Watercolor; Illustration: *Our Navy, Its Growth and Achievements*, Part II, opposite p. 12; Made into chromolithographic set; Location of watercolor unknown III 1 a 34

1893 Plate 5: *Miantonomoh, Newark*; Watercolor; Illustration: *Our Navy, Its Growth and Achievements*, Part II, opposite p. 48; Made into chromolithographic set; Location of watercolor unknown III 1 a 435

1893 Plate 6: *Kearsage, Constitution*; Watercolor; Illustration: *Our Navy, Its Growth and Achievements*, Part II, opposite p. 122; Made into chromolithographic set; Location of watercolor unknown III 1 a 436

1893 Plate 7: *Alarm, Philadelphia, Vesuvius*; Watercolor; Illustration: *Our Navy, Its Growth and Achievements*, Part II, p.55; Made into chromolithographic set; Location of watercolor unknow III 1 a 437

1893 Plate 8: *Machias, Massachusetts, Marblehead*; Watercolor; Illustration: *Our Navy, Its Growth and Achievements*, Part II, opposite p. 64; Made into chromolithographic set; Location of watercolor unknown III 1 a 438

1893 Plate 9: *Enterprise, Pennsylvania, South Carolina, Hornet*; Watercolor; Illustration: *Our Navy, Its Growth and Achievements*, Part II, opposite p. 84; Made into chromolithographic set; Location of watercolor unknown III 1 a 439

1893 Plate 10: *Philadelphia, Petrel, Vesuvius*; Watercolor; Illustration: *Our Navy, Its Growth and Achievements*, Part II, opposite p. 79; Made into chromolithographic set; Location of watercolor unknown III 1 a 440

1893 Plate 11: *Colorado, Hartford, Franklin, Powhatan*; Watercolor; Illustration: *Our Navy, Its Growth and Achievements*, Part II, opposite p. 108; Made into chromolithographic set; Location of watercolor unknown III 1 a 441

1893 Plate 12: *Bennington, Katahdin, Iowa*; Watercolor; Illustration: *Our Navy, Its Growth and Achievements*, Part II, opposite p. 12; Made into chromolithographic set; Location of watercolor unknown III 1 a 442

1893 Plate 13: *Type of Monodnock, Type of Cannonicu, Passaic, Ajax, Naugatuck, New Ironsides, Nantucket*; Watercolor; Illustration: *Our Navy, Its Growth and Achievements*, Part II, p. 144; Made into chromolithographic set; Location of watercolor unknown III 1 a 443
In the list of illustrations, this plate is listed: *Monitors, Passaic, Monodnock, Nantucket, Keokuk, New Ironsides*

1893 Plate 14: *Detroit, Monterey, Oregon*; Watercolor; Illustration: *Our Navy, Its Growth and Achievements*, Part II, opposite p. 90; Made into chromolithographic set; Location of watercolor unknown III 1 a 444

1893 Plate 15: *S.S. New York, Vamose, New Hampshire, Dolphin*; Watercolor; Illustration: *Our Navy, Its Growth and Achievements*, Part II, opposite p. 26; Made into chromolithographic set; Location of watercolor unknown III 1 a 445
In list of Illustrations, this plate is listed: *New Hampshire Dolphin, Chicago and New York (Liner)*.

1893 Plate 16: *Dispatch, Atlanta, Yorktown*; Watercolor; Illustration: *Our Navy, Its Growth and Achievements*, Part II, opposite p. 102; Made into chromolithographic set; Location of watercolor unknown III 1 a 446

1893 Plate 17: *Portsmouth, Constellation, Bancroft, Saratoga*: Watercolor; Illustration: *Our Navy, Its Growth and Achievements*, Part II, opposite p. 60; Made into chromolithographic set; Location of watercolor unknown III 1 a 447

1893 Plate 18: *Cincinnati, Terror, Indiana*; Watercolor; Illustration: *Our Navy, Its Growth and Achievements*, Part II, opposite p. 114; Made into chromolithographic set; Location of watercolor unknown III 1 a 448

1893 Plate 19: *Concord, Stiletto, Columbia*; Watercolor; Illustration: *Our Navy, Its Growth and Achievements*, Part II, opposite p. 122; Made into chromolithographic set; Location of watercolor unknown III 1 a 449

1893 Plate 20: *Brooklyn (New) and Brooklyn (Old)*; Watercolor; Illustration: *Our Navy, Its Growth and Achievements*, Part II, p.129; Made into chromolithographic set; Location of watercolor unknown III 1 a 450

1893 Plate 21: *Amphitrite, Puritan, Montgomery, Ericsson*; Watercolor; Illustration: *Our Navy, Its Growth and Achievements*, Part II, opposite p. 34; Made into chromolithographic set; Location of watercolor in F. D. Roosevelt Library at Hyde Park III 1 a 451

1893 Plate 22: *Raleigh, Castine, Maine*; Watercolor; Illustration: *Our Navy Its Growth and Achievements*; Part II, opposite p. 140; Made into chromolithographic set; Location of watercolor unknown III 1 a 452

1893 Plate 23: *Texas, Olympia, Minneapolis*; Watercolor; Illustration: *Our Navy Its Growth and Achievements*; Part II, opposite p. 144; Made into chromolithographic set; Location of watercolor unknown III 1 a 453

1893 Plate 24: *Naval Review; Foreign Lines; American Lines*; Watercolor; Illustration: *Our Navy Its Growth and Achievements*; Made into chromolithographic set; Location of watercolor unknown III 1 a 454

1892 Plate 1: *Boston, Baltimore*; Watercolor; Made into chromolithographic set, "Old Naval Prints"; Location of watercolor unknown III 1 a 455

1892 Plate 2: *Atlanta, Chicago, Yorktown, Boston*; Watercolor; Made into chromolithographic set, "Old Naval Prints"; Location of watercolor unknown III 1 a 456

1892 Plate 3: *Charleston, San Francisco*; Watercolor; Made into chromolithographic set, "Old Naval Prints"; Location of watercolor unknown III 1 a 457

1892 Plate 4: *Richmond, New York, Cushing*; Watercolor; Made into chromolithographic set, "Old Naval Prints"; Location of watercolor unknown III 1 a 458

1892 Plate 5: *Miantoinomoh, Newark*; Watercolor; Made into chromolithographic set, "Old Naval Prints"; Location of watercolor unknown III 1 a 459

1892 Plate 6: *Kearsage, Constitution*; Watercolor; Made into chromolithographic set, "Old Naval Prints"; Location of watercolor unknown III 1 a 460

1892 Plate 7: *Alarm, Philadelphia, Vesuvius*; Watercolor; Made into chromolithographic set, "Old Naval Prints"; Location of watercolor unknown III 1 a 461

1892 Plate 8: *Machias, Massachusetts, Castine, Marblehead*; Watercolor; Made into chromolithographic set, "Old Naval Prints"; Location of watercolor unknown III 1 a 462

1893 Plate 9: *Enterprise, Pennsylvania, South Carolina, Hornet*; Watercolor; Made into chromolithographic set, "Old Naval Prints"; Location of watercolor unknown III 1 a 463

1893 Plate 10: *Philadelphia, Petrel, Vesuvius*; Watercolor; Made into chromolithographic set, "Old Naval Prints"; Location of watercolor unknown III 1 a 464

1893 Plate 11: *Colorado, Hartford, Franklin, Powhatan*; Watercolor; Made into chromolithographic set, "Old Naval Prints"; Location of watercolor unknown III 1 a 465

1893 Plate 12: *Machias, Katahdin, Iowa*; Watercolor; Made into chromolithographic set, "Old Naval Prints"; Location of watercolor unknown III 1 a 466

1893 Plate 13: *Type of Monadnock, Type of Canonicus, Passaic, Naugatuck, New Ironsides Nantucket*; Watercolor; Made into chromolithographic set, "Old Naval Prints"; Location of watercolor unknown III 1 a 467

1893 Plate 14: *Detroit, Monterey, Oregon*; Watercolor; Made into chromolithographic set, "Old Naval Prints"; Location of watercolor unknown III 1 a 468

1893 Plate 15: *S.S. New York, Vamose, New Hampshire, Dolphin*; Watercolor; Made into chromolithographic set, "Old Naval Prints"; Location of watercolor unknown III 1 a 469

1893 Plate 16: *Dispatch, Atlanta, Yorktown*; Watercolor; Made into chromolithographic set, "Old Naval Prints"; Location of watercolor unknown III 1 a 470

1893 Plate 17: *Portsmouth, Constellation, Bancroft, Saratoga*; Watercolor; Made into chromolithographic set, "Old Naval Prints"; Location of watercolor unknown III 1 a 471

1893 Plate 18: *Cincinnati, Terror, Indiana*; Watercolor; Made into chromolithographic set, "Old Naval Prints"; Location of watercolor unknown III 1 a 472

1893 Plate 19: *Concord, Stiletto, Columbia*; Watercolor; Made into chromolithographic set, "Old Naval Prints"; Location of watercolor unknown III 1 a 473

1893 Plate 20: *Brooklyn (New) and Brooklyn (Old)*; Watercolor; Made into chromolithographic set, "Old Naval Prints"; Location of watercolor unknown III 1 a 474

1893 Plate 21: *Amphitrite, Puritan, Montgomery, Ericsson*; Watercolor; Made into chromolithographic set, "Old Naval Prints"; Location of watercolor unknown III 1 a 475

1893 Plate 22: *Raleigh, Castine, Maine*; Watercolor; Made into chromolithographic set, "Old Naval Prints"; Location of watercolor unknown III 1 a 476

1893 Plate 23: *Texas, Olympia, Minneapolis*; Watercolor; Made into chromolithographic set, "Old Naval Prints"; Location of watercolor unknown III 1 a 477

1893 Plate 24: *Naval Review, 1893; Foreign Lines, American Lines*; Watercolor; Made into chromolithographic set, "Old Naval Prints"; Location of watercolor unknown III 1 a 478

1893 *Unidentified Square-Rigged Vessel*; Watercolor 33.6x52.6 cm.; *Goodspeed's Catalogue* of June 1956; Location unknown II 1 F c 479

1893 *Three Battleships of the Great White Fleet*; Watercolor; 48.5x73.6 cm.; Private Collection III 2 c d 480

1893 *Yachts, Vigilant and Valkyrie*; Watercolor; Museum of the City of New York I 1 A a c d 481

1893 *The Gallant Vigilant Showing the Way Home*; Pen, ink drawing; Illustration: *New York Herald*; September 10, 1893; Location unknown I 1 A a b 482

1893 *The Vigilant and the Colonia at the Start*; Pen, ink drawing; Illustration: *New York Herald*, September 12, 1893; Location unknown I 1 A a b 483

1893 *The Vigilant Nearing the Finish*; Pen, ink drawing; Illustration: *New York Herald*, September 12, 1893; Location unknown I 1 A a b 484

1893 *Starboard Side View of the Valkyrie with Full Spinnakers*; Pen, ink drawing; Illustration: *New York Herald*, September 24, 1893; Location unknown I 1 A a b 485

1893 *Yacht Valkyrie, Her Owner*; Illustration: *New York Herald*, 9/24/1893; I 1 A a 486

1893 *The Vigilant in the Doldrums*; Pen, ink drawing; Illustration: *New York Herald*, October 6, 1893 Location unknown I 1 A a b 487

1893 *Together the Vigilant and the Valkyrie Start Away*; Pen, ink drawing; Illustration: *New York Herald*, October 8, 1893; Location unknown I 1 A a b 488

1893 *The Vigilant Finishing in Front*; Pen, ink drawing; Illustration: *New York Herald*, October 8, 1893; Location unknown I 1 A a b 489

1893 *Starting Away Together*; Pen, ink drawing; Illustration: *New York Herald*, October 10, 1893; Location unknown I 1 A a b 490

1893 *The Valkyrie's First Tack*; Pen, ink drawing; Illustration: *New York Herald*, October 10, 1893; Location unknown I 1 A a b 491

1893 *The Vigilant Rounding the First Mark*; Pen, ink drawing; Illustration: *New York Herald*, October 10, 1893; Location unknown I 1 A a b 492

1893 *At the Second Turning Point*; Pen, ink drawing; Illustration: *New York Herald*, October 10, 1893; Location unknown I 1 A a b 493

1893 *Five Miles from the Finish*; Pen, ink drawing; Illustration: *New York Herald*, October 10, 1893; Location unknown I 1 A a b 494

1893 *Crossing the Line a Winner*; Pen, ink drawing; Illustration: *New York Herald*, October 10, 1893; Location unknown I 1 A a b 495

1893 *The Vigilant in the Lead*; Pen, ink drawing; Illustration: *New York Herald*, October 12, 1893; Location unknown I 1 A a b 496

1893 *America's Cup Stays in America*; Pen, ink drawing; Illustration: *New York Herald*, October 14, 1893; Location unknown I 1 A a b 497

1893 *Rent in Valkyrie's Spinnaker*; Pen, ink drawing; Illustration: *New York Herald*, October 14, 1893; Location unknown I 1 A a v 498

1893 *Yacht, Vigilant*; Watercolor; Illustration: *Yacht Races for America's Cup*; Frontispiece; Location unknown; I 1 A c 499

1893 *Yacht, Valkyrie*; Watercolor; Illustration: *Yacht Races for the America's Cup*; p. 13; Location unknown I 1 A a 500

1893 *America*; Pen, ink drawing; Illustration: *Yacht Races for the America's Cup*; p. 14; Location unknown I 1 A a 501

1893 *The Yacht, Maria*; Pen, ink drawing; Illustration: *Yacht Races for the America's Cup*; p. 15; Location unknown I 1 A a 502

1893 *English Yacht, Cambria*; Pen, ink drawing; Illustration: *Yacht Races for the America's Cup*; p. 28; Location unknown I 1 A a 503

1893 *Yacht, Sappho*; Pen, ink drawing; Illustration: *Yacht Races for the America's Cup*; p. 32; Location unknown I 1 A a 504

1893 *Yacht, Henrietta*; Pen, ink drawing; Illustration: *Yacht Races for the America's Cup*; p. 36; Location unknown I 1 A a 505

1893 *Yacht, Fleetwing*; Pen, ink drawing; Illustration: *Yacht Races for the America's Cup*; p. 37; Location unknown I 1 A a 506

1893 *Yacht, Vesta*; Pen, ink drawing; Illustration: *Yacht Races for the America's Cup*; p. 41; Location unknown I 1 A a 507

1893 *Yacht, Rebecca*; Pen, ink drawing; Illustration: *Yacht Races for the America's Cup*; p. 42; Location unknown I 1 A a 508

1893 *Yacht, Magic*; Pen, ink drawing; Illustration: *Yacht Races for the America's Cup*; p. 44; Location unknown I 1 A a 509

1893 *Yacht, Halcyon*; Pen, ink drawing; Illustration: *Yacht Races for the America's Cup*; p. 45; Location unknown I 1 A a 510

1893 *Yacht, Madeline*; Pen, ink drawing; Illustration: *Yacht Races for the America's Cup*; p. 53; Location unknown I 1 A a 511

1893 *Yacht, Gracie*; Pen, ink drawing; Illustration: *Yacht Races for the America's Cup*; p. 60; Location unknown I 1 A a 512

1893 *Yacht, Fanny*; Pen, ink drawing; Illustration: *Yacht Races for the America's Cup*; p. 61; Location unknown I 1 A a 513

1893 *Yacht, Mischief*; Pen, ink drawing; Illustration: *Yacht Races for the America's Cup*; p. 62; Location unknown I 1 A a 514

1893 *Yacht, Priscilla*; Pen, ink drawing; Illustration: *Yacht Races for the America's Cup*; p. 71; Location unknown I 1 A a 515

1893 *Yacht, Bedouin*; Pen, ink drawing; Illustration: *Yacht Races for the America's Cup*; p. 75; Location unknown I 1 A a 516

1893 *Yacht, Miranda*; Pen, ink drawing; Illustration: *Yacht Races for the America's Cup*; p. 77; Location unknown I 1 A a 517

1893 *Yacht, Galatea*; Pen, ink drawing; Illustration: *Yacht Races for the America's Cup*; p. 94; Location unknown I 1 A a 518

1893 *Yacht, Mayflower and Yacht, Galatea*; Pen, ink drawing; Illustration: *Yacht Races for the America's Cup*; p. 94; Location unknown I 1 A a 519

1893 *Yacht, Atalanta*; Pen, ink drawing; Illustration: *Yacht Races for the America's Cup*; p. 98; Location unknown I 1 A a 520

1893 *Yacht, Mayflower*; Pen, ink drawing; Illustration: *Yacht Races for the America's Cup*; p. 99; Location unknown I 1 A a 521

1893 *Yacht, Thistle*; Pen, ink drawing; Illustration: *Yacht Races for the America's Cup*; p. 108; Location unknown I 1 A a 522

1893 *Yacht, Volunteer*; Pen, ink drawing; Illustration: *Yacht Races for the America's Cup*; p. 109; Location unknown I 1 A a 523

1893 *Yacht, Madge*; Pen, ink drawing; Illustration: *Yacht Races for the America's Cup*; p. 124; Location unknown I 1 A a 524

1893 *Yacht, Irex*; Pen, ink drawing; Illustration: *Yacht Races for the America's Cup*; p. 125; Location unknown I 1 A a 525

1893 *Yacht, Gloriana*; Pen, ink drawing; Illustration: *Yacht Races for the America's Cup*; p. 130; Location unknown I 1 A a 526

1893 *Vigilant and Colonia Race*; Pen, ink drawing; Illustration: *Yacht Races for the America's Cup*; p. 142; Location unknown I 1 A a 527

1893 *Jubilee and Pilgrim Race*; Pen, ink drawing; Illustration: *Yacht Races for the America's Cup*; p. 144; Location unknown I 1 A a 528

1893 *Valkyrie, Satanita and Brittania*; Pen, ink drawing; Illustration: *Yacht Races for the America's Cup*; p. 173; Location unknown I 1 A a 529

1893 *Yacht, Valkyrie and her owner*; Pen, ink drawing; Illustration: *Harper's Weekly*; September 24, 1893; Location unknown I 1 A a 530

1894 *Two Fishing Dories with Five Fishermen and a Sailboat*; Watercolor 35.5x52 cm.; Private collection II 2 a c 531

1894 *Catboat, Acorn*; Watercolor; 48.5x38 cm.; *Old Print Shop Catalogue* of June 1965; Location unknown I 1 A c 532

1894 *Unidentified Yacht*; Watercolor; 33.5x66 cm.; *Goodspeed's Catalogue* of June 1956; Location unknown I 2 A c d 533

1894 *Raising the Halyard*; Watercolor; 52.6x38 cm.; Sotheby Parke Bernet Galleries Sale 3823, #70, 1975; Location unknown I 2 A c 534

1894 *Madeline*; Pen, ink drawing; Illustration: *The Yachts and Yachtsmen of America*, by Henry Mott, 1894, Fig. 101; Location unknown I 1 A a 535

1894 *Fleetwing*; Pen, ink drawing; Illustration: *The Yachts and Yachtsmen of America*, Fig. 94; Location unknown I 1 A a 536

1894 *America (As She Was)*; Pen, ink drawing; Illustration: *The Yachts and Yachtsmen of America*, Fig. 90; Location unknown I 1 A a 537

1894 *Cygnet*; Pen, ink drawing; Illustration: *The Yachts and Yachtsmen of America*, Fig. 88; Location unknown I 1 A a 538

1894 *Maria*; Pen, ink drawing; Illustration: *The Yachts and Yachtsmen of America*, Fig. 89; Location unknown I 1 A a 539

1894 *Sloop Yacht, Corsair*; Pen, ink drawing; Illustration: *Outlook Magazine*, June 9, 1894; Location unknown I 1 A a 540

1895 *Beacon Light off the Point at New Bedford*; Watercolor; 16.5x32.5 cm.; Sold at Kennedy Gallery; Location unknown V 2 F b 541

1895 *Two-Mast Bluenose Schooner*; Watercolor; 43x53 cm.; Providence National Band II 1 F c d 542

1895 *Running In*; Racing vessel and sailing ship; Watercolor; 26x36.7 cm.; Sold by Kennedy Gallery; Location unknown I 2 c d 543

1895 *Cup Defender*; Watercolor; New York Yacht Club I 2 A c 544

1895 *Starboard Quarter of Racing Yacht*; Watercolor; 28x36.7 cm.; Private collection I 2 A c d 545

1895 *Sailing Ship in Full Sail*; Watercolor; 28x35.5 cm.; Private collection II 2 f 546

1895 *Shipwreck*; Watercolor; 45.5x61 cm.; Private collection IV 2 c d 547

1895 *Full Moon*; Night Scene with two-mast ship; Pen, ink drawing; Illustration: *Book of the Fair*; May 1895; Location unknown V 2 C c 548

1895 *Outward Bound*; Two-mast sailing ship sailing out of harbor; Pen, ink drawing; Illustration: *Book of the Fair*; May 1895; Location unknown V 2 C c 549

1895 *Rigging of a Yacht*; Pen, ink drawing; Illustration: *Handbook of International Yacht Race*, 1895; Location unknown I 2 e 550

1895 *Rigging of a Yacht*; Pen, ink drawing; Illustration: *Handbook of International Yacht Race*, 1895; Location unknown I 2 e 551

1895 *Fisherman in Dory*; Watercolor; 35x26.5 cm.; Sotheby, Parke Bernet Galleries; Sale 3823 #70; 1975; Location unknown II 2 C d 552

1895 *Yachting Scene*; Port view of racing vessels with reviewing fleet in background; Watercolor; 35.5x53 cm.; Mystic Seaport I 2 c d 553

1895 *Full-Masted Sailing Ship in Full Sail*; Staten Island Quarantine in background; Watercolor; 25.5x35.5 cm.; Private collection II 2 F b 554

1896 *One-Mast Sailing Ship with Dory*; Watercolor; 52x34.3 cm.; Private collection II 2 F c 555

1896 *Going Out in the Skiff Through Surf*; Watercolor; 36.7x55.2 cm.; Sotheby, Parke Bernet Galleries Sale 3687 #70; 1974; Location unknown V 2 H c 556

1896 *Cup Defender Flying the Iselin Signal*; Watercolor; New York Yacht Club I 2 A c 557

1896 *Two Men on Beach Bluefishing with Dory in Foreground*; Watercolor; 35.5x56 cm.; Private collection II 2 A c d 558

1896 *Sailboat Passing Lighthouse*; Watercolor; 35.5x25.5 cm.; Sotheby, Parke Bernet Galleries Sale 3804; #690; 1975; Location unknown I 2 A c 559

1896 *Workboat*; Watercolor; 24x32.5 cm.; Private collection II 1 A c d 560

1896 *Going Out*; Watercolor; 23x34.2 cm.; Sold at Kennedy Gallery; Location unknown VII 561

1896 *Two Sailboats Off Sandy Shore with Two Large Rocks*; Watercolor; 25.5x35.5 cm.; Private collection II 2 A c d 562

1897 *Robbins Reef*; Watercolor; Private collection V 2 F b 563

1897 *Lifeboat Going Out to Ship in Distress*; Watercolor; Private collection IV 2 c d 564

1897 *Sailing Ship at Low Tide Near Pier*; Watercolor; 25.5x18 cm.; Private collection V 2 B c d 565

1897 *Sailing Ship on the High Seas*; Watercolor; 25.5x18 cm.; Private collection II 2 f c d 566

1897 *Seaweed Covered Rocks with Breakers*; Watercolor; *Goodspeed's Catalogue*; Location unknown V 2 B b 567

1897 *Coming Ashore*; Watercolor; 33x26 cm.; *Child's Gallery*, March 1969; Sales Bulletin, Location unknown VII 568

1897 *Rescue Boat Coming to Aid of Distressed Vessel*; Watercolor; Private collection IV 2 c d 569

1898 *Hauling One into the Dory*; Watercolor; 30.5x49.5 cm.; Sold at Kennedy Gallery; Location unknown II 2 C c d 570

1898 *Two Sailboats*; Watercolor; 30.5x47 cm.; Private collection; I 2 c d 571

1898 *Beach Scene*; Watercolor; 23x38 cm.; Private collection V 2 B c d 572

1898 *Two Sailboats off Highlands, New Jersey*; Watercolor; 25.5x34.2 cm.; Private collection I 2 A b 573

1898 *Starboard View of New York Under Full Steam*; Watercolor; 35.5x54.5 cm.; Mystic Seaport VII 574

1898 *Ocean Steamers, City of New York*; Illustration *Harper's Weekly*, March 30, 1889; p. 254; Location unknown II 1 G a 575

1898 *Hand Lining for Cod*; Watercolor; 30.5x48.5 cm.; Private collection; Exhibited at Penobscot F. S. Cozzens Exhibition 1976 II 2 C a 576

1898 *Sailing Ship Going From a Large Two-Masted Ship with Sails Down*; Watercolor; 61x51 cm.; Sold By Sporting Gallery; Location unknown II 2 F c 577

1898 *The Open Sea*; Watercolor; Private collection V 2 H c 578

1898 *U.S. Destroyer*; Watercolor; Private collection III 2 C d 579

1898 *Columbia vs. Shamrock; Leeward and Return October 20, 1899*; Watercolor; 34.2x49.5 cm.; Sold by Old Print Shop; Location unknown I 1 A a b 580

1899 *Sunset on the Kill Van Kull*; Watercolor; Made into chromolithograph by H. D. Turner for the *Staten Island News* Independent Supplement, October 27, 1898 V 2 C b 581

1899 *Small Beach Scene*; Watercolor; 30.5x51 cm.; Staten Island Institute of Arts and Sceince V 1 B c 582

1899 *Naval Victory; Battle of Santiago*; Watercolor; 51x101.5 cm.; Admiral's Office, Washington Naval Yard, Washington D.C. III 2 a b 583

1899 *Naval Victory; U.S. and Spanish Fleets Engaged in Combat; Fleet Entering Manila Bay*; Watercolor; 51x101.5 cm.; Admiral's Office, Washington Naval Yard, Washington, D.C. III 2 a b 584

1899 *With Topmast Housed; In Rough Weather*; Watercolor; Illustration: *Yachting Wrinkles*, p. 13; Location unknown I 2 A c 585

1899 *America, Maria*; Pen, ink drawing; Illustration: *Yachting Wrinkles*, p. 38; Location unknown I 1 A a 586

1899 *The Cutter, Oriva*; Pen, ink drawing; Illustration: *Yachting Wrinkles*, p. 49; Location unknown I 1 A a 578

1899 *Madge*; Pen, ink drawing; Illustration: *Yachting Wrinkles*, p. 83; Location unknown I 1 A a 588

1899 *Vesta*; Pen, ink drawing; Illustration: *Yachting Wrinkles*, p. 85; Location unknown I 1 a a 589

1899 *Sloop, Gracie*; Pen, ink drawing; Illustration: *Yachting Wrinkles*, p. 133; Location unknown I 1 A a 590

1899 *Schooner, Sappho*; Pen ink drawing; Illustration: *Yachting Wrinkles*, p. 134; Location unknown I 1 A a 591

1899 *Yacht, Vigilant*; Watercolor; Illustration: *Yachting Wrinkles*, p. 224; Location unknown I 1 A a 592

1899 *Yacht, Valkyrie*; Watercolor; Illustration: *Yachting Wrinkles*, p. 243; Location unknown I 1 A a 593

1900 *Clippership, Sweepstakes*; Watercolor; 26.5x41.3cm; Sold by Old Print Shop, June 1958; Location unknown II 1 F a 594

1900 *Life Line*; Watercolor; 45.5x71cm; Sold at Sloan Auction Gallery, February 18, 1978; Location unknown IV A c d 595

1901 *Two Racing Yachts*; Pencil sketch; Mystic Seaport Museum; Exhibited at F.S. Cozzens Exhibition at Penobscot Marine Museum in 1976; I 2 A c d 596

1901 *Fishing Boat Aground with Two Fishermen Ashore*; Watercolor; 34.2x50cm, Sold by Kennedy Gallery; Location unknown II 1 A c d 597

1901 *Beach Scene*; Watercolor; 16.5x25.5cm, Private collection V 2 B c d 598

1901 *Columbia, Shamrock; Second Race*; Watercolor; Exhibited at F.S. Cozzens Exhibition at Penobscot Marine Museum in 1976; Private collection I 1 A a b 599

1901 *Columbia vs. Shamrock October 3, 4, 1901*; Watercolor; 30.5x51cm. Old Print Shop Catalogue June 1970; Location unknown I 1 A a b 600

1901 *Unidentified Sailing Vessel in Tow of Tug*; Watercolor; 30.5x51cm. Old Print Shop Catalogue June 1970; Location unknown II 1 F c d 601

1901 *Cod Fishing*; Watercolor; 26.5x43cm; Newcastle Galleries; Location unknown II 2 A c d 602

1902 *Schooners Clifford N. Carver and Inez N. Carver*; Watercolor; Penobscot Marine Museum in 1976 II 1 F c d 604

1902 *Seascape with Sailing Ships Off Shore*; Watercolor; 17x29cm, Sold at R. A. Bourne Galleries, July 14, 1973; Location unknown V 2 A c d 605

1902 *Two Vessels in Heavy Seas; Steam Freightship and Sailing Vessel Meeting at Sea*; Watercolor; 40.5x45.5cm; Mystic Seaport Museum II 2 F G c d 606

1903 *Two Sailboats off the Highlands, New Jersey*; Watercolor; 23x32cm; Private collection V 2 A b 607

1903 *Preparations for a Cup Race; Reliance, Race Committee Boat; Debris and Barrels in Water*; Watercolor; New York Yacht Club I 1 A c d 608

1903 *Stern View of the Vigilant*; Watercolor; Seawanhaka Corinthian Yacht Club I 1 A c d 609

1903 *Port View of the Aloha*; Watercolor; Seawanhaka Corinthian Yacht Club I 1 A c d 610

1903 *Schooner*; Watercolor; 22x38cm; Sold by R.A. Bourne Galleries July 14, 1971; Location unknown II 2 F c d 611

1903 *Three-Mast Sailing Ship Passing Lighthouse*; Watercolor; Private Collection II 2 F c d 612

1903 *Sailing Ship*; Watercolor; Private collection II 2 F c d 613

1903 *Beach Scene*; Watercolor; 38x28 cm.; Private collection V 2 B b 614

1903 *Schooner and Steam Vessel Meeting in Rough, Foggy Weather*; Watercolor; 36.2x54.5 cm.; Private collection; Exhibited at F.S. Cozzens Exhibition at Penobscot Marine Museum 1976 II 2 A c d 615

1903 *Yacht, Mischief*; Pen, ink drawing; Illustration: *Rudder Magazine*, March 1903; Location unknown I 1 A a 616

1903 *Yacht, Valkyrie*; Pen, ink drawing; Illustration: *Rudder Magazine*, March 1903; Location unknown I 1 A a 617

1903 *Yacht, Gorilla*; Pen, ink drawing; Illustration: *Rudder Magazine*, March 1903; Location unknown I 1 A a 618

1903 *Yacht, Hesper*; Pen, ink drawing; Illustration: *Rudder Magazine*, March 1903; Location unknown I 1 A a 619

1903 *Yacht, Iroquois*; Pen, ink drawing; Illustration: *Rudder Magazine*, March 1903; Location unknown I 1 A a 620

1903 *Yacht, Intrepid*; Pen, ink drawing; Illustration: *Rudder Magazine*, March 1903; Location unknown I 1 A a 621

1903 *Yacht, Ariel*; Pen, ink drawing; Illustration: *Rudder Magazine*, March 1903; Location unknown I 1 A a 622

1903 *Yacht, Fortuna*; Pen, ink drawing; Illustration: *Rudder Magazine*, March 1903; Location unknown I 1 A a 623

1903 *Yacht, Yampa*; Pen, ink drawing; Illustration: *Rudder Magazine*, March 1903; Location unknown I 1 A a 624

1903 *Yacht, Elmira*; Pen, ink drawing; Illustration: *Rudder Magazine*, March 1903; Location unknown I 1 A a 625

1904 *Sailing Dory*; Watercolor; 35.5x28 cm.; Old Print Shop Catalogue, June 1966; Location unknown II 2 C c d 626

1904 *Large Two-Mast Fishing Boat with Five Men on Board*; Watercolor; 34.1x50 cm.; Sold by Kennedy Gallery; Location unknown II 1 A a 628

1904 *Fishing Boat Aground*; Watercolor; 34.2x50 cm.; Kennedy Gallery; Location unknown II 2 A a 628

1904 *Beached Coastal Schooner*; Watercolor; Penobscot Marine Museum; Exhibited at F.S. Cozzens Exhibition, 1976 II 1 A c d 629

1904 *Brigantine, Aloha*; Watercolor; Sold at Sotheby, Parke Bernet Gallery, Sale #320, 1941; Location unknown II 1 F c d 630

1904 *Two Fishing Schooners*; Watercolor; Penobscot Marine Museum; exhibited at F.S. Cozzens Exhibition at Penobscot Marine Museum in 1976 II 2 A c d 631

1905 *Sloop Yacht, Pluck and Luck*; Watercolor, gouache; 20.6x24.3 cm.; Peabody Museum; Exhibited at F.S. Cozzens Exhibition at Penobscot Marine Museum, 1976 I 1 A a 632

1905 *Yacht of the Seas*; Watercolor 30.2x49.5 cm.; Sold at Kennedy Gallery; Location unknown II A c d 633

1905 *Whaler in Port*; Watercolor; 44.5x32.5 cm.; Sold at Kennedy Gallery; Location unknown II 2 B c d 634

1905 *Fishermen at Work*; Watercolor 21.5x26,5 cm.; Sold at Newcastle Gallery; Location unknown II 1 A c d 635

1905 *Sandbagger Racing Sloop*; Pencil sketch; Peabody Museum; Exhibited at F.S. Cozzens Exhibition at Penobscot Marine Museum, 1976 I 2 A c d 636

1905 *Sandbagger Racing Sloop; Just So*; Pencil sketch; Peabody Museum; Exhibited at F.S. Cozzens Exhibition at Penobscot Marine Museum, 1976 I 2 A c d 637

1905 *Four-Mast Schooner*; Watercolor; 53x28 cm.; Private collection II 2 F c d 638

1906 *Bringing in the Rescue Boat*; Watercolor; Private collection IV 2 c d 639

1906 *Tug Pulling Three-Masted Sailing Vessel*; Watercolor; 51x76 cm.; Sold at Sotheby, Parke Bernet Galleries, Sale 3804 #690, 1975; Location unknown II 2 F c d 640

1906 *Capsize to Windward*; Pen, ink drawing; Illustration: *Rudder Magazine*, March 1906; Location unknown I 2 A c d 641

1906 *Must Go*; Pen, ink drawing; Illustration: *Rudder Magazine*, March 1906; Location unknown I 2 A c d 642

1906 *Pluck and Luck*; Pen, ink drawing; Illustration: *Rudder Magazine*, March 1906; Location unknown I 1 A c d 643

1906 *Susie S.*; Pen, ink drawing; Illustration: *Rudder Magazine*, March 1906; Location unknown I 1 A c d 644

1906 *A Friendly Brush*; Pen, ink drawing; Illustration: *Rudder Magazine*, March 1906; Location unknown I 2 A c d 645

1906 *Mollie C.*; Pen, ink drawing; Illustration: *Rudder Magazine*, March 1906; Location unknown I 1 A c d 646

1906 *Lobstermen in Dory in Quiet Water*; Watercolor; 30.5x53 cm.; Private collection; Exhibited at F.S. Cozzens Exhibition at Penobscot Marine Museum 1976 II 2 A c d 647

1907 *Morning with a Sea Fog; West Bank Light*; Watercolor; 24x40.5 cm.; Sold at Kennedy Gallery; Location unknown V 2 F a c 648

1907 *Terminal Moraine on Staten Island*; Watercolor; Private collection V 2 B b 649

1907 *Two Sailboats*; Watercolor; Private collection I 2 A c d 650

1907 *Stern View of Schooner Meeting Motor Vessel in Severe Weather Conditions*; Watercolor; 23x35.5 cm.; Private collection II 2 G c d 651

1907 *Two Men Beaching a Dory with Sailboat in Background*; Watercolor; 21.5x33 cm.; Private collection II 2 C c d 652

1907 *Sailing Yacht, Port Side, With Private Signal of Charles F. Adams II*; Watercolor 38x61 cm.; Private collection I 2 A c d 653

1907 *Beach Scene with Sailboat in Background and Rowboat on Sand*; Watercolor; 23x36.7 cm.; Private collection V 2 B c d 654

1907 *Sailing Vessel*; Watercolor; 34.2x21.5 cm.; Private collection II 2 F c d 655

1907 *South Beach, Staten Island*; Watercolor; Sold at Sotheby, Parke Bernet Galleries, Sale #3678B, 1974; Location unknown V 2 B b 656

1908 *Cod Fishing on the Newfoundland Banks; Nantucket to Grand Banks*; Watercolor; 33x58 cm.; New York Historical Society II 1 A b 657

1908 *Two Men in Dory with Distress Signal on Upturned Oar*; Watercolor; 40.5x71 cm.; Private collection IV 2 c d 658

1908 *Sailboats*; Watercolor; 28x53 cm.; Private collection I 2 A c d 659

1908 *Enyole Beach, Mass.*; Watercolor; 33x58.5 cm.; Sold at Kennedy Gallery; Location unknown V 2 B c d 660

1908 *Starboard View of Tamerlain*; Watercolor; Seawanhaka Corinthian Yacht Club I 1 A a c d 661

1908 *Cod Fishing Scene*; Watercolor; Seawanhaka Corinthian Yacht Club II 2 A c d 662

1908 *Beach Scene; Large Promontory on Left*; Watercolor; Private collection V 2 B c d 663

1908 *Sailing Vessels at Sea*; Watercolor; Private collection II 2 F c d 664

1908 *Large Sailing Vessel*; Vatercolor; Private collection II 2 F c d 665

1908 *Stern View of Pilot Vessel Meeting Motor Vessel*; Watercolor; 23x35.5 cm.; Private collection V 2 G c d 666

1908 *Sea Fog; Six Men Unloading Surfboat on Beach and Loading a Donkey-Drawn Cart; Early Morning*; Watercolor; 28x56 cm.; Private collection; V 2 B c d 667

1908 *Bow View of Two-Mast Sailing Vessel with Another in Deep Trough in Background*; Watercolor; 33x58.5 cm.; Private collection II 2 F c d 668

1908 *Beaching a Fishing Boat*; Watercolor; Penobscot Marine Museum; Exhibited at F.S. Cozzens Exhibition at Penobscot Marine Museum in 1976 II 2 a c d 669

1908 *Lost Fishermen*; Watercolor; Penobscot Marine Museum; Exhibited at F.S. Cozzens Exhibition at Penobscot Marine Museum in 1976 VII 670

1908 *Fishing in a Storm*; Watercolor; Penobscot Marine Museum; Exhibited at F.S. Cozzens Exhibition at Penobscot Marine Museum in 1976 II 2 A c d 671

1908 *Codfishing Scene*; Watercolor; Mentioned by Harper in *Early Painters and Engravers of Canada*; Location unknown II 1 A b c 672

1909 *The Half Moon and the Clermont in the Hudson River*; Watercolor; 15.3x38 cm.; New York Historical Society V 1 D a b 673

1909 *Two Men in a Dory with Upturned Oar and Sailing Vessels in Background*; Watercolor 30.5x48.5 cm.; Private Collection IV 2 c d 674

1909 *Tonging for Clams*; Watercolor; 21.5x34.2 cm.; Old Print Shop Catalogue December 1969; Location unknown II 2 A c d 675

1909 *Castle Garden, New York Bay*; Watercolor; 25.5x36.7 cm.; Old Print Shop Catalogue November 1867; Location unknown V 2 A b c 676

1909 *A Quiet Night, Tompkinsville Night Scene*; Watercolor; 23.5x38 cm.; New York Historical Society V 2 C b c d 677

1909 *Marine Coast Scene with Ship*; Watercolor; 32x57.2 cm.; Sold by R. A. Bourne Auction Galleries; Sale September 19, 1973; Location unknown V 2 A c d 678

1910 *No Wind*; Watercolor; 30.5x23 cm.; Sold at Kennedy Gallery; Location unknown VII 679

1910 *Stone Pier with Sailboats*; 28x48.5 cm.; Private collection V 2 A b c 680

1910 *Seascape*; Watercolor; 28x49 cm.; Sold at Sotheby, Parke Bernet Galleries, Sale 1580 #236A in 1955; Location unknown VII 681

1910 *The Landing*; Watercolor; 19x61 cm.; PB84 Auction Gallery #27; November 28, 1978 IV 2 c d 682

1910 *Beach Scene with Two Boatmen and Two Dories*; Watercolor; John H. Carver Collection, Penobscot Marine Museum; Exhibited in F. S. Cozzens Exhibition in 1976 II 2 C c d 683

1910 *Ship on the High Seas*; Watercolor; 28.8x44.5 cm.; PB84 Auction Galleries October 10, 1979; Location unknown II 2 F c d 684

1910 *Ship Passing Pilot Boat*; Watercolor; John H. Carver Collection; Penobscot Marine Museum; Exhibited in F. S. Cozzens Exhibition at Penobscot Marine Museum in 1976 V 2 H c d 685

1910 *Two Men in a Dory*; Watercolor; 28.8 x 44 cm.; Sold at PB 84 Auction Galleries October 10, 1979; Location unknown II 2 C c d 686

1910 *Beachscape*; Watercolor; 28x49 cm.;Sotheby, Parke Bernet Galleries Sales #1580, #236B 1955; Location unknown VII 687

1910 to 1915 *Large Stone Mountain Outside Atlanta, Georgia*; Location unknown VII 688

1911 *Yacht, Avenger*; Watercolor; Seawanhaka Corinthian Yacht Club I 1 A a c d 689

1911 *Two Sailing Ships and Tug*; Watercolor; 23x34.2 cm.; Private collection II 2 F c d 690

1911 *Sailboat with Another in Background*; Watercolor; 36.7x24 cm.; Private Collection I 1 A c d 691

1911 *Large Square-Rigged Sailing Vessel with Three Smaller Schooner-Type Vessels and Two Dories*; Watercolor; 59.5x34.2 cm.; Private Collection II 2 F c d 692

1911 *Two-Mast Sailing Vessel with Man in Dory in Foreground*; Watercolor; 23x28 cm.; Private collection II 2 f c d 693

1911 *Square Rigger Headed Dead-on with Freighter; Sailing Vessel in Background*; Watercolor; 30.5x45.5; Chesapeake Bay Eastern Yacht Club II 2 F c d 694

1911 *Sailing Vessel in America's Cup Race Scene; Port Quarter View with New York Yacht Club Official Boat in Right Foreground*; Watercolor; 30.5x51 cm.; Chesapeake Bay Eastern Yacht Club I 1 A a b 695

1911 *Rocks and Surf*; Watercolor; 53x76 cm.; Provident National Bank V G c d 696

1912 *Schooner Hard, a Port with Tramp Steamer in Background*; Watercolor; 40.5x61cm.; Private collection II 2 F c d 697

1912 *The Red Beacon Near the Point*; Watercolor; 35.5x61 cm.; Old Print Shop Catalogue, June 1967; Location unknown V F b c 698

1912 *Rock Jetty with Storm Signals Flying; Men in Sou'westers*; Watercolor; 56x35.5 cm.; Private collection V 2 B c d 699

1912 *Any Ole Beach Near No Man's Land*; Watercolor; 35x59.5 cm.; Old Print Shop Catalogue, June 1968; Location unknown B c d 700

1913 *Home From Cathay*; Watercolor; 38x48.5 cm.; Private collection II 2 F c d 701

1913 *Chesapeake and Shannon*; Watercolor; Museum of the City of New York III 1 c d 702

1913 *Square Rigger in a Calm*; 35.5x55.2 cm.; Old Print Shop Catalogue, June 1967; Location unknown II 2 F c d 703

1913 *Large Three-Mast Sailing Ship*; Watercolor; 68.5x52 cm.; Private collection II 2 F c d 704

1913 *Old Galleon*; Watercolor; Private collection II 2 F c d 705

1913 *Seascape*; Watercolor; 29x44.5 cm.; Sold by Newcastle Galleries; Location unknown V 2 H c d 706

1913 *The Breakers; Seacoast with Beach, Rocks, Sailboat*; Watercolor; 28x48.5 cm.; The Staten Island Institute of Arts and Science V 2 B c d 707

1914 *Beach Scene*; Set of three with trick signature; Watercolor; 15.3x20 cm.; Rocks, breakers and three mast schooner; Signed "Fred" in red, "S." in grey, and "Cozzens" in grey; Private collection V 2 B c d 708

1914 *Beach Scene*; Set of three with trick signature; Watercolor; 15.3x20 cm.; Signed "Fred" in grey; "S." in red, and "Cozzens" in grey; Private collection V 2 B c d 709

1914 *Beach Scene*; Set of three with trick signature; Watercolor; 15.3x20 cm.; Cove with sailing craft; Signed "Fred" in grey, "S." in grey and "Cozzens" in red; Private collection V 2 A c d 710

1914 *When the Cynthia Ann Came Ashore in, 14; A Life-Saving Crew with its Breeches Buoy Attached to the Vessel; Sailing Vessel Aground with Waves Breaking It Up*; Private collection; Exhibited in F. S. Cozzens Exhibition in Penobscot Marine Museum in 1976 IV 1 a 711

1914 *Great South Bay, Sayville, L. I.*; Watercolor; 24.1x43.5 cm.; Doyle Auction Gallery September 19, 1979; Location unknown VII 712

1915 *Fall River Line Steamer, Priscilla*; Watercolor; 38.7x74 cm.; Private collection II G a c d 713

1915 *Passenger Liner off Fort Wadsworth; Battery Weed on Shore*; Watercolor; Staten Island Historical Society; Loaned to Exhibition called, "Treasurers of Staten Island" held by the Staten Island Institute of Arts and Science, October 15, 1952 II 2 G b c d 714

1915 *Sloops, Resolute and Vanitie in a Trial Match off Sandy Hook in 1914*; Watercolor; Massachusetts Institute of Technology; Department of Naval Architecture I 1 A a b 715

1915 *Rounding the Lightship; Ambrose Light-Ship Outside the Hook*; Watercolor; 63.5x43 cm.; Private collection II 2 F b c d 716

1915 *Steamship Liner Aground in Fog with Viewers on Beach and Jetty*; Watercolor; Private collection; Exhibited at F. S. Cozzens Exhibition at Penobscot Marine Museum in 1976 II 2 G c d 717

1916 *Beached Dutch Boat*; Watercolor; 25.5x33 cm.; Inscribed "To Mrs. Ernest V. Hubbard" Private collection V 2 B c d 718

1916 *Schooner Yacht, Mermaid*; Watercolor; 32x48.5 cm.; Peabody Museum; Exhibited at F. S. Cozzens Exhibition at Penobscot Marine Museum in 1976 I 1 A c d 719

1917 *Barque, New Bedford; American Whaling Ship*; Watercolor; 13.5x30.5 cm.; Peabody Museum; Exhibited at F. S. Cozzens Exhibition held at Penobscot Marine Museum in 1976 II 2 B c d 720

1917 *Steam Yacht, Sylvia*; Watercolor; 33.7x49.5 cm.; Peabody Museum; Exhibited at F. S. Cozzens Exhibition at Penobscot Marine Museum in 1976 I 1 A a c d 721

1917 *Two Sailboats on Beach*; Watercolor; 25.5x42 cm.; Private collection V 2 B c d 722

1918 *Clipper Ship*; Watercolor; Private collection II 2 F c d 723

1918 *New York Harbor and the Statue of Liberty*; Watercolor; 38x61 cm.; Museum of the City of New York V 2 C c d 724

1918 *Yachts in Moonlight*; Watercolor; Made into chromolithograph; Exhibited at F. S. Cozzens Exhibition at Penobscot Marine Museum in 1976 V 2 I c d 725

1918 *Challenge*; Watercolor; Illustration: *Valentine's Manual*, Vol. III, 1919; Location unknown II 1 F c d 726

1918 *Ship, New Hampshire*; Watercolor; Illustration: *Valentine's Manual*, Vol. III, 1919; Location unknown II 1 F c d 727

1918 *Ship, William H. Macy*; Watercolor; Illustration: *Valentine's Manual*, Vol. III, p. 220; Location unknown II 1 F c d 728

1918 *Ship, Young America*; Watercolor; Illustration: *Valentine's Manual*, Vol. III, p. 38; Location unknown II 1 F c d 729

1918 *Schooner, Emma Knowleon*; Watercolor; 48.9x73.6 cm.; Sotheby Parke Bernet Galleries #430 February 2, 1979; Location unknown II 1 A a 730

1918 *Schooner, Edith Olcott*; Watercolor; 48.9x73.6 cm.; Sotheby Parke Bernet Galleries #431, February 2, 1979; Location unknown II 1 A a 731

1919 *Two-Mast Sailing Ship with Dory*; Watercolor; 51x68.5 cm.; Provident National Bank II 2 F c d 732

1919 *Teaship, Oriental*; Watercolor; Made into chromolithograph; Illustration: Commissioned by Great Northern Railway Company; Location unknown II 2 F c d 733

1919 *Ship, Andrew Jackson*; Watercolor; Illustration: *Valentine's Manual*, Vol. III, 1919; Location unknown II 1 F c d 734

1919 *U.S.S. George Washington*; Watercolor; Illustration: *Valentine's Manual*, Vol. IV, 1920; Location unknown III 1 a c d 735

1919 *Clipper ship, Samuel Russell*; Watercolor; Illustration: *Valentine's Manual*, Vol. IV, 1920; Location unknown II 1 F c d 736

1919 *Three-Mast ship, N.B. Palmer*; Watercolor; Illustration: *Valentine's Manual*, Vol. IV, 1920; Location unknown II 1 F c d 737

1919 *Ship, Hoaquah*; Watercolor; Illustration: *Valentine's Manual*, Vol. IV, 1920; Location unknown II 1 F c d 738

1919 *Ship, Aloha, Private Yacht of Commodore Curtis who Donated Her to the U.S. Navy*; Watercolor; Illustration: *Valentine's Manual*, Vol. IV 102; Location unknown I 1 A c d 739

1919 *Ship, U.S.S. Noma, Private Yacht of Vincent Astor who Donated Her to the U.S. Navy*; Watercolor; Illustration: *Valentine's Manual*, Vol. IV, 1920; Location unknown I 1 A a c d 740

1919 *Steam Yacht, Corsair*; Watercolor; Illustration: *Valentine's Manual*, Vol. IV, 1920; Location unknown I 1 A c d 741

1919 *Ship, Columbia*; Watercolor; Made into a calendar by the State Street Trust Company of Boston; Location unknown VII 742

1920 *Ambrose Lightship*; Watercolor; 35.5x45.5 cm.; Private collection V F a c 743

1920 *Indian Camp View*; Watercolor; Sold by R. A. Bourne Galleries; Private collection VI 744

1920 *Indian Camp View*; Watercolor; Sold by R. A. Bourne Galleries; Private collection VI 745

1920 *Indian Camp View*; Watercolor; Sold By R. A. Bourne Galleries; Private collection VI 746

1920 *Shipwreck; Abandoning the Ship*; Watercolor; 41.3x65.5 cm.; Old Print Shop Catalogue, June 1968; Location unknown IV 2 c d 747

1920 *Sand Dunes*; Watercolor; 51x70 cm.; Provident National Bank V B c d 748

1921 *Bluenose Schooner, John M. Emory*; Watercolor; 68.5x81 cm.; Private collection II 1 A c d 749

1921 *Eskimo Village, Alaska*; Watercolor; 34.2x49.5 cm.; Sold at Kennedy Gallery; Location unknown VI 750

1921 *Delawanta Esperanta Running Under Her Lea*; Watercolor; Exhibited by Cozzens in American Watercolor Society Exhibition, 1921; Location unknown II 1 G c d 751

1921 *Beach Scene*; Watercolor; 23.5x35 cm.; Sold at Kennedy Gallery; Location unknown V 1 B c d 752

1922 *Hudson River Canal Boats*; Watercolor; Illustration: *Valentine's Manual* #6, 1922; Location unknown II 1 E c d 753

1922 *Clippership, Dreadnaught*; Watercolor; Private collection II F c d 754

1923 *Three-Mast Ship in Becalmed Sea*; Watercolor; 25.5x35.5 cm.; Private collection II 1 F c d 755

1923 *Beach Scene*; Watercolor; 35.5x53 cm.; Private collection V 2 B c d 756

1923 *Serapis and Bonhomme Richard*; Watercolor; Penobscot Marine Museum; Exhibited at F. S. Cozzens Exhibition at Penobscot Marine Museum in 1976 VII 757

1924 *Mt. Steward, British Sailing Vessel*; Watercolor; 20x33 cm.; Private collection II 2 F c d 758

1924 *Ship Flying the Pennant, T B A*; Watercolor; 20x30.5 cm.; Sold at Kennedy Galleries; Location unknown II 1 F c d 759

1924 *Ship, Sweepstakes*; Watercolor; 25.5x40 cm.; Sold at Kennedy Galleries; Location unknown II a F 760

1924 *Sovereign of the Seas*; Watercolor; 24x33 cm.; Sold at Marine Arts Co.; Location unknown VII 761

1924 *Small Coastal Schooner*; Watercolor; Inscribed "Presented to my old sailor friend, Ex-Gov. Sulzer"; New York Historical Society II 1 F c d 762

1925 *Ship, Thames; Owned by Isaac Hicks*; Watercolor; Museum of the City of New York II 1 F c d 763

1925 *Pirate Ship*; Penobscot marine Museum; Exhibited at F. S. Cozzens Exhibition at Penobscot Marine Museum in 1976; II 1 F c d 764

1925 *Ship, Mayflower*; Watercolor; Penobscot Marine Museum; Exhibited at F. S. Cozzens Exhibition at Penobscot Marine Museum 1976 II F c d 765

1925 *Brig, Alert*; Watercolor; Penobscot Marine Museum; Exhibited at F. S. Cozzens Exhibition at Penobscot Marine Museum in 1976 II F c d 766

1925 *Barque, Andrew Hicks*; Penobscot Marine Museum; Exhibited at F. S. Cozzens Exhibition at Penobscot Marine Museum in 1976 II F c d 767

1925 *Constitution and Guerriere*; Watercolor; Penobscot Marine Museum; Exhibited at F. S. Cozzens Exhibition at Penobscot Marine Museum in 1976 III 1 a 768

1925 *Unidentified Ship Awaiting Pilot*; Watercolor; Penobscot Marine Museum; Exhibited at F. S. Cozzens Exhibition at Penobscot Marine Museum in 1976 VII 769

1925 *Full Rigged Ship, Bangalore*; Watercolor; Penobscot Marine Museum; Exhibited at F. S. Cozzens Exhibition at Penobscot Marine Museum in 1976 II 1 F c 778

1926 *Port Side of Schooner Flying the NYYC Pennant with Motor Boat Flying the Atlantic Yacht Club Pennant*; Watercolor; 35.5x53 cm.; Private collection I 1 A c d 771

1926 *Staten Island Athletic Club Boathouse*; Pen, ink drawing; Exhibited at Staten Island Institute of Arts and Science Exhibition, July 8, 1976 V 2 A a b 772

1926 *Constitution and Java*; Watercolor; Penobscot Marine Museum; Exhibited at F. S. Cozzens Exhibition at Penobscot Marine Museum in 1976 III 1 a 773

1926 *Staghound*; Pencil sketch; 53.7x30.8 cm.; Newport Marine Museum II 1 c d 774

1927 *Westhampton Beach, Long Island*; Watercolor; 17x25.5 cm.; New York Historical Society V B a 775

1927 *Ship Foundering*; Watercolor; Private collection IV 1 A c d 776

1928 *Stone Jetty with Cabin Showing Brooklyn, New York on Opposite Shore*; Watercolor; Private collection V i A c d 777

1928 *Ship, America*; Watercolor; Museum of the City of New York I 1 A a c d 778

1928 *American Privateer, War of 1812*; Watercolor; Museum of the City of New York III 2 a c d 779

1928 *Burning of the Frigate, Philadelphia, Tripoli 1804*; Watercolor; Museum of the City of New York III 1 a b 780

1928 *Ship, Constitution*; Watercolor; Museum of the City of New York III 1 c d 781

1928 *Ship, Flying Cloud*; Watercolor; Museum of the City of New York II 1 F c d 782

1928 *Yacht, Gimcrack*; Watercolor; Museum of the City of New York I 1 A a c d 783

1928 *Ship, Half-Moon*; Watercolor; Museum of the City of New York II 1 F c d 784

1928 *Ship, Andrew Hicks*; Watercolor; Museum of the City of New York II 1 F c d 785

1928 *Yachts, Mischief and Atalanta*; Watercolor; Museum of the City of New York I 1 A a c d 786

1928 *Whaler, Charles W. Morgan*; Watercolor; Museum of the City of New York II 1 B c d 787

1928 *Ship, Niagara, Perry's Flagship*; Watercolor; Museum of the City of New York I 1 A a 788

1928 *Adrien Block's Onrust*; Watercolor; Museum of the City of New York II 1 F c d 789

Ship, N.B.Plamer; Watercolor; Museum of the City of New York II 1 F c d 790

Pinta, Nina and Santa Maria; Watercolor; Museum of the City of New York II 1 F c d 791

Adrien Block's Quest; Watercolor; Museum of the City of New York II 1 F c d 792

Resolute and Shamrock; Watercolor; Museum of the City of New York I 1 A a c d 793

The Royal George; Watercolor; Museum of the City of New York II 1 1 c d 794

Thermopylae and Snark; Watercolor; Museum of the City of New York II 1 F c d 795

Trimountain; Named for the hills of Boston; Watercolor; Museum of the City of New York II 1 F c d 796

Unidentified Early Dutch Ship; Watercolor; Museum of the City of New York II 1 F c d 797

Whaler, Wanderer of New Bedford; Watercolor; Museum of the City of New York II 1 B a 798.

Mystery ship; Watercolor; Museum of the City of New York VII 799

16th-century Spanish Galleon; Watercolor; Museum of the City of New York II 2 F c d 800

Unidentified Marine Scene; Watercolor; Museum of the City of New York VII 801

Brig, Topaz and Brig, Alert; Watercolor; 28x38cm; BIAP Survey; Location unknown II1 A 803

Brigantine, Experiment; Watercolor; 28x38cm; BIAP Survey; Restricted II 1 A a b 803

Small Share Scene with Three-Mast Ship; Watercolor; Grandson of the artist V2Fcd 804

Rock, shore, surf; Watercolor; Grandson of the artist V 2 B c d 805

Fishing Sailing Vessel; Watercolor; Grandson of the artist II 2 A c d 806

Marsh Scene with Building; Watercolor; Grandson of the artist V J c d 807

Small Sailboat Coming into Prince's Bay, Staten Island; Watercolor; Grandson of the artist I 2 A a c d 808

Marine Scene; Watercolor; Grandson of the artist VII 809

Sailboat on Water at Night; Watercolor; 25.5x36.5cm; Private collection V2 C c d 810

Marine Scene; Watercolor; Private collection VII 811

Lighthouse at Prince's Bay, Staten Island; Watercolor; Private Collection V F a c d 812

Marine Scene; Watercolor; Private collection VII 813

Clipper Ship and Yachts Offshore; Watercolor; 35x54.5cm; Sold at Kennedy Gallery; Location unknown II 2 A c d 814

Tale of the Grounded Ship; Watercolor; 25.5x35.5cm; Sold at Kennedy Gallery; Location unknown IV 2 c d 815

Pride of the Trade; Watercolor; Sold at Kennedy Gallery; Location unknown II 2 F c d 816

Out to Sea; Watercolor; Sold at Kennedy Gallery; Location unknown VII 817

Achusnet River; Watercolor; Sold at Kennedy Gallery; Location unknown V 2 D a b 818

Sovereign of the Seas; Watercolor; 20.6x31cm; Sold at Kennedy Gallery; Location unknown II 1 F c d 819;

Large Ship; Man in Dory on Left; Watercolor; Private collection II 2 F c d 820

Homeward Bound; Watercolor; 33x58.3cm; New York Historical Society II 2 F c d 821

Private Chapel at Town.of Fort Wadsworth, Staten Island; Watercolor; Commissioned by owner Cuthbert Mills; Location unknown VI 822

Mills Homestead at Arrochar, Staten Island; Watercolor; Commissioned by Cuthbert Mills; Location unknown VI 823

Fort Wadsworth; Watercolor; Commissioned by Cuthbert Mills; Location unknown VI 824

Four Yachts; Watercolor; Royal Canadian Yacht Club I 2 c d 825

Large Paddle-Wheel Steamer Passing Hong Kong; Watercolor; Private Collection II 2 G a 826

New York Harbor with Tug and Ferry; Watercolor; Private collection II J b 827

Sandy Hook; Watercolor; Private collection V 2 A c d 728

Two Fishermen in Sailboat; Watercolor; Private collection II 2 A c d 829

Beach and Water; Watercolor; Private collection V B c d 830

Lobsterman Examining his Traps; Watercolor; Private collection II 2 A a c d 831

Whaling Ship Caught in the Ice; Sold at Childs Gallery, 1973; Location unknown II 2 F c 832

Ship, Columbia; Commissioned by the Great Northern Railroad; Watercolor; Location unknown II 2 F c d 833

Bass Fishing with Plug from Beach; Watercolor; Old Print Shop Catalogue, January 1973; Location unknown V B c d 834

New York Skyline from the Bay; Given by the artist to Harriet Slater and then to the Dominie of the Ascension Church on Staten Island; Location unknown V C a c d 835

Spanish Galleon with Painted Sails; Watercolor; Commissioned by W.C.Hubbard; Location unknown II 2 F c d 836

Shoreline with Churches and Large, Three-Masted Ship; Watercolor; 51x76cm.; Sold by Sporting Gallery; Location unknown II 2 A c d 837

Duck Shooting; Watercolor; 26.5x44.5cm.; Sold by Sotheby, Parke, Bernet Galleries #388 in 1942; BIAP Survey; Location unknown V D E c d 839

Fishermen; Watercolor; 32x56cm.; sold by Sotheby, Parke Bernet Galleries #388 in 1943; Location unknown V 2 A c d 839

Fishermen Putting Out to Sea; Watercolor; 47.7x71.7cm.; Sold by Sotheby, Parke Bernet Galleries #71 December 12, 1975; Location unknown II 2 A c d 840

Tug Pulling Three Masted Sailing Vessel; Watercolor; 50.8x76.1cm.; Sold by Sotheby, Parke, Bernet Galleries #690 November 7, 1975; Location unknown II 2 F c d 841

Sailboat Passing Lighthouse; Watercolor; 43.5x26.2cm.; Sold by Sotheby, Parke Bernet Galleries; Location unknown II 2 f c d 842

Sailboat Off Rocky Coast; Watercolor; 34.5x26.2cm.; Sold by Sotheby, Parke Bernet Galleries #688 November 7, 1975; Location unknown I 2 A c d 843

High Sail; Watercolor; 32x25.5cm.; Sold by Raydon Gallery; Location unknown VII 844

Large Rock on Beach with Breakers; Watercolor; Provident National Bank V 2 c d 846

Tug; Watercolor; Private Collection II 2 L c d 847

Steam vessels; Watercolor; Private collection VII 848

Rescue Boat; Watercolor; IV 2 c d 849

Beaching a Dory; Watercolor; Private collection II 2 C c d 850

Destroyer; Watercolor; Private collection III 2 c d 851

Rescue Boat with Five Men; Watercolor; Private Collection IV 2 c d 852

Three-Masted Sailing Ship; Watercolor; Private collection II 2 F c d 853

Sailing Ship Taking Grain and Food to Europe During W.W.I; Watercolor; Great-grandson of the artist II 2 M a 854

Stone Pier at Clifton with People on Dock in Dirty Weather Gear; Watercolor; Great-Grandson of the artist V A a b 855

Marine Scene; from collection of Captain Arthur H. Clark to L. Francis Herreshoff VII 856

Marine Scene; From collection of Capt. A. H. Clark to L. Francis Herreshoff VII 857

Marine Scene; From Collection of Capt. A. H. Clark to L. Francis Herreshoff VII 858

Marine Scene; From Collection of Capt. A. H. Clark to L. Francis Herreshoff VII 859

Marine Scene; From Collection of Capt. A. H. Clark to L. Francis Herreshoff VII 860

Marine Scene; From Collection of Capt. A. H. Clark to L. Francis Herreshoff VII 861

Shipping Scene Along the East River Docks; Watercolor 45.5x30.5cm; Museum of the City of New York V 3 C b 862

Hauling in the Dory; Watercolor; 44.5x72.4cm; Sold at Kennedy Gallery; Location unknown II 2 C c d 863

Coastline; Watercolor; Private collection V 2 B c d 864

Lifeboat with Figures Trying to Free Lifeboat from Sand; Watercolor made into chromolithograph; Location unknown; Chromolithograph in Lyman Ammen Museum IV 2 c d 865

Shipping Off Coast Under Full Sail; Watercolor; 34.5x26.2cm; Sotheby Parke Bernet Galleries #688, November 7, 1975; Location unknown II 2 F c d 866

Marine Scene; Watercolor; Mariner's Museum, Newport News, Va. VII 867

The Maria Outsailing the America; Watercolor; Reproduced in the Lawson *History of the America's Cup* by Winfield M. Thompson and Thomas W. Lawson. Caption reads," In the Stevens Mansion, Hoboken, New Jersey." 868

H.M.S. Victory; Watercolor; Private collection III 1 a b c d 869

Shore Scene with Small Boat; Watercolor; Private collection V 2A 870

1907 *Hard Down*; Watercolor; 18"x14"; Private collection V 2 G871

1907 *Whale Rock*; Watercolor; 18"x14"; Private collection V G872

1887 *Sailing Ship*; Watercolor; 35"x20"; Sold by B. Rinaldi, Pleasant Valley, N.Y. I 2 B 873

Harbor Scene; Watercolor; 17"x22"; Sold by Barridoff Galleries May 7, 1980 2 F c d 874

1894 *Meeting the Pilot*; Watercolor; 14"x20³/4"; Sold R.A. Bourne August 12, 1980 II2cd 875

Sailboat; Watercolor; Sold by R.A. Bourne August 12, 1980 I 2 A c d 876

1898 *Sailing Cargo Ship with Tug*; Watercolor, 8"x10"; Private collection II 2 F c d 877

1899 *Two-Mast Sailing Ship with Steamsail in Rear*; Watercolor; 10½"x10"; Private colleciton II 2 F c d 878

1889 *Ocean Steamer, City of New York*; Pen and ink drawing; Illustraion *Harper's Weekly*, March 30, 1889; Location unknown II 2 G b c d 879

1909 *Surf Boat*; Watercolor, 14½"x20"; Private collection IV 1 c d 880

1915 *U.S.S. Portsmouth*; Watercolor; 12½"x20"; Private collection III 1 c d 881

Beached Boat; Two Sailing Ships in background; Two men on shore; Watercolor; Private collector IV 2 c d 883

1907 *Yachts Racing*; Watercolor; 13½"x21½"; B.I.A.P. Survey; Owner Restricted; I 1 A c d 884

1892 *Two Coasting Vessels Approaching Land and Fog*; Watercolor; 12"x21"; B.I.A.P. Survey; Owner restricted II 2 F c d 885

1906 *Tug Towing Two-Mast Sailing Vessel*; Watercolor; 14"x23½"; B.I.A.P. Survey; Owner restricted II 2 F K c d 886

That's Her; Watercolor; 12½"x22¼"; Sold by Nina Hellman, April 1977 V 2 c d 887

1891 *Sheets Lifted*; Watercolor; 10"x14"; B.I.A.P. Survey; Owner restricted I 2 B c d 888

1906 *Sea Scene with Rocks*; Watercolor; 8"x18"; B.I.A.P. Survey; Owner restricted V A c d 889

1895 *Sailing Steamer at Sea with Full Moon*; Watercolor; 11½ x 29½"; B.I.A.P. Survey; Owner restricted II 2 c d 890

1904 *Marine Ship*; Sailing dory; Watercolor; 14"x11"; Old Print Shop Portfolio, Vol. 25

1894 *Homeward Bound*; 10"x13½"; B.I.A.P. Survey; Owner restricted II 2 c d 892

1886 *High Sail*; Watercolor; Sold by Raydon Gallery, N.Y.C. V 2 c d 893

Fishing Boat with Two Seamen; Watercolor; Museum of Fine Arts, St Petersburg, Florida II 1 A c d 894

1895 *Fishermen in Dory*; 13³/4"x10½; Sotheby Parke Bernet Sale, 1975; Location unknown II 2 A C C d 895

1909 *Castle Garden, New York Bay*; Watercolor; 10"x14"; Old Print Shop Portfolio, Vol. 27; Location unknown VI b 896

1893 *Columbia Naval Review,1893*; Watercolor; Old Print Shop Portfolio, Vol. 27; Location unknown III 1 a b 897

Duck Shooting; Watercolor, 10½"x17½"; Sotheby Parke Bernet, Sale 1942; Location unknown I 2 B c d 898

Fishermen; Watercolor; 12½"x22" Sotheby Parke Bernet, Sale 1942; Location unknown II 2 A c d 899

High Sail; Watercolor; 12½"x10"; Sold by Raydon Gallery, New York City; Location unknown V c d 900

Under Full Sail; Watercolor; 11½"x8³/4"; Old Print Shop Portfolio, Vol. 30; Location unknown V c d 901

1907 *Two Racing Vessels*; Watercolor, 14"x23"; B.I.A.P. Survey; Owner restricted I 1 A 2 c d 902

1888 *Buoyant Sea*; Watercolor, 14"x20"; Raydon Gallery, N.Y.C.; Location Unknown

1876 *Buoyant Sea*; Watercolor; Raydon Gallery, N.Y.C.; Location unknown V c d 904

1892 *Two Fishermen in Sou'westers Landing a Dory in Surf*; Private collection V c d 905

1891 *Four Fishermen in Sou'westers Sailing Two Dories Through the Fog*; *Lobstertraps in Dories*: Private Collection V c d 906

1895 *Two Fishermen in Dory in Sou'westers Sailing a Sailing Vessel in Fog*; Private collection V c d 907

1891 *Abandoned Dinghy on Beach Being Broken Up in Surf*; Private collection V c d 908

1893 *Tug Boat Covered with Ice in Open Sea*; Private collection V c d 909

1907 *Whale Rock*; Watercolor; 23½x12½; Private collection V 2 G b a 915

1907 *Sou'wester Scene*; Chromolithograph; Private collection V c d 916

1904 *Schooner in Full Sail*; Sold at Christie's New York, March 27, 1981; Location unknown II 2 B c d 917

1887 *Sailing Ship*; Watercolor 35"x20"; Sold B. Rinaldi, Pleasant Valley, N.Y.; Location unknown II 2 c d 918

1887 *Tug Scene*; Watercolor; 15"x19"; Private collection II 2 L 919

1898 *Two Schooners in Choppy Water with Buoy and Tug*; Watercolor; 12½"x19½"; Private collection II 2 F 920

1906 *Early Morning or Early Evening Scene of Sailboats in Harbor*; Watercolor; 10½"x16"; Private collection I 2 B 921

1919 *Aloha; Fitted Out for Wartime during Battle Drill*; Watercolor; 11"x17"; Private collection I 1 A a b 922

1919 *Noma*; Watercolor; 11"x17"; Private collection I 1 A a b 923

1911 *Racing Scene No. 8*; Watercolor; 13"x16"; Private collection I 1 A c d 924

1921 *Westhampton, Long Island*; Dark water with marsh, tree and bulkhead view; watercolor; 9"x14"; Private collection V B K 925

1892 *Miantonomah*; Watercolor; 10½"x16"; Private collection III 1 926

1893 *Vesuvius*; Watercolor; 11½"x16"; Private collection III 1 927

1905 *Monterey with Oregon and Detroit*; Watercolor; 11½"x15½"; Private collection III 1 928

1926 *Staten Island Athletic Club Boathouse*; Watercolor; 12"x9"; Staten Island Institute of Arts and Science V 929

1888 *The New Hoboken Ferry Boat, Bergen*; Pen, ink; Illustration: *Harper's Weekly*, Supplement, January 5, 1889 II 1 J e d 930

1888 *The Obelisk in Central Park*; Pen, ink; Illustration: *Harper's Weekly*, February 12, 1881 II 1 A G a b 931

1888 *Trial Trip of the New Mexico*; Watercolor; Exhibited in Staten Island Institue of Arts and Science, April 1926; *Museum Bulletin*; III 1 932

1888 *In Harbor*; Watercolor; Exhibited in Staten Island Institute of Arts and Science, April 1926; *Museum Bulletin* V 2 c 933

1910 *Lemon Creek*; Watercolor; 11³/4"x8¼"; Private collection V 2 A b 934

1914 *Sailing Ship on the High Seas*; Watercolor; 13½"x10½"; Private collection II 2 F c d 935

1898 *Three Men Oystering in Dory*; 12"x15"; Private collection II 2 A c d 936

1887 *The Blanche*; Pen, ink drawing; Illustration: *Harper's Weekly*, September 10, 1887; Annual Meet of the American Canoe Association; Location unknown I 1 A c d 282.01

1887 *The Carrier Pigeon, The Veteran Cook's Canoe*; Pen, ink drawing; Illustration: *Harper's Weekly*, September 10, 1887; Annual Meet of the American Canoe Association; Location unknown VII I 1 A c d 282.02

1887 *The Pecowsic, a Winner of Two Races*; Pen, ink drawing; Illustration: *Harper's Weekly*, September 10, 1887; Annual Meet of the American Canoe Association; Location unknown I 1 A c d 282.03

1887 *The Upset Sailing Race*; Pen, ink drawing; Illustration: *Harper's Weekly*, September 10, 1887; Four drawings on one full page; Annual Meet of the American Canoe Association; Location unknown I 1 A c d 282.04

1889 *Corsica, Commerce on the Great Lakes*; Pen, ink drawing; Illustration: *Harper's Weekly*, April 14, 1889; Location unknown II 1 b c 292.01

1889 *The John Craig, Commerce on the Great Lakes*; Pen, ink drawing; Illustration: *Harper's Weekly*, April 13, 1889; Location unknown II 1 b c 292.02

1889 *The Neosho, Commerce on the Great Lakes*; Pen, ink drawing; Illustration: *Harper's Weekly*, April 13, 1889; Location unknown II 1 b c 292.03

1889 *The New York, Pennsylvania and Ohio Railroad Dock at Cleveland, Ohio Showing the Operation of the Brown Patent Movable Bridge Tramway System for the Rapid Handling of Coal and Oil*; *Commerce on the Great Lakes*; Pen, ink drawing; Illustration: *Harper's Weekly*, April 13, 1889; Location unknown II 2 b c 292.04

1889 *The Cumberland*; *Commerce on the Great Lakes*; Pen, ink drawing; Illustration: *Harper's Weekly*, April 13, 1889; Location unknown II 2 b c 292.05

1889 *The Pewabic of Whitney Line*; Built in 1862; Lost by Collision with her Sister Ship, the Metier on Lake Huron; *Commerce on the Great Lakes*; Pen, ink drawing; Illustration: *Harper's Weekly*, April 13, 1889; Location unknown II 2 b c 292.06

1889 *The Mineral Rock Built in 1852*; *Commerce on the Great Lakes*; Pen, ink drawing; Illustration: *Harper's Weekly*, April 13, 1889; Location unknown II 2 b c 292.07

Date unknown; *Trial Trip of the New Mexico*; Watercolor; Listed in Staten Island Institue of Arts and Science *Bulletin* of April 1926, as appearing in an exhibition of paintings and sculpture in April 1926 at the Institute, #36 III 1 a

Date unknown; *In Harbor*, #37 in an exhibition of paintings and sculpture at the Staten Island Institute of Arts and Science, April 1926 V 2 c

Bibliography

Abbott, Edith R. *The Great Painters in Relation to the European Tradition*, New York: 1927

Action By The Navy, Catalogue of Exhibition of Lyman Allen Museum, March 4 to April 15, 1943

A L A Portrait Index, 1906

Albion, Robert Greengalgh, with Pope, Jennie Barnes. *The Rise of New York Port*, 1815-1860, Charles Scribner's Son, N.Y. 1939

American Art Annual, Ed. Florence N. Levy, The Macmillan Company; Indices from Vol. 1, 1888 to 1907; 1910 list of illustrators in 1900, 1916 exhibitions, 1911, Vol. XXV, 1928; Vol. XXVI, 1929

American Art Gallery Sales; 1882 Catalogue

American Art Union; Exhibition Catalogue

American Heritage Magazine, August 1958

American Magazine of Art, publication of American Federation of Art, Washington, D.C. 1909-1953 Vol. XXIII, November, 1931; *American Painters of the Sea*

American Watercolor Society; Exhibition Notices and Catalogues, l880 Spring, December 1881, January 1882, February, 1883, February, 1884, and 1921

Antiques Magazine, March 1932, November 1960

Antiquarian Magazine Index

Appleton's Cyclopedia of American Biography, 1888; James Grant Wilson and John Fiske, editors; 6 vols. Appleton and Co., N.Y., 1889-1894

Arnot Art Gallery, Catalogue of the Permanent Collection, Elmira, N.Y.

Art Bulletin, Index. Vol. 1, 1913-1948

Art Digest, September 1928

Art Index, Wilson, 1933 to date, New York

Art Institute of Chicago:
  Catalogue of a Century of Progress, Exhibition of painting and sculpture, 1933
  Catalogue of Exhibition, 1910
  Catalogue of International Exhibition of Watercolors, April, 1940

Art News Annual, published by the Metropolitan Museum of Art

Art of the World As Illustrated in the Painting of World's Columbian Exhibition, 2 vols. 1894

Art Quarterly, published by Detroit Institute of Art, Detroit, Michigan

Art Work On Staten Island, 12 section pamphlet; W. H. Parish Publishing Company, 1894

Bard, James and John, Harold Sniffen, and Alexander C. Brown, Publication of the Mariners Museums, #18, 1949

Barker, Virgil, *American Painting*, A Critical Introduction to American Painting, New York, Whitney Museum of American Art, 1931

Bayles, Richard M., ed.,*History of Richmond County (Staten Island) New York: From the Discovery to the Present Time*, New York, L.E. Preston and Company, 1887

Bayley, F.W., *Little Known American Portrait Painters*, 1915-1917

American Neptune, Beck, Horace P., *An American Heritage*, Vol XXV, January 1965

Benizet, Emmanuel, Ed., *Dictionnaire Critique et Docementaire Des Peintres, Sculpteurs, Dessinateurs et Graveurs*, 8 vols., Third ed., Paris, 1960

Benjamin, Samuel, *Fifty Years of American Art*, l882-1879

Bicentennial Inventory of American Painting, Smithsonian Institution, 1976

Biographical Sketches of American Artists, Michigan State Library, Lansing, Mich., 1924 ed.

Boating Almanac, published by Bromley, G. W. and Co., Inc., N.Y.C.

Bolton, Robert Jr., *History of the County of Westchester*, New York, 1848

Book of the Fair, with original and special literary contributions and illustrations; Issued by Tompkins F. and A.M. #471, Copyright 1895, by Press Unz and Company

Bowen, Franc C., *America Sails the Seas*, Robert McBride

Bowker, R. R. , *American Art Directory*, New York; originally called *American Art Annual*

Bowman, W. D., *Yachting and Yachtsmen*, 1929

Brenton, Christian, *Impressions of Art at the Panama Pacific Exposition*, New York, 1916

Brewington, M. V. and D., *Marine Paintings and Drawings in the Peabody Museum*, Salem, Massachusetts, 1969

Brittanica Encyclopedia of American Art, Simon and Schuster, 1973

Brockmeyer, Henry, *Masterpieces of Centennial International Exposition*, 3 vols., 1876-78

Brooklyn Art Association; Exhibition Catalogue, March 1881

Brooklyn Museum of Art, *The Coast and the Sea*, A Survey of American Marine Painting; November 1948 to January 1949, Catalogue

Bryant's Dictionary of Painters and Engravers, G. C. Williamson, ed., 3 vols., 1918-1919

Buchman, David L., *Steamboat Days on the Hudson*, New York, 1907

Burke, J. and Howe, N., Eds, *American Authors and Books, 1640 to Present Day*

1878 Business and Regular Directory of Long Island

Canadian Illustrated News, Montreal, June 10, 1880

Catalogue of Marine Prints and Paintings in Mariners Museum, Newport News, Virginia

Century Magazine, August 1893

Champlin, John D. and Perkins, C., *Cyclopedia of Painters and Painting*, 1913 ed.

Chapelle, Howard, *The History of American Sailing Ships*, Bonanza Books, New York, 1935

Chapelle, Howard, *The Search for Speed Under Sail*, 1700-1855, Bonanza Books, New York MCMLXVII

Chatterton, C. Keble, *Old Ship Prints*, London, 1927

Childs, Charles D., "Marine Painting, Flood Tide," *Antiques Magazine*, July 1954

Cook, Clarence, *Art and Artists Of Our Times*, 3 vols, New York, 1888

Clark, Arthur Hamilton, *The Clipper Ship Era*, 1910

Clark, Arthur Hamilton, *A History of Yachting, 1600-1815*

Clute, John Jacob, *Annals of Staten Island From Its Discovery to The Present Time*, New York, Press of Charles Vogt, 1887

Comstock, Helen, "American Watercolor Before 1860", *Panorama II*, August-September, 1948

Corcoran Gallery of Art, *Catalogue of Paintings*, 1920

Cowdrey, Bartlett, compiler; National Academy of Design, *Exhibition Record*, Compilation of artists and their works as read in American Academy of Fine Arts and American Art Union, 1953

Cozzens, Frederic Swartwout,
  Arcadia, A Sojourn Among The Bluenoses, Derby and Jackson, 1859
  Country Life and Mrs. Sparrowgrass, Scribner's Monthly, December 1916
  Fitz-Hallock Green, A memorial read before the New York Historical Society, 1868
  Mr. and Mrs. Nicholas Longworth, 1857, Cincinnati
  Memory of Brig. Gen. James S. Wadsworth and Col. Peter A. Porter, Memorial read before the Century Club, December, 1864
  Prismatics, pseudonym, Richard Haywards, New York, Appleton and Company, 1853
  The Sayings of Dr. Bushwacker and Other Learned Men, New York, A Simpson and Company, 1867
  Sayings Wise and Otherwise, Published by D.G. Mitchell, New York, 1880
  The Sparrowgrass Papers of Living in the Country, New York, Derby and Jackson, 1856
  Wine Press, 1854 to 1861
  Private Theatricals and Weathercocks, New York, American Book Exchange, 1880
  The Sound of a Voice or the Song of the Debardeur, Philadelphia, J.B. Lippencott, 1891

Cozzens, Frederic Shiller,
  American Yachts, Their Clubs and Races, a series of watercolor sketches with an accompanying volume of text by J.D.J. Kelley, New York; C. Scribner's Sons, 1884, 2 vols.
  Old Naval Prints, a scarce and unusual collection of 24 prints in color depicting 75 ships, New York, National Military Publishing Company, 1893-94, Copy. 1894
  Old Naval Prints, a scarce and unusual collection of 24 prints in color depicting 75 ships; Boston, Armstrong and Company, Copy. 1892-94; American Publishing Company, Hartford, Connecticut
  Our Navy, Its Growth and Achievement, text by J.D.J. Kelley; watercolors by Fred. S. Cozzens, Hartford, Connecticut; American Publishing Company, 1892
  Our Navy, Its Growth and Achievement, text by J.D.J. Kelley; watercolors by Fred. S. Cozzens; Hartford, Connecticut; American Publishing Company, 1897
  Typical American Yachts, Plates by Fred. S. Cozzens; text by J.D.J. Kelley, New York, C. Scribner's Sons, 1886
  Yachts and Yachting, with over 110 illustrations; New York; Cassell and Company, Ltd., 1887
  Yachts and Yachting, with over 135 illustrations; New and revised editions, New York, Cassell and Company, Ltd., 1888

Creer, Davis Jean, *Thomas Birch*, University of Delaware, 1858

Cumulative Book Index, New York, Wilson

Cutler, Carl C., *Greyhounds of the Sea; The Story of the American Clipper Ships*, New York; Halcyon House, 1930

Daggett's New York Directory, 1841, 42, 46, 54

Daily Graphic, June 19, 1875, November 2, 1975

Five Centuries of Marine Painting, Catalogue, Detroit, Institute of Art; March 5- April, 1942

Dictionary of American Biography, Johnson, Allen, Editor; Charles Scribner, New York, 21 vols. American Council of Learned Societies, 1931

Dictionary of National Biography, London, 1921-1922

Directory of Artists

Dunbar, Seymour, *History of Travel in America*, Tudor Publishing Company, New York, 1937

Dunlap, G. D., American Heritage; *American Cup Defender*

Dunlap, William, *A History of the Rise and Progress of the Arts of Design in the United States*, 2 vols., New York, 1834. New Edition illustrated; edited by Frank W. Bayley and Charles E. Goddspeed, 3 vols. Boston, 1918

Durham House, Inc., Stamford, Connecticut; *A Portfolio of Great American Yachts*, 1971

Encyclopedia Britannica, Cambridge, England, University Press, 1953

Erskine, Clara, Clement Waters and Laurence Hutton, Editors; *Artists of the Nineteenth Century and Their Work*, Boston, 1881

Fielding, Mantle, *Dictionary of American Painters, Sculpters and Engravers*, With an addendum containing corrections and additional material on the original entries by James F. Carr, 1965

Fifth Avenue Art Galleries, *Catalogue*, November 26, 1915 #82

Forest and Stream, Part II

Gardner, Albert Ten Eyck and Stuart P. Feld, *American Painting*, Catalogue of the collection of the Metropolitan Museum of Art, New York, 1965

Gilbert, Dorothy, *Who's Who in American Art*, American Federation of Art

Glen, Grace H. *Reminiscences of Old Bay Ridge*, 1962

This Month At Goodspeed's, Catalogue; September 1935; April 1937, 1940; October 1944; February 1946; June 1956

Goodrich, Lloyd, *American Watercolor and Winslow Homer*, Minneapolis, Minn. 1945

Gottesman, Rita Suswein, *The Arts and Crafts in New York, 1800-1804*, New York Historical Society, 1965

Groce and Wallace, *New York Historical Society Dictionary of Artists in America 1564-1860*, Yale University Press, 1957

Grossman, Emery, *Art and Tradition*, New York 1967

Groves, Algernon, *Dictionary of Artists who have Exhibited in the Principal London Exhibitions of Oil Paintings from 1760 to 1880*

Goulding's Directory, New York City; 1876-77; 1877-78; 1878-79; 1880-81

Green, Samuel and Benjamin Wheeler, *Art in America*, A Critical and Historical sketch, 1880

Hamer, Philip, *A Guide to Archives and Manuscripts in the United States*, National Historical Publication Commission

Hamilton, Sinclair, *Early American Book Illustration and Wood Engravers, 1670-1870*, Princeton University, 1968

Hanson, H.I., Cruising Association Library, *Catalogue*, 1927

Harper, J. Russell, *Early Painters and Engravers in Canada*, University of Toronto Press, 1970

Harper's Cyclopedia of United States History

Harper's Monthly Magazine, 1869, Vol. 39, July 1879, Sept. 1879, Oct. 1879

Harper's Weekly, Vol. 25, 1862; July 4, 1868; August 1870; June 29, 1878; September 27, 1879; September 4, 1879; September 27, 1879; October 25, 1879; February 19, 1880; April 10, 1880; July 17, 1880;

July 31, 1880; August 7, 1880; September 8, 1880; October 8, 1880; February 12, 1881; February 19, 1881; September 27, 1881; October 6, 1881; December 9, 1882; September 4, 1886; March 19, 1887; May 28, 1887; July 30, 1887; August 13, 1887, September 10, 1887; December 8, 1888; March 30, 1889; January 5, 1889; August 2, 1890; Vols. 33 and 35, 1891; March 19, 1892; September 24, 1893; August 26, 1899

Hendricks, Samuel F., *Staten Island Athletic Club Decennial Celebration at Club Grounds, West Brighton, Staten Island*, September 5, 1887

Herreshoff, L. Francis, *Rudder Magazine*, June 1944

Herringshaw's National Library of American Biography, American Publishing Association, 1909, Vol. 2

History of National Academy of Design, Columbia University Press

History of the World's Fair, Being a complete and authentic description of the Columbian Exposition from its inception, Providence

Hitchcock, Ripley, ed., *The Art of the World*, illustrated in the paintings and architecture of the World's Columbian Exposition; 10 vols., New York, 1893

Holmes, William H., National Gallery of Art, *Catalogue of Collections*, Smithsonian Institute, 1926

Howat, John K., *The Hudson River and Its Painters*, Viking Press, 1972

Hubbard, Nathaniel Tuthill, *Autobiography*, 1875

Hunt's New York City Directory, 1890

Illustrated America Magazine, July 5, 1890

Illustrated America, Supplement, 1890

Illustrated News, May 7, 1853

Illustrated Official Signal Program and Handbook of the International Yacht Races, 1895

Illustrated Sketch Book of Staten Island, 1886, published by Staten Island Amusement Company

Impressions of Art at the Panama Pacific Exposition, 1916

International Auction Records, Vols. 1 to 6, 1967-1972; Vol. 5, 1971

International Directory of Arts, 1967-1970, 2 vols.

International Exhibition of Watercolors, Art Institute of Chicago, April 1940

Irving, Pierre M., *Life and Letters of Washington Irving*

Isham, S., *History of American Painting*, Macmillan, 1905; rewritten in 1927 by Royal Cortissez

Jacobson, Anita, *From Sail To Steam; The Story of Antonio Jacobsen*, Manor Publishing Company, New York, 1972

James, Sidney, *They Taught Themselves; American Primitive Painters of the Twentieth Century*, New York 1942

Johnson, Allen and Malone, Dumas, *Dictionary of American Biography*, Charles Scribner's, New York, 20 vols. and index

Joubert #15, Banquero, Manila, P.I.

Kelley, James Douglas, Jerrold, *American Yachts, Their Clubs and Races*, Charles Scribner's Sons, New York 1884

    Boat Sailing in Fair Weather and Foul, Outing Publishing Company, 1896

    Our Navy, Its Growth and Achievement, 1892, American Publishing Company, Hartford, Connecticut

    Typical American Yachts, C. Scribner's Sons, New York, 1886

    Yachts and Yachting; New York, Cassell and Company, Ltd. 1887

Kenealy, Ahmed, John; *Yacht Races for the America's Cup*; 1851-1893 New York Outing Company, Ltd., 1894

    Yachting Wrinkles, New York Outing Company, Ltd., 1899

Koehler, S. R. *United States Directory and Year Book*, compiler 1882-1884, New York and London

Kouwenhoven, John A. *Adventures of America, 1857-1900*, Harper's Brothers, 1936

Kraut, John Allen, *Pageant of America; A Pictorial History of United States; Annals of American Sport*; New Haven, Yale University Press 1929

Krist, Robert, "Fort Wadsworth" *The Staten Island Historian*, XVIII 17-18 July-September, 1957 XVIII, 25-28, October-December, 1957

Kurtz, C. M., *Art Gallery Illustration*; World Columbia Exposition, Philadelphia, George Barrie, 1893

Lamb's Biographical Dictionary of the United States, 1900

Landgren, Michael, *Years of Art; The Story of the Art Student's League of New York* 1940

Leng, Charles W. and William T. Davis, *Staten Island and It's People*, Lewis Historical Publishing Company, Inc., 1930

Leslie's Magazine, June 7, 1879

Levy, Florence, *See American Art Annual*

Lippencott's Magazine, "Leaves From the Journal of Frederic S. Cozzens," May, 1980

McKay, Richard, *Some Famous Sailing Ships and Their Builder, Donald McKay*, G. Putnams Sons, New York, 1928

Magazine of Art, Vol. 29 November 1946

MacMillan Book of Boating, Published by William N. Wallace, 1972

Mallett's Index of Artists, New York, 1931; D. T. Mallett, Supplement

Marlor, Clark, S.; *A History of the Brooklyn Art Association*, with an index of exhibitors; Vol. VII; James F. Carr, New York, 1970

A Maritime Exhibition of 19th-Century Ships, February 6, 1955; Wilmington Society of Fine Arts

Metropolitan Museum of Art, *Catalogue of Paintings*, 1922-26

Monroe, Isobel and Kate; *Index to Reproductions of American Paintings*, see Krout, John Allen

Montclair Art Museum, *Exhibition Catalogue*, 1973

Morgan, John Hill, *Early American Painters*

The Monthly Illustrators for the Second Quarter of 1895, Vol. 4, Published by Harry C. Jones, New York, 1895

Morris, Charles V.; *Athletes and Athletics, Staten Island's Claim to Fame*, Tercentenary Booklet, Staten Island, New York, Staten Island Tercenternary Committee, 1961

Morris, Ira K., *Memorial History of Staten Island*, New York, Memorial Publishing Company, 1898

Morrison, John H., *History of American Steam Navigation*, New York, 1903

Morse, Mrs., "Impressions of the Fifties," *Patman's Magazine*, January 1906

Mott, Frank Luther, *History of American Magazines, 1741-1930*, 5 vols.

Mynell, Wilfred, *Modern Art and Artists, Some Modern Artists and Their Work*, The Modern School of Art

Museum of Fine Arts, *Catalogue of Paintings*, 1921

National Cyclopedia of American Biography, New York, White, 1898

National Union Catalogue, Pre-1956 Imprint

New York City Directory and Registry of Merchants

New York Times Index, 1880-1905, May 16, 1926; June 13, 1926; August 31, 1928; December 3, 1972

New York Watercolor Club; early catalogue

New York World; September 1, 1928

New York Herald; September 10, 1893; September 12, 1893; October 6, 1893; October 8, 1893; October 10, 1893; October 12, 1893; October 14, 1893; August 30, 1928; August 31, 1928; December 25, 1928

New York Historical Society; Vol. LVI October 1972

The New International Encyclopedia, New York, Dodd, 1914

The New York Public Library, *Catalogue of Paintings*, New York, 1912

Official Catalogue Of Exhibitors, Universal Exposition. St. Louis, U.S.A. 1904; Division of Exhibits, Dept. B. Art

Outlook, Vol. 49; June 9, 1894

Outing Magazine, April 1886; May, 1886; June 1886; July 1886; August, 1886; September, 1886; October, 1886; November, 1886; December, 1886; February, 1887; Spring, 1900 issues

Parton, James, *Parton's Lives of Illustrious Men*, The Arundel Press, New York, 1881

Parke Bernet Galleries, *Auction Catalogues*, January 28, 1929, October 16,1974

Patterson's Illustrated Nautical Dictionary, Unabridged, Captain Howard Patterson, New York, 1891

Pennsylvania Academy of Fine Arts, *Exhibition Records*, 1807-1870

Picturesque Staten Island, published, 1886; Pamphlet by Staten Island Amusement Company

Piscatorial Pictorials of America, See Montclair Art Museum

Poole's Index to Periodicals, 1802-1888, Vol. 1 to 6

Portfolio of the Old Print Shop; #10, Vol. 27; May 1942; February 1946; June-July 1963; June-July 1970

Preston's History of Staten Island, Another title for Bayles' History

Punchinello, Vol. 1; April 2 to September 24, 1870 and Vol. 2; October 1 to December 24, 1870

Randolph, Arthur D.F. *Leaves from the Journal of F.S. Cozzens*; See under Lippencott's Magazine

Rauschenbush, D.D., *International Directory of Arts*, 1961

Rhodes, *1850 Directory of New York City*

Richmond Borough Guide, 1913

Richmond, John P., *Yachting in Richmond County*, Tercentenary Booklet, Staten Island Tercentenary Committee, Staten Island, New York

Robinson Atlas of the City of Yonkers, 1887

Robinson, Frank T., *Living New England Artists*, 1888

Roosevelt, Franklin Delano, *The Old Navy; 1776-1860*, Catalogue of an exhibit from the naval collection of Franklin Delano Roosevelt, Washington, D.C.

Rowan, Col. E.M., *History of Fort Wadsworth*, Tercentenary Booklet, Staten Island Tercentenary Committee, 1961

Rudder Magazine, March, 1903; March 1906; June, 1944

Rutledge, Anna Wells, compiler and editor, *Cumulative Record of Exhibition Catalogues of the Pennsylvania Academy of Fine Arts, 1897-1878*, American Philsophical Society, 1955

Sail and Paddle Magazine, March 1889

St. Louis Fair; *St. Louis Louisiana Purchase Exposition with a Complete List o the Awards by the International Jury*, Universal Exposition, St. Louis, 1904

Salmagundi Sketch Club; *Catalogues of Annual Black and White Exhibitions*, 1881

History of Westchester County, 1886; 2 vols.

Scribner's Monthly, December, 1916; Vol. 5, 1915-18; Vol. 4, 1915-18; Vol. 1, 1887-91

Seaboard Magazine, September 1928; October, 1928

Sears, Clara E. *Highlights Among the Hudson River Artists*, Boston, 1947

Sheldon, George William, *Recent Ideals of American Art*, 1888

Simmons, William, "The Sandbaggers", *Rudder Magazine*, March, 1906,

Sketchbook of Staten Island, 1886

Smith, B. H. and H. du Boulay, *The Complete Yachtsman*, 5th Ed., 1928

Smith, Ralph Clifton, *A Biographical Index of American Artists*, Baltimore, Williams and Wilkins Company, 1930

Standard Directory of Richmond County, 1895-96

Stanton, Samuel Ward, *American Steam Vessels*, New York, 1895

Staten Island Advance, August 31, 1928; August 30, 1928

Staten Island And Its People See Leng and Davis

Staten Island Institute, *The Island and the Bay in Art from 1776 to the Present*, Proceedings of the Staten Island Institute of Arts and Science, XIX, 3-25, Fall 1956

Trow's Consolidated Directory of the North and South Shores of Staten Island, 1882

Staten Island Historian, October-December 1972; January-March 1974

Staten Island News Illustrated, October 17, 1898; October 27, 1898, March 11, 1899; October 27, 1898

Staten Island Magazine, 1880

Stephens, W.P., *American Yachting*, Macmillan Company, New York, 1904

Stone, H.; William Taylor, William Robinson, *The America's Cup Races*, W.W. Norton and Company, New York, 1970

Sullivan, E.R.; *Yachting*; 2 vols., Badminton Library, 1895

Sun and Shade, Photo-gravure Company, New York

Transit, 1967 Student Year Book, Rensellaer Polytechnic Institute

Thackery, William Makepeace, *Letters of*, Vol. 3 and Vol. 4

Thieme and Becker, *Allemeines Lexicon der Bilden*, Kunstler, Leipsig, 1907

Treasures of Staten Island, an exhibition of paintings and from the homes of Staten Island; September to October, 1952; Staten Island Institute of Art and Science

Tremble, Alfred, *Representation Works of Contemporary American Artists*, New York, 1887

Trow's Directory of Staten Island; Business and Residential Directory, 1856; 1857; 1877; 1878; 1879; 1881; 1882-83; 1884; 1887-88; 1890-92; 1895; 1897; 1898; 1899; 1900; 1903; 1905; 1907; 1912; 1917; 1927; 1933

Tuckerman, Henry, *Book of the Artists*, New York, 1867

United States Art Directory, 1882-84

United States Catalogue, 4th ed., Wilson, 1928

United New York and New Jersey Sandy Hook Pilot's Benevolent Association, *Pilot Lore, From Sail To Steam*, Supervised by Edward L. Allen 1922

Valentine's Manual of Old New York, Vol. 3, New Series, 1919; Vol. 4, 1920; Vol. 6, 1922; Vol. 4, 1927

Valintiner, W.R. and Robinson, Frances; *Five Centuries of Marine Painting*, Detroit Institute of Art, 1942

Villiers, Alan J., *Men, Ships and the Sea*, National Geographic Society, Washington, D.C., 1962

Vollmer, Hans, *Allgemeiner Lexicon der Bildenden Kunstler*, Jahrunderts, 1961

Walker, John and James McGuire, *Great American Painting from Simbert to Bellows*, Oxford University Press, 1943

MacMillian Book of Boating, Wallace, William 1972

Walton, William, *The Army and Navy of the United States, From the Period of the Revolution to the Present Day*

Webb's Consolidated Directory of the North and South Shores of Staten Island, 1882-83; 1890-91; 1892-93

Weitenkamff, Frank, *American Graphic Arts*, Reprint, 1970; Original, 1924

Westchester County Bibliography

Westchester County Historical Society Quarterly Bulletin, Vol. 7, No. 1, 1931

White, James L. and Company, *The National Cyclopedia of American Biography*, see *National Cyclopedia*

Whitney Museum; *Watercolors and Pastels in Second Bicennial Exhibition*, February, 1938

Who's Who In American Art, See Gilbert, Dorothy

Wilmerding, John, *A History of American Maritime Painting*, Salem, Massachusetts, 1968
    Fitz Hugh Lane, New York, 1971

Wilmington Society of Fine Arts, *Exhibition Notice*, 1955

Wilson, H.W., Art Index, *Historical Abstracts and or American History and Life*, Ann Arbor, Mich., January, 1929

Wilson, James Grant, *Bryant and His Friends*, 1886

Wilson, James Grant and John Fiske, *Appleton's Cyclopedia of American Biography*, See *Appleton's Cyclopedia of American Biography*

Worchester Art Museum, *Catalogue of Paintings and Drawings*

World, September 1, 1928, December 28, 1869

Worth, Claud, *Yacht Navigation and Voyaging*, New York, 1927 *Yachting Magazine*, 1880; issues to 1920;

Yachting Magazine, 1880; Issues to 1920

Yonkers City Directory

Index

Acknowledgments

I gratefully acknowledge my indebtedness in my research to the following:

Warren Adelson, Elizabeth Anderson, Robert Albion, Odette M. Appel, Ann Abid, Laura Antoinette, Bruno Adissi, Doris B. Adams, Mabel Abbott, Wm. A. Baker, Thomas F. Beck, Barbara Butturff, R. Gordon Barton, Frank O. Braynard, Richard A. Bourne, E. John Bullard, Gerard Boardman, Georgia Baumgardner, Larned Bradford, Harold E. Brown, J.N. Bartfield, Chester A. Baker, Max Berman, Dorothy Burden, Phyllis Barton, David Berreth, A.K. Baragwanath, Nancy Blood, Elizabeth Bland, C. Baxter, Therese Brown, Jeffrey E. Brown, M.V. Brewington, William A. Baker, Arthur D. Baker, Frederick Den Broeder, Jeanne Borden, Ann Balko, Mrs. John N. Brown, Abagail Booth, Thomas B. Card, Jack Cowart, Paul Clifford, James Gould Cozzens, Clement E. Conger, Edward Cortise, Herve Cras, George Crosette, Louise Cozzens, Raymond Cozzens, V.R. Cozzens, Barbara Connor, Cecelia Chin, Butler Coleman, Harriet Cabot, Michael Cohn, Theresa Cederholm, James Cheevers, Herbert Cahoon, Phillis Cochrane, James D. Conyers, Herbert Cutler, Eugenie Candau, Miller M. Cragon Jr., Howard Chapelle, Robert E.S. Clark, Elizabeth C. Coogan, Carl Crossman, James F. Carr, Elizabeth Culler, Christine Childs, Herbert Davidson, Elaine Dee, Alice B. Dibble, Howell Dodd, E. Dowling, Edwin H. Dwight, Lamia Daumato, Lydia Davis, Virginia H. Dunstan, Carolyn J. Diskant, Robert M. Doty, Briggs Dalzell, Thea Ellison, Arpi Ermoyen, Ida G'Everson, Alma G. Ellis, Robert Ehrgott, Linda Ferber, J. Leo Finn, Norman Flayderman, S.K. Feldman, Stephanie Farrell, Mary Ellen Florence, Roger Fromm, Ann Fernandez, Robert Fitzgerel, Brenda Finn, Jaime French, E. McSherry Fowble, Albert Fach, Mrs. Stuart Fleming, Robert Fleming, C.D. Graham, Donald Gormley, Mrs. G. Grote, Neil R. Gahagan, Lucien Goldschmidt, Melanie Gifford, M. Goransen, Susan Grady, Ellen R. Goheen, Frank H. Goodyear, Freida Gray, Donald T. Gibbs, Jane des Grange, Elizabeth Gustison, Louis Goldenberg, Trudy R. Gray, William Geohegan Donald Gibbs, Frances Whiting Hatch, Marie Higgins, Edwin B. Hooper, Morgan Holmes, Margaret Holzinger, Henry D. Hill, Stuart C. Henry, Edward B. Hutton, William Henry Harrison, L. Francis Herreshoff, Richard B. Holman, A. Sidney Herreshoff, A. Griswold Herreshoff, Clarence De W. Herreshoff, Mr. Harlihane, Llewellyn Howland, John K. Howat, Barbara Haskell, J.P. Hennings, Sally Hume, A. Hill, Sara B. Hinnegan, Lynda Hartmann, Sohei Houri, Frederick Hicks, C.R. Hickman, Aggie Hoover, W.E. Ireland, Robert Bruce Inverarity, William R. Johnson, Robert F. Johnson, Mary G. Jewett, Caryl Johnson, Waldo C.M. Johnson, J. Johnson, Melvin H. Jackson, P.H. Johnson, Coral Jensen, I. Johnson, Virginia Jones, Rolf Kepl, Margaret A. Keller, Kathryn Kearney, L.W. Kinley, Karl Kortum, James A. Knowles, Margaret Kaufman, Janet Kennedy, Marjorie Kerr, Adm. John D.H. Kane Jr., Samuel Leitman, John Lindenbush, Lawrence Lane, Reginald A. Lombard, Mills B. Lane, Marcia Laszlo, John L. Lockhead, John F. Leavitt, Phyllis K. Lunderberg, Dr. Langley, Martin Leifer, Sally Lumm, Barbara Levy, Garnett McCoy, Helen McCormack, L.G. McCann, Andrew McWilliams, Loring McMillen, Frederick Meylert, Clark S. Marlor, Gertrude MacIntyre, R.B. Moody, Edgar de N. Mayhew, F.R. Morro, Rev. Marion L. Matics, Willa R. Moore, Ruth S. Magurn, Mary G. Makras, James E. Mooney, Mary Jean Madigan, Edwin N. MacConomy, Howard S. Mott, Bruce Matheson, C.S. Murphy, Joseph F. Michels, Alice Melrose, Robin L. Michel, P.H. Moreno, J.H. Mayne, Betty Monkman, Dianne MacEllwinen, D. Denise Minault, John Metkus, Josephine Mollock, Elizabeth Montgomery, Kathleen Mende, Milo M. Naeve, Robert Nikirk, Kenneth Newman, Nathaniel Cushing Nash, Albert C. Nolte Jr., Marian B. Owen, William V.O'Connor, Molly O'Connor, F.N. Owens, Joseph Outerbridge, Wayne O'Leary, Catherine Perry, Sybille Pantazzi, Hugo Poisson, Katherine Paris, Hugh Powell, Joseph Proctor, Laird U. Park Jr., Even Petley-Jones, Thelma Paine, Karin Peltz, Patricia Pierce, Mary Ann Pitassy, Philip Purrington, R.J. Prattle, Arthur Priedetis, R. Quarum, Walt Reed, Sue Rames, Gary Reynolds, Mary Riordan, Carol Robbins, Helmut Ripperger, Ann S. Rogerson, F.L. Rath, Angela Russell, Wanda Randall, Charles Reese, Betty Reese, Kenneth C. Rogers, Donald Reichert, Florette Robinson, Critchell Rimington, Caroline Rollins, Rita Rawley, Mrs. John Rianhart, Sue W. Rames, Robert Schoelkopf, H.R. Bradley Smith, Christopher Simon, Paul Schweizer, Billie Sass, Janice Strickland, Abby Shaw, Dorothy Struth, Susan Strickler, W.W. Sullivan, Victor D. Spark, Philip Cadwick Foster Smith, Henry Steinmeyer, Milton Swanson, Mildred Steinbach, Gisela Severino, Harold Samuels, Ruth Shevin, Clyde Singer, Robert Sharp, D.P. Snowden, Jerome Irving Smith, Philip C.F. Smith, Ann Somerville, J.W.D. Symons, Alice Simkins, Steven Straw, Jamie Suits, Edward Stackpole, Susan Soloman, Paul E. Seufer, Harold Sniffen, Ida Standerwick, Robert G. Stone, Flora K. Scheib, Walter B. Stearns, Chauncey Stillman, Mr. and Mrs. Rudolph Schaefer, William T. Talbot, Carolyn Tannehill, R. Tucker, L.G. Traynor, E. Berkeley Tompkins, Helen Traina, Harold Togesen, Gale R. Thompson, Nicki Thiras, Robert Vose, S. Morton Vose, Gudmund Vigtel, Muriel L. Vaughn, Alfred G. Vanerbilt, Amelia Volkhart, L. Hoyt Watson, John Wilmerding, Maudine B. Williams, Madeline Wordell, Dansy Williams, James L. Whitehead, Beatrice Welch, George D. Wintress, Richard P. Widdebombe, Nelson C. White, Virginia Wolven, S. Wollman, Rev. L.J. Winterbottom, Alice Wilson, Rudolph Wunderlich, Patricia Yannes, William Young, Kathleen Zimmerman, E. Zimbelman.